HEART·LIFE·MUSIC

HEART·LIFE·MUSIC

KENNY CHESNEY

WITH
HOLLY GLEASON

WILLIAM MORROW
An Imprint of HarperCollins*Publishers*

Pages 339–340 constitute an extension of this copyright page.

Without limiting the exclusive rights of any author, contributor or the publisher of this publication, any unauthorized use of this publication to train generative artificial intelligence (AI) technologies is expressly prohibited. HarperCollins also exercise their rights under Article 4(3) of the Digital Single Market Directive 2019/790 and expressly reserve this publication from the text and data mining exception.

HEART LIFE MUSIC. Copyright © 2025 by Kenny Chesney. All rights reserved. Printed in the United States of America. No part of this book may be used or reproduced in any manner whatsoever without written permission except in the case of brief quotations embodied in critical articles and reviews. For information, address HarperCollins Publishers, 195 Broadway, New York, NY 10007. In Europe, HarperCollins Publishers, Macken House, 39/40 Mayor Street Upper, Dublin 1, D01 C9W8, Ireland.

HarperCollins books may be purchased for educational, business, or sales promotional use. For information, please email the Special Markets Department at SPsales@harpercollins.com.

hc.com

FIRST EDITION

Designed by Nancy Singer
Endpaper photographs by Allister Ann (back) and courtesy of the author (front)

Library of Congress Cataloging-in-Publication Data has been applied for.

ISBN 978-0-06-342310-7

25 26 27 28 29 LBC 5 4 3 2 1

CONTENTS

STARS / 1

CHICKEN AFTER CHURCH / 4

SOMETHING FRIED / 12

SPLASHKETBALL / 17

TENNESSEE RIVER / 25

FARMER, HOLT, AND HOBBY / 30

BLUEGRASS / 35

THE TURF / 48

WHAT DID I JUST SEE / 55

ACUFF-ROSE / 59

CAPRICORN / 69

ROCK IN YOUR SHOE / 76

PUT A SMILE ON IT / 81

DALE / 86

WILDEST DREAMS / 90

TURNING THE TIDE / 105

8 SECONDS / 113

SEXY TRACTOR / 123

THE ISLANDS / 129

SEA CHANGE / 137

IT'S ALL HAPPENING / 147

WHO THE F IS KENNY CHESNEY? / 153

LIVING IN FAST FORWARD / 161

BACK WHERE I COME FROM / 170

I GO BACK / 174

WHEN THE SUN GOES DOWN / 177

KEG IN THE CLOSET, KENNY IN THE KEYS / 181

DIVER DOWN / 188

BEER IN MEXICO / 191

BE AS YOU ARE / 196

DRAFTED / 208

THE ROAD, RADIO, POETS, AND PIRATES / 219

WE DO! / 231

MOMENT OF FOREVER / 234

LUCKY OLD SUN / 238

THE WALL / 244

BOYS OF FALL / 247

GRACE / 256

SHE COMES FROM BOSTON / 263

WHEN I SEE THIS BAR / 270

REVIVALS / 280

NOISE / 283

SPIRIT OF A STORM / 286

GET ALONG / 297

DA PONCH AND DA RUBA GIRL / 299

WEGMAN / 306

HERE AND NOW / 311

UNTHINKABLE NEWS / 320

THE HALL REVEALED / 325

Acknowledgments / 333

Rights and Attributions for Photographs and Lyrics / 339

To the curious, the seekers.

♦

To every dreamer I have known
may Lady Luck take you home
I pray for every wannabe
Dreamin' big and livin' free . . . like me.
—Troy Jones, "Like Me"

HEART•LIFE•MUSIC

STARS

As a kid, I'd lie out in the yard at night, staring up at the sky, wondering what in the world was up there. I could see all those stars, hanging in the darkness; it made me think about all the things that could be beyond this moment. Curious as to all the things that might exist between my patch of grass and the entire cosmos, it made me dream.

In those early years, we lived so far beyond the city limits, everybody had gardens by their house. We didn't have streetlights, or a lot of traffic, only a lot of yard, dirt, and night sky. Whether I was living with my mom, Grandma Lucy and Grandpa JB, or on my own, I loved to lie in the cool grass and listen to the quiet.

My mom and dad divorced before I was one; Karen Grigsby and Dave Chesney were entirely too young to be married. For me, I don't remember any of that. Even when I was a little kid, all I recall is the extra love of being with my mom's parents.

No matter where we lived, there was always lots of Grigsby love.

When I was old enough to be out in the early evenings, I'd listen to the quiet, counting the stars. Nobody worried about me, because there was nowhere to go. No matter where we lived, those grass patches were my consistent escape.

As I wandered back in the house, I'd spend time trying to catch lightning bugs; I had a jar with a lid with holes in it. It was fun chasing the flickering lights as they flew around. I loved to catch those fireflies, because putting them in the jar felt like I was holding stars in my hand.

Lying on my back, hands behind my head in the thick grass, I'd feel the hill's curve under my body. You'd be amazed at what you see that far out. No lights from Knoxville, only endless blackness and stars forever. Staring into it, I felt a peace, but also a curiosity rumbling that's never stopped.

That's where this dream started, or at least the idea of dreaming. Being a child who didn't have much to draw on—growing up in a rural town—didn't stop me. I was dreaming to dream. It wasn't this dream of making music, certainly. Letting my mind wander and drift was enough, it opened a lot of windows along the way.

I grew up in a really small town. Luttrell is 3.9 square miles, populated by 915 people according to the 2000 census and 812 in 1970. Built in a valley between Copper Ridge and Clinch Mountain, Luttrell's part of what is considered "the Ridge and Valley" Appalachians.

State Route 131 and State Route 61 intersect in Luttrell. But other than taking us to Plainview, Blaine, or Maynardville, which was the Union County seat, they're both two-lane rural highways when they roll through our town. They run by Norris Lake, along the Clinch River, but there were bigger highways in East Tennessee.

I only knew the roads I was used to going down, to school, church, and sometimes to see my dad. For me, those roads didn't lead any farther than the park where I played ball, school, church, and the places we went running errands. It was a small world; even as a child, I knew that much. How I knew, I don't know. But the stars made me wonder. I sensed those roads went places I'd like to see.

What you don't realize when you're staring at the sky is how much the Virgin Islands or Jamaica; some village in the hills of Italy; Stowe, Vermont; Brownsville, Texas; or Mount Clemens, Michigan, are like the towns where I grew up. Every kid in places that aren't even dots on the map probably stares into that same night sky, wondering those same things.

It's not that you want to leave, it's that you want to know.

And dreaming—even when you're just drifting around in your own head—is really about whatever that might be. You don't have to know in that moment, because you believe if you keep looking, you'll figure it out.

Other than Knoxville to see the Christmas lights, I didn't really go anywhere.

CHICKEN AFTER CHURCH

I was raised in a community where we leaned on church, school, sports, and one another. In our family, music was a thread that ran through everything. For three years when I was small, we lived with my mom's parents, Lucy and JB (as in John Beecher Grigsby); those memories are filled with music.

My mom and my grandma were in the hospital at the same time, having me and my Aunt Missy, who's six days older. Missy and I grew up like brother and sister, running around and going to school together.

It made us a close family. Love really held us together.

When I was three and we were living with my mom's parents, Santa paid me a visit. Under the tree wrapped in colorful paper was a plastic guitar with my name on it. There was also a cheap kid's microphone for me to play with, because everybody thought the way I experienced music was cute.

There's a picture from Christmas morning of Mom and me with my guitar on in the living room. I thought I'd won the big door prize. Not knowing how to play didn't dampen my enthusiasm one bit. Having sat in my little chair next to Aunt Missy—or on the sofa next to Grandpa JB—watching *Hee Haw* rocking to the music, I'd seen plenty of people playing guitars on TV.

In that child's way, I knew what to do. I actually held the fretboard properly with my left hand. That was all I needed. It felt good. Having that strap on my shoulder, plus the neck in my hands, felt so natural. I could play along with whoever was on TV—or the record player—as if it was me up there.

Music was everywhere. You didn't think about it.

Starting with church, music spoke to me. I grew up going to a Southern Baptist church. Cedar Ford Baptist isn't a big towering church, like people think of when they think of those big Southern superchurches. More of a humble, rectangle-shaped brick building, there was plenty of room for all the believers. White walls, wood trim, three sets of pews, and a cross over the altar. What I knew more than those details is Cedar Ford Baptist had an awful lot of faith inside.

Very structured, the services were scripture readings, a sermon that was almost a "teaching," meant to help people use the *Bible* to lead their life. Church was meant to inspire us. Grandpa JB, who'd spent his life working as an engineer with the TVA, was a deacon at my church.

Now and then, Grandma Lucy took me to the church where she grew up in Snake Holler, Tennessee. A building with a dirt floor, their worship was all the fire and brimstone you hear so much about. I wasn't more than four or five. That preacher'd get so worked up, he'd spit as he witnessed. Every phrase a fleck of spit would fly out of his mouth like punctuation. Everything about it scared the hell out of me.

I loved the church music. The hymns were almost follow-the-bouncing-ball simple, so everyone could join in. Most people did.

"Amazing Grace," "How Great Thou Art," especially my favorite, "Just as I Am." That hymn made me feel whatever I was doing, there was a place for me. That was the promise.

Around Easter, when we sang "He Arose," Mom would get to giggling, and we'd all catch it. I was never sure whether it was the syntax of it, what happens if you separate the syllables into "a rose," or something else. But it tickled Mom so much, we'd start laughing, too.

Cedar Ford Baptist is probably the first place I truly "heard" music and realized the way it can lift you up. When everyone is singing, you'd be lighter through all the faith and heart flowing through those hymns. Whatever was on your soul, it faded. You felt energized, even joyful. When people were sad, singing somehow made it seem like it would get better.

My mom and her whole family loved music. Church had something to do with it.

When Missy and I were old enough for kindergarten, my grandmother went to work in the school cafeteria so she could be there if we needed her. All I knew was Grandma Lucy would fuss over us and made sure we got the biggest piece of pizza when we came through the line.

One of my first memories of music was getting ready to go to school. Because the three of us were all headed to Luttrell Elementary, we'd wake up early to get ready. That morning rush was the first time I heard bluegrass music.

Every morning, *The Cas Walker Farm and Home Hour* aired on WBIR-TV. Walker owned a bunch of supermarkets in Knoxville and East Tennessee, so he had this local TV variety show every morning from 5:00 to 6:00 a.m. He'd been Knoxville's mayor, but mostly he was a character who was shameless, outrageous, and funny. He'd talk about what was going on in town, what was coming up, what he was trying to sell at his store. He also booked local musicians. Dolly Parton played his show when she was young.

Bluegrass was a big piece of it. Some of the biggest names, including Bill Monroe and Jimmy Martin, knew it was a good place for their fans to see them. The way those bluegrass harmonies bent into each other, plus the picking, made me stop cold and stare at the TV. It was music from another planet.

Having heard harmony in church, which was nothing like this, I thought, *Wow! What's this?* No idea who was playing, I couldn't move. That sound absorbed me, reached inside, and set a hook. Mandolin, banjo, fiddle, even the acoustic guitars were unlike anything I'd ever experienced. Another window opened in my imagination.

Local morning shows were a pretty regular thing in the South when I was growing up. Later I learned when my mom and her identical twin sister, Sharon, were young, my grandfather would buy them matching dresses, then take them to sing at talent shows, revivals, and churches. Known as the Grigsby Twins, they sang on Cas Walker's show a few times, and *Mull's Singing Convention*, a gospel show broadcast on Saturday afternoons all over East Tennessee between cartoons and football.

It's amazing how things you don't know growing up can become part of who you are.

Mom loved secular music, especially country music. There was always something playing around the house. We didn't get in the car, either, without the music being turned up.

Hearing this voice wail "Jeremiah was a bullfrog . . ." lit me up. "Joy to the World" by Three Dog Night became one of my most favorite songs. When it came on, I'd be beside myself. Music as a life force ran through everyone on the Grigsby side.

When I was young, when Mom picked me up from school or practice, she'd be shaking her head to some song. She loved Merle Haggard and Glen Campbell, Con Hunley, who was from Knoxville. She might be playing Alabama, the Statler Brothers, or the Oak Ridge Boys, who'd started out gospel and went country; they all had three- and four-part vocals.

Mom also loved George Jones. The whole family, Grandma Lucy especially, loved Jones. The kind of country singer whose electric, raw voice got under all our skin and made everybody almost shake, smile, feel whatever he was singing. Whether novelty ("The Race Is On") or heartbreak ("The Window Up Above"), we agreed he was the best.

Jones's voice was straight lightning. He sang songs that were so fierce, so sad, or so funny, you wanted to turn them up when they came on because you wanted to hear every bit of emotion. It didn't matter which feeling, when George Jones sang, it ran through you. Being young, I did like the funny songs that made me laugh, but like my entire family, I liked it all.

My first concert ever, I went with Mom, Aunt Sharon, and their Uncle Ken, who was my Grandma Lucy's younger brother. After a big Thanksgiving dinner, they decided they were going to the Knoxville Civic Coliseum. Smart move having a concert on Thanksgiving because it gives people something to do other than dishes.

And this show was the Super Bowl of country music. It's hard to imagine Merle Haggard, George Jones, and Conway Twitty on the same bill. That was a lot of heat.

Extra special, because I'd heard them coming home from school, going to the grocery store, and in Grandma's kitchen as she was making dinner. Growing up where I did in the '70s, Haggard, Jones, and Conway were in the air all the time.

Twisted into the DNA of our being, they were larger than life. Those men sang our lives and we sang along. But on this Thanksgiving, they were going to be right there in Knoxville and singing for all of us. *In person.*

The show was sold out, but Aunt Sharon might've known someone or heard something. So, without tickets, we were going. We decided to drive down to the Coliseum to see what might be available.

"You never know," Mom said, and she's right. You don't.

I know how many times over the years we release tickets we've been holding right before doors open. Or if I know people want to get in, I'll try to open up seats somewhere that may not be ideal, but they're "in." For me, I never want anybody left out, because I've been there: Thanksgiving night in Knoxville.

Since the show didn't have a lot of production, someone decided to sell tickets behind the stage. They were cheap, too. Maybe we couldn't see the faces when the stars were singing, but we saw all the action behind the stage! We got the music, the concert, *and* to see the workings of how a show happened. As a curious nine-year-old, seeing all the people walking around, bringing instruments, adjusting equipment was fascinating.

Haggard went on first. Smooth as a singer but also rugged, you could see why the men loved him. My mother loved everything about the way he sang "Mis'ry & Gin" especially, but all these hits—"Mama Tried," "If We're Not Back in Love by Monday," and "If We Make It Through December"—that came one after another. The whole building was singing along, stories that you could feel meant something to them.

George Jones went on second. He walked out and sang fire with all those songs we knew, bending notes and wringing out feelings I wasn't old enough to understand. The Jones Boys played in their matching polyester suits, but knew where to push the songs. "She Thinks I Still Care," "The Race Is On," "White Lightning," "The Window Up

Above" sounded so much more urgent in concert; Jones's voice went straight into all of us.

Looking back now, I laugh, because there's such a difference in the way I do things at our shows. Before I go on, I've got loud music playing, this huge video intro that we've shot all over the world with lots of my friends on the massive screens. It's almost a show before the show, pumping people up, showing them how much fun we're about to have. That's the way I like to do things, especially in stadiums. But this was simple: a band, a few lights, these stars.

When Conway Twitty went onstage, my mind was blown. The lights went off. Total darkness. Then this man's voice came out of the speakers into the black—"Ladies and gentlemen, Conway Twitty."

No music, nothing. One spotlight clicked on: Conway was standing there in blue pants and a hot pink shirt. He looked down into the audience, said, "Hello, darling," in that massive molasses voice, and the place went fucking crazy! Absolutely out of their skins wild.

I stood there. Overwhelmed. I can't tell you what he sang or how he moved because it's a blur. In that moment, without ever truly understanding why, I was so swept away in this sensation of Conway's songs and people responding, I was gone. Internally I said, "Wow! That's what I want to do."

SOMETHING FRIED

It wasn't until we went on vacation to Myrtle Beach that I started to know what I was dreaming. That first trip, I thought I was going to jump out of my skin I was so excited to see what was beyond the Smoky Mountains, my grandparents' house, and church.

Mom told me about the ocean, the sand, how people from everywhere, well, really everywhere around the mid-South, all went to the beach to have fun. She told me they'd be walking around, taking in all that seaside town had to offer with such delight, I couldn't wait to see it.

I could feel everyone's energy in the car. We were doing something new, something beyond the grown-ups' obligations. My mother, who hadn't gone to the beach until she was in her twenties, loves the water as much as I do. So, taking her kids to have fun where we could splash and play really made her happy.

Talking about where they were going to go, what we were going to eat, I knew it was going to be unlike anything I'd experienced. We had the music playing in the car, sometimes all of us singing along. Six hours driving there felt like forever.

But it faded away once we got close. Because we were driving, I saw the scenery change; all these roadside stands with signs that read "Boiled Peanuts." Salty, soft, there was nothing that had that texture or taste anywhere else.

Getting closer to the beach, we rolled down the windows. From ten miles away, we could smell the ocean in the air. That first time we drove onto the main road where the hotels and motels were, I felt the breeze coming off the ocean rushing between them; the blasts of wind made me turn my face toward them, and the warm air with a bit of salt stung my skin.

We checked into a hotel called the Reef, which was brand newish, sixteen stories high and right on the beach. White concrete with big windows in all the rooms, it felt fancy. All the guests shared that same energy we felt: exhaling, letting go, loving life.

That was part of what drew me to Scooter Carusoe's "Anything but Mine." The way a day at the ocean, especially in a tourist town, leaves you with the slight hint of sunburn, tired but feeling so at peace with the world. That tug of how it feels to be in the water all day, run around the boardwalk, then go find dinner and drift into the night seemed like the way to live.

After that first trip, I would be so excited knowing we were going to go that I almost felt electric by the time we'd hit the road. My mom, who loves life more than anyone, would sometimes decide we were going to go for two days. Start very early, hit the beach, spend the night, go back to the ocean the next day, and head home.

You couldn't get me out of the ocean or the pool. Running in and out of the waves, feeling the power of the sea push you, then pull back and away was the greatest feeling. Splashing around, playing games in the pool was great fun, too. A friendly kid, I'd get down to the pool, looking around to see who I could play with.

Every day, my mother would have to come down to the beach to drag me out of the ocean because it was time to go eat something fried. I had never had a hush puppy in my life until we went on that first trip to Myrtle Beach. That crunch around the balls of corn meal was salty, delicious, and comforting all at once.

One time, I wouldn't come out of the pool. Mom loved beach music, and a band called Fat Jacks was playing on the deck nearby. The sun was out. People were dancing around at the pool to songs by The Temptations, The Tams, the Drifters, and The Embers. That music was so smooth and rhythmic, with lots of harmonies and good songs. Seeing her with her big smile, dancing and so happy even as she wanted me out of the water, is such a memory.

Moments like that are where my sense of happiness got defined. No matter what else happened, how hard people worked, when we got to the beach, it was all in on the fun. Mom in her bikini, her cute hairdo and that musical laugh that was contagious, who wouldn't have fun when she's clearly loving the experience?

Those sights and smells were so basic, but they made me happy as a kid. And those sounds—music spilling out of people's radios driving or walking by, pouring out of the local storefronts, laughter, especially the waves hitting the beach and pulling back into the ocean—carried me into my adult life, to this very moment.

SOMETHING FRIED / 15

Those are things my mom and I have in common. We love the water, especially the ocean, whether hanging out around it, jumping in it, or sailing somewhere on it. We both love music, too. She gave me those gifts without even telling me, by sharing these experiences with me. That gift of positive energy, too, came straight from the source. She gave me her love of sunlight, taught me that it's the energy we take with us—all those things have been infused in my soul and in my music even before I was making music.

SPLASHKETBALL

Dad was a coach. He loved sports, creating teams based on people's strengths and honing those things so they could win. Getting a bunch of athletes on the court or field to play hard was his passion. My competitiveness and love of sports comes from him.

When Dave Chesney wasn't coaching basketball or baseball—his first loves—he taught history and civics as well as PE. My father was a big believer in getting an education, to understand how to put a plan in action. No matter what you were going to do, having the fundamentals of critical thinking let you make stronger decisions.

He felt strongly that whatever you do, do it completely. He wasn't one of those parents who put pressure on me. It was never about "the parent's ego." More about strategy, how you're attacking the game. His biggest bit of advice was probably, "Play with older kids, people who are better than you."

When you're the smallest one, you're struggling to keep up. You don't want to be the one who blows it. Then when you play with people your own age, it's a whole other thing because your skills are sharper.

Dad lived in West Knoxville, a world away from my life out beyond the city limits.

He had an apartment and a blond cocker spaniel named Brandy, who'd run up to me when I walked in the door. His life was different. Weekends with Dad weren't everyone sitting down to supper at six o'clock, *M*A*S*H* or *Hee Haw* on the three channels, and doing the dishes when we finished.

Cable was being installed in Knoxville. It was the earliest days of ESPN and *SportsCenter*, and that was all we watched. I remember Bob Ley, a journalist. Listening to him, I felt smarter and wanted to hear what he had to say.

Dad, also, had some of the greatest friends in the world, who included me. All single and in their thirties, they were living life wide open, without ties and having fun.

Jim Cogdill owned the local Dodge dealership. Back then, he didn't have kids, but he had a youthful sense of "What can we get into today?" I can't decide looking back if he treated me like part of the club, or if my presence gave them permission to do some of the stuff we got into.

John Staley, "Doc," was a doctor coming into his own. He'd been a local sports star growing up; played second base at the University of Tennessee. Not quite a legend, but people who knew sports in East Tennessee knew Doc.

Jim had a house with a pool, where everybody got together. Eleven, twelve years old, we'd go over there and play splashketball, basically basketball in the pool; it was very physical, competitive stuff. Listening to them trash talk one another, they let me play like one of the grown-ups. I loved that camaraderie.

Sometimes we'd go to the movies, see the pictures people were talking about. *Smokey and the Bandit* was one of our favorites.

I was consumed with sports. We had the best basketball hoop in the neighborhood, and I also played Pee Wee Football. Baseball, though, was the sport I had the best chance of playing, because being smaller wasn't as much a factor.

After a day in the pool, we'd figure out dinner; the men would cook steaks or throw something on the grill. Sports was on the TV all day, all night. Talk was about who was playing, which players were working, which teams were falling apart—that was our native language.

On those weekends when there were home games at UT, we'd all pile into Jim Cogdill's van and head to Neyland Stadium. Cogdill had a box, top section, first row. Dad and I would go, with Jim and whoever else he invited, and watch the Vols play.

The first time I walked in, it was Tennessee against Notre Dame. It was the loudest place I had ever been. Here was this stadium I'd seen on TV, packed with almost 70,000 cheering fans, all losing their minds for the Vols! Only that day, I was walking with my dad into the stands and finding our seats. I had so much adrenaline running through me, I could hardly breathe.

There was a famous local broadcaster named John Ward. He brought University of Tennessee football and the games to life for every fan across the state. He was massive to us, because he was our eyes when we listened to the radio, the energy and emotion. When he called a game, you felt like you were there. Now I was here, seeing it for myself.

There was a real sense of ownership in East Tennessee. We didn't have an NFL team; in many ways, that made our Vols' passion more intense. It was literally a piece of our identity. My friendship with Dad's friends was forged over college sports, rivalries, and talking smack. There is a bond that comes from this that's unbreakable.

To this day, I call Cogdill and Staley every Saturday morning "to get my bets in." I've been in Italy in the middle of dinner and walked out of a restaurant, had a taxi driver pull over to the side of the road outside Cabo, and been heading to sound check for the Rock & Roll Hall of Fame induction and sat in the car, making sure my bets were in before the games started.

This isn't big-time gambling. It's almost two decades of fifty-dollar wagers on the line and over/under. Not so anybody makes money, but bragging rights. I am, as I write this, $7,850 in the hole in fifty-dollar bets, but it's really about those bragging rights. I may get that number "paid" down, but that's not what Staley or Cogdill wants: the bigger the hole, the better the smack talk.

Bragging rights with those guys? Everything. Always was, and still is.

One summer in middle school, I went to Dean Smith's Basketball Camp at the University of North Carolina. It was my first time away from home by myself, an adventure. We slept in the dorms, ate in the cafeteria, and spent days completely consumed by drills, scrimmages, strategy, and how to improve as athletes, players, and teammates.

The conditioning exercises made us stronger. But even more, playing with kids who were committed to basketball enough to leave home for a week creates a different kind of focus. It was fun. It felt like the future. It also exposed me to people from a lot of different places, mostly from the South; everybody checking into Granville Towers had a different journey to get there.

That stoked my curiosity about people's lives.

Something else struck me. Sitting in the dining room during dinner, a crazy music video came on TV. Tom Petty, whose music I knew, was wearing the biggest top hat I'd ever seen. The guitar sound was pulled out of shape, sounded hollow. I leaned closer.

"Don't Come Around Here No More" was a trippy Alice-in-Wonderland video with all the sizes out of perspective. The guitars at the end, circling and thrashing, whirled almost like a tornado.

It made an impression. His whole *Southern Accents* made an impression. Lyrically, melodically, it was great rock music, but had a country soul to it. That was my life. It was his life in Gainesville, Florida, but it was East Tennessee through and through. That album and also "The Waiting" from *Hard Promises* had all the frustration, the urgency that rises from being judged without being known.

He spoke to me from a place I'd lived. Sitting in that lunchroom chaos, transfixed by Petty's strange video, I wanted to know more. Sparks land when you don't expect them.

We lived on a gravel cul-de-sac called Mynatt Circle Road. A dead end in Union County with a lot of land behind us, it was great for getting on our dirt bikes, taking off for whatever adventures nine-, ten-, and twelve-year-olds get into.

When you lived where we did, especially before *Pac-Man*, PlayStation, even MTV, let alone having the whole world on your phone, all we had in our lives was school, church, sports, and family. For me, a basketball hoop or my baseball glove was how I lived every day of my life.

When I was five and six years old, Mom took me to John Tarleton Park for Pee Wee Football. A bunch of little kids running around, we got to play a couple games at Gibbs High, where I eventually went to school. We practiced every day; those "big games" were the payoff. Playing kids in different uniforms, those practices gave us confidence and that thrill of competition embedded deeply. We were fighting for our team's "name."

My mom could tell how much I wanted to play. As soon as I was big enough to get on the field, she'd signed me up. There weren't enough practices, games, and scrimmages to consume me. When I wasn't playing organized sports, I was at the Wilsons' across the way.

Matt and Lance Wilson were twin brothers, about a year or two younger. Their dad was a coach, and they were really athletic. I could always get some kind of pickup game going with them. Our moms would turn us out to play—and we did. Until dark or dinner.

When I was seven or eight, Mom took me to Gibbs Ruritan Park and put me in Little League. I met Tim Holt, light blond hair and skinny, there. His dad was one of the coaches, so he was young, but already a seriously good athlete. He played third base or shortstop, and I was second base, perfect for becoming friends.

Sponsored by Harbison Auto Parts, who paid for our maroon jerseys with the white letters, our team had players from across the Knox–Union County line. Suddenly, I had friends who didn't go to Luttrell Elementary.

That meant two sets of friends: the kids I went to school with and the kids I played with in the rec leagues. Sports friends *and* school friends. Tim didn't live far from me. We'd get on our bikes and hang out.

Who knew Tim Holt would grow up, get a real job, then work with me on the road?

The smells of the ballpark, the oil and leather of my glove take me back. I can still smell the dirt in my socks, the sweat in my ball cap, even the humidity and mist that would settle as we played. I close my eyes—it's all right there.

When we were twelve or thirteen, the Wilson kids went to the state tournament in Memphis. Joanne Wilson, their stepmother, took us all. Even if I wasn't playing, we were friends. She took us to Graceland, Elvis's home. When we saw his guitar-shaped swimming pool, we were awestruck. Not a big house, it was where the King of Rock & Roll lived.

Joanne Wilson, who played guitar, saw the way I loved music. She taught me my first few chords. I'd pick up her guitar, and she showed me D, G, A, and E. I wanted to play, and didn't have my own guitar, but I knew that little bit. I was curious from singing in church, around school, even out in the yard.

Showing me how to place my fingers on the fretboard, to position the guitar across my body, I wanted to learn more. I didn't realize how important it was, just that I was hungry to know how to play a little.

TENNESSEE RIVER

My mom had me while she was finishing her senior year of high school. A young mother, she started her life with a lot of responsibility. First she was working at St. Mary's Hospital as a secretary, typing up the doctors' comments on patients' files. Then she decided after a few years to go to beauty school and become a hairdresser. She had that gift of fixing people up—literally, as well as their soul—so she put her talents to use.

I joke I lost my hair from her practicing on me when I was little. It's not a coincidence, I'm sure of it. I had very fine light blond hair when I was in grade school. Mom decided to give me a permanent to practice, though she swears it was to make my hair seem fuller. All those solutions and chemicals smelling to high heaven made my scalp burn and my eyes water, but she needed someone to work on.

A few years later, it wasn't funny when I was in high school and saw clumps of my hair when I took off my helmet. I'd be in the locker room, looking around, not sure what to think. It's disorienting, even embarrassing when you realize your hair is falling out. To this day, I'm certain it was those chemicals.

Dealing with the reality of losing my hair as a senior in high school sucked. There's nothing you can do. Once the shock wore off, then the panic, I realized a full head of hair is not what makes you *you*.

What makes you *you* is your ability to show up and be present. Finding something good in the day even when you're not feeling it is what defines you. I watched my mom go to the beauty shop every day, whether her feet hurt, her back ached, or she didn't feel well. She knew hairdressing was actually the business of making people feel good; such a people person to begin with, she was the best at getting someone in her chair and making them feel pampered.

From the moment she started, people would be soaking up those positive vibrations as she fussed over them. She showed me that good energy multiplies. It draws people to you, because there's nothing better than someone who makes you feel good.

Union County, Tennessee, was too far from most everywhere to draw the big concert tours. Sometimes we'd get an act who'd been beating the road up and wanted to make sure they got every last bit of cash before they ended their tour. That's when they'd finally get around to Knoxville. Occasionally, before a tour would've found its stride, they'd come through trying to tighten their show up; it was almost a dress rehearsal before they got to the major markets. Mostly, we didn't get to see the really big stars.

That's just how it was. I never thought about it.

That summer after Conway, Jones, and Haggard played

Thanksgiving night, there was a festival that was put together literally in a field in Maynardville, Tennessee. Long before all the massive three-day country festivals people are used to today, things like this didn't happen, especially not a few miles down the road.

For all of us in East Tennessee, the news that Alabama was coming to play near us was easily the biggest thing happening that year. I've forgotten the other acts, because all that mattered to any of us was the fact Alabama was playing.

Like George Jones, me and my mom—really my whole family—loved Alabama. They were rare because they felt more like us than fancy stars. They didn't dress up, wore their T-shirts and jeans. They had long hair and beards. They didn't seem to think they were better or different than us.

And their songs reflected that, too. They'd played in Myrtle Beach bars, so they understood making music to let working people have a good time, dance, and let off some steam.

I even loved the slow songs. Randy Owen's voice was strong, believable, and their harmonies reminded me of church. Everything about them spoke to who we were as people—a hairdresser, a lunch lady, a TVA worker, a young mom—when we'd hear them in the car.

When I heard they were coming so close—we lived less than fifteen miles from where this field on Highway 33 was—I started the begging and bargaining with Mom. I'd say I wore her out, but the truth is Mom wanted to go as badly as I did. Never mind the show was in a field on somebody's property, a quarter horse farm that was called Red Gate. I didn't care, I wanted to be there.

Traffic backed up for miles. We lived close and went early enough, so we weren't trapped in our car. Listening to WIVK—they were playing all the Alabama songs to get us pumped up for the show. Once we got close, people were directing the drivers into another, adjacent field where all the cars were lined up in neat rows. With our ten-dollar tickets in hand, we walked through the grass, talking excitedly, to where the entrance was.

It was one of those clear nights, no clouds anywhere above us, you could see the stars up in the sky. Just looking up, as we sat there with all the people, was gorgeous. All of a sudden, instead of constellations, a helicopter comes into view and moves closer, hovering over the audience.

I looked up. Randy Owen was waving from inside the helicopter to all of us. One of the most crazy, badass things I'd ever seen. Maybe ten or eleven years old, I remember going, "My God! This is the coolest thing ever . . ." I don't think anybody heard me because they were all looking up, cheering, and waving, too.

The helicopter landed in the field off to the side of the stage. A door popped open, and the band scrambled out; hunching low under the blades, it was Randy, Teddy Gentry, Jeff Cook, the three cousins who'd formed the band in Fort Payne, Alabama, and Mark Herndon, their drummer. Like something in a movie, like something rock stars would do. We lost our minds.

That move took the anticipation up 100 percent. Now they were superheroes, landing in a field in their helicopter. Who does that? We know they're going to get up and play all these songs for thousands of people who can't get enough of their music. My pulse raced, my head swiveled around. I wanted to experience everything that was happening.

They came onstage and played "Old Flame," then "Feels So Right." Swaying in time, everyone was humming or singing along. It wasn't rowdy, but a coming together of people who understood one another. It was a community built on people knowing that this music was about so much more than show business or being famous, it was about life, hard work, falling in love to last, and throwing down on the weekends.

They played all the songs we had listened to since their records came out. "Tennessee River" with its big chorus had everybody clapping in time; swept up in a song that was all about something that really was part of our lives.

I'll never get over the feeling. If Conway turned my head around, Alabama created space where I could jump up and down, feel part of it. One of those things I still think about when I'm onstage, that excitement I felt when I was a boy. In that field with ten thousand or more people like me, all crammed in and surfing the moment to the same songs with complete and total abandon, we were one.

We knew there was the Rolling Stones. We knew there was The Beatles. But they weren't us, and they didn't understand who we were.

But that night in East Tennessee, there was Alabama! That was *it*. They were not only the biggest band in the world to us, which they were in many ways, but they were ours! They looked like people we knew and sang songs that could've been what happened to us that day. They understood who we were. They reveled in all the stuff we did, because once upon a time, they did it, too. Southern, small-town, family-oriented, Sunday dinner, local high school team, and being damn proud of it, was what "My Home's in Alabama" meant to us.

FARMER, HOLT, AND HOBBY

Youth football practice was at Gibbs Ruritan Park. We didn't have goalposts, only white chalk yard markings. It wasn't a big community or a fancy park. Ten and eleven years old, we loved getting out there, doing drills and playing our Wednesday and Saturday night games against teams including Farragut, Halls, Carter, Powell, and Central.

Tim and I joke that David Farmer was always six feet tall, which isn't true. But there are young athletes who stand out. That was Farmer. When we started playing football with him in the rec leagues, he brought a whole other way of attacking the game.

Farmer lived seven, eight miles away, in Corryton, so we didn't become good friends until I started Gibbs freshman year. But playing on a youth league team, we knew each other.

That's the thing about small towns and being in the country: You may not hang out every day, but the sports kids all know one another. When it's time for high school, we were already friends. With communities the size we lived in, you know the bonds forged from a team's coming together are going to last.

I knew about Daryl Hobby (who started working with us helping Tim with merch in 2006) long before I met him. A senior when I was a freshman, he was the Eagles' catcher. An unbelievable athlete, he helped us go to a state championship. I was on the bench, but it was awesome. This was high school sports, where you wanted to annihilate the other schools for bragging rights, which mattered.

Towns lean on those teams, and the teams lean on the towns. When you're young, you can't wait until you're old enough to be on that field. I can't explain how excited we were on Fridays to go to school, because the football players wore their team jerseys all day in anticipation of that night.

To feel a part of something bigger than me or my family for the first time was overwhelming. We'd all worked so hard to be in this club, because not everybody who starts practices makes it.

Two-a-day football practices in really hot, humid weather is a lot. People were throwing up from dehydration and how hard we pushed ourselves. My junior year, Mom got up the second morning and made me a big breakfast of eggs and bacon. She was so proud, she wanted to fuel me for the day.

Big mistake. I got out there, during the first drills, and that whole breakfast came back up. I went, "Okay, lesson learned." We were sweating, soaking through our pads and jerseys; running hard, tackling, doing drills, getting knocked down, getting back up.

When you get knocked down, there's a bigger reason to get up than yourself. You've got a team counting on you. To learn, but even more to feel that at such a young age, is a gift. It was my first time feeling that. Head Coach Randy Carroll really instilled that, to believe in the team; he knew we were young, but these lessons would stay with us as adults.

Like getting on the bus and going to an away game. All of us—the coaches, the players, the cheerleaders—would get on that bus, and drive to Maynardville, Halls, Tazwell, and Seymour. We'd be fired up, whether they were bigger schools or not, whether we won or not, because we were going as one.

You learn about depending on others, picking up where someone may be struggling. You absorb that idea. I took those lessons into my life, especially the idea that everyone on the team matters because the team is ultimately who wins.

There comes that moment, too, when you realize no matter how bad you want to play, high school is as far as you'll go. That's why people crowd those bleachers, to remember their own moments and celebrate all the kids who've committed so much to it.

There's a picture of me in my uniform with my parents, one of the few of my mom and dad together. It was Senior Night, our last home game. All the seniors take this picture with their folks. My parents are both staring at me, because they'd never seen me that upset. I knew playing football was ending for me shortly.

My final game was awful. An afternoon match-up called the Bragging Bowl, it was played in November at Gatlinburg-Pittman High School. One of those traditions that meant everything to us, even if no college recruiter would care, we were playing for our school.

When that game was over, that was it. We won, 14–6 maybe.

I sat in front of my locker for the longest time. I finally took my shoulder pads off, and took the moment in. I didn't want to leave. I knew I wasn't going to play competitively like that ever again—and it gutted me.

I was so lost in my thoughts, I didn't hear Coach Carroll come in. This man had put us through hell, tested us on a daily basis, pushed hard and showed us what we were capable of. I am so grateful that he, as well as Coach Edmonds, Coach Walker, and Coach Anderson, pushed us.

Aware someone had sat down on the bench next to me, I was still. Coach didn't say a word. He didn't have to. We sat there, soaking in the enormity of the moment. We both knew it was over for me as a player. With a lump in my throat, I got up and looked at Coach Carroll, who'd been a driving force in my life for the last two years.

He smiled and nodded, saying "Good job" without a word.

We hugged. You can't stop a moment like that, you can't even make it pause. How many times had he done that? His showing up meant the world to me. I was losing something so important in my life, but I was keeping the lessons, which would sustain me in ways nobody would ever imagine.

My life as a football player was done.

"We gotta go," Coach Carroll said. "We gotta go."

BLUEGRASS

Summers and sports run together, measured as much by the bands we loved—Steve Miller in my friend David Farmer's basement, hearing Skynyrd and AC/DC blasting out of David and Bobby Ogle's boom box as they worked on cars in the driveway next door to Farmer's house, going to see this new country traditionalist Randy Travis, who wasn't much older than us, with Tim Holt.

That summer before college, David Farmer and I decided to lifeguard at Norris Lake, at Hickory Star Boat Dock and Marina. His family introduced me to water-skiing and life on the lake. They had a houseboat. David and I decided to stay on it that summer. Hang out, listen to music, get a tan, and get ready for college.

That whole summer is tethered to Steve Miller's "The Joker." When I hear it, I'm there.

Farmer and I figured we'd learn something about business in college, then figure out how to apply it. East Tennessee State in Johnson City wasn't as big as the University of Tennessee, but it was away from home. My cousin Sherry was going there.

With my mother working ten, twelve hours a day, I'd gotten used to being alone in our apartment, taking care of myself, doing my laundry.

My freshman year, I'd go home on Friday for football games. Part of me was holding on to who I was. But I wanted something different than Knoxville.

Sherry Monteith was a year ahead of us at Gibbs. She had David and I meet her at Poor Richard's Deli for our first beer. That was our introduction to college life. Poor Richard's became our St. Elmo's Fire—the place you met up with people, went for lunch or to see what was happening.

Marketing seemed like a good major. Not sure what I wanted to do, communications worked everywhere. ETSU also had something no other college in America had: an accredited program in bluegrass and old-time music. Created by respected bluegrass multi-instrumentalist Jack Tottle, it drew on the region's musical roots.

That took me back to being in my grandma's house when I was small, loving that music on the early morning television; it echoed in my soul. The idea bluegrass music was an actual course? I couldn't believe it. Having that kind of respect, it made me want to learn to be a better musician. Who knows? Maybe even play for tips somewhere.

I thought about being a music major. My first class in music theory squashed that idea; it was harder than any chemistry class I'd ever taken. Looking back, I wish I'd stuck with it.

Turns out dropping that music theory class was a very important decision.

Jack Tottle, Princeton-educated and a founder of the Lonesome River Boys, created the ETSU Bluegrass Band for students to play bluegrass and old-school country. Barry Bales, Tim Stafford, and Adam Steffey, who'd play with Alison Krauss in Union Station, were in the program, so I was playing "with better kids," like Dad said.

The first band I was ever in, people were patient. Tottle wanted everyone to join in, so we weren't all music majors. I was green. Barry Bales gave me the nickname "Timing," because I had none. Not a good trait for the acoustic guitar player.

Intimidated, because these were great musicians, I knew I could learn from them. Dad was right about better players. Even though I wasn't ready, being with them—the way they played—was inspiring.

Jack Tottle recognized how badly I wanted to learn. No master plan, just a real love of this music. I'd go to his house two, three nights some weeks, announcing, "Okay, I'm coming over and we're gonna play."

Our friendship was about learning and playing. I still don't do it very well, but we spent almost a whole semester on Doc Watson–style picking. I learned Doc's "Deep River Blues." We'd sit, Jack showing me where the thumb plays the bass and fingers play the melody. Complicated, but I was proud when I could almost do it.

Not very good, I was committed to getting better. I wanted to play well enough to fit in, maybe write songs. Music was now all I cared about. I didn't see it coming, but ultimately, it consumed me.

I'd joined Lambda Chi because a couple guys there played music; once I started playing for tips, I wasn't around enough to be a member. There was a keg upstairs, though, where you could always draw a beer, memorialized when Brett James and I wrote "Keg in the Closet."

Around this time, a girl in my twice-a-week persuasion class named Amy sat near me. I wanted to ask her out, persuade her if you will. I thought I'd impress her with a song. Back then, you had to write it, record it on a cassette, and give it to the person. Not thinking about class schedule, I left the song on her desk on a Thursday.

That meant waiting all weekend. Four long days.

When I got to class on Tuesday, she was seated as far from where she'd been sitting as possible. BOOM! My first taste of musical rejection, served ice-cold. No explanation, no thanks for trying. Part of me thought it was hilarious, the other decided to work on my songwriting.

I'd sit on the porch of that apartment Farmer and I shared with Tim Holt and play my guitar, sing, and get some fresh air and sunshine.

One day, a girl who lived in our complex named Sherry Odum walked up to me. "You know there's a place down on the Nolichucky

River, an old house they've turned into a Mexican restaurant where people are doing exactly what you're doing right now, right?"

I didn't.

"Chucky's Trading Post has tables in the front, pool tables in the back. People sing for tips. You should call them," she continued.

I did and was told, "You have to audition."

We set a time. I had a white truck, drove maybe thirty minutes to where that house hung out over the river. Turning the engine off, I was energized. It felt like my life was going to be different. I pulled my guitar out of the back and went inside.

I can't remember the lady's name, but she asked me to play something. I played "Tuesday's Gone" by Lynyrd Skynyrd, "Deeper Than the Holler" by Randy Travis —who was as big as they got—and probably a Hank Jr. song, because it seemed like a more country place.

I also did a James Taylor song, because who didn't like James Taylor? A great singer-songwriter, it showed her I knew what that kind of music was, too. She studied me for a few seconds, half smiling.

"How much material do you have?"

"About an hour, maybe a little more."

"You're gonna need four," she said flatly. "Forty-five minutes on, fifteen off. People are eating, so a lot will talk when you play. You can't take it personal."

"Yes, ma'am."

"You think you can work up some more material?"

I nodded.

"Call me when you do."

That gave me a reason to pull together a catalogue of songs I loved. It would be me, on a stool, with a guitar. Sure, it was a corner of a Mexican restaurant, but it was my world to create through the songs I chose. I played too loud because I wanted people to listen. I was booked to be background music for people who wanted to have conversations and eat their enchiladas.

But I wanted them to stop and watch me. The ones who weren't offended came up and talked with me. We'd have conversations about different artists, songs they wanted to hear. There were so many requests for "Margaritaville," I made a sign: "Requests $1, 'Margaritaville' $20." I can't tell you how many twenties I got.

With my tip jar, some nights I'd leave with $200. That was a lot of money. I could hit Taco Bell on the way home, hit Taco Bell all month and have some cash in my pocket. More importantly, it gave me a direction. The more I played, the more natural it felt. I quit going home on the weekends because I wanted to stay and play music.

One week night turned to two, eventually weekends, which is where the real money was made. Chucky's had a six-channel board. I started to learn what all the inputs did, how to make things sound as good in the room as possible. I wanted to understand how to get the most out of what was available.

I found other places to play. I'd rent a basic sound system, drive to Galax, Virginia, set up, and play until after midnight. I'd tear down, drive back to the music store, park, and grab a couple hours' sleep until they opened. When they did, I'd turn in the equipment, get my deposit, hit the McDonald's drive-through on my way to class. I was living the life.

I had the ETSU Bluegrass Band and the opportunities Jack Tottle created. We played the Carter Family Fold in Hiltons, Virginia, the first family in country music's homestead, a few times. I don't think most of us kids "got" it when we were there. Over the years, I've thought about what Mother Maybelle, A.P., and Sarah Carter created; how Maybelle took her daughters and gave the Carter Family an enduring legacy.

I made good friends in the Bluegrass Band. Talking endlessly about JD Crowe and the New South or The Seldom Scene, Marcus Smith, Shawn Lane, and I would rehearse all week to go to the Down Home. Wednesday night's "Open Hoot" meant anyone could sign up to play for thirty minutes. Some of the best bluegrass musicians had come through there, so it was a big deal.

The three of us were learning. It was Keith Whitley, Ricky Skaggs, Tony Rice; also Doyle Lawson and Quicksilver, The Seldom Scene. They were progressive bluegrassers, but it was also the music in my grandma's living room getting ready for school. My childhood soundtrack was suddenly the coolest music of all.

Like all college towns, there was a music scene. Tall Paul played an Ibanez guitar; a really good musician, fun to watch. Alex Ogburn played an Ovation guitar left-handed and de-tuned; with his rock star hair, he could play anything. There was Plain Jane Has No Date, a jammy rock band with the best marketing concept *ever*: Every week

APPEARING AT THE DOWN HOME
Thursday, October 11th
8:00 p.m.

MARCUS SMITH   KENNY CHESNEY   SHAWN LANE

or two, they became Plain Jane *Has* a Date, and on those nights, the beer would be free for a couple hours. Also, Stinky Finger, probably East Tennessee's version of punk, but more garage rock. Their T-shirts said, "I saw Stinky Finger"—and everybody wanted one.

And me. I was the country guy. At ETSU, "the Tree Streets" are where the Greek houses are, and a bar named Quarterback's BBQ with music nightly. It also had no ventilation and no windows, so two o'clock in the afternoon was like two in the morning.

Somebody knew somebody who wanted me to play for the guy who owned the place. By then, I had good enough chops, I could play for hours. Music had become my identity; yes, I was getting a degree in marketing, but barely. I needed to graduate, with grades enough to squeak by.

I played for the owner an hour.

"Can you start tomorrow night?"

With that, I was playing music every night. Quarterback's was crazy, because it was near campus. Back when restaurants allowed smoking, the place was literally a smoker. You'd breathe it in, knowing it wouldn't exhale out. Even my perspiration smelled like nicotine.

I'd get done at one or two, collect my money, count my tips, and talk to people for a few minutes. Then I'd drive back to the apartment. Tim and David used to say they could smell me coming in like a walking ashtray.

I'd go directly to the shower, throwing my clothes in a pile on the porch. I'd stand and let that hot water hit me. Twenty, thirty minutes, whatever kind of soap, or shampoo, it didn't matter.

I couldn't have been happier. I was soaking up everything I could. I was saving my money. I went to Classic Recording Studio in Bristol, Virginia, where the Carter Family recorded, and made some demos. I ran a thousand cassette tapes, called it *Good Old Boy at Heart* to sell, or use to try to get my foot in the door.

I didn't know why, but I knew I needed them. I was friends with a guy named Todd Daniel, my mom knew the whole family. Zane Daniel was a lawyer, a community-minded man who had a way of pulling people together. One of those people was Con Hunley, who'd had some hits on Warner Brothers.

Con had the voice, the charisma, the song sense. He was "in" the music business. To be at the Daniels' house, alongside someone who was releasing records, I realized regular people with talent could get into the music business. Watching Con play piano, singing his hits, struck me.

Maybe it didn't set me on my path, but when I went to Nashville, I thought about Con. If he could, why couldn't I? If he went to Nashville, what was stopping me? I should try to get some meetings.

I wasn't ready. I probably knew that, but I wanted to get started. I figured if I did some meetings before I was out of school, I'd have a head start. So, I'd get Tim or David to ride over to Nashville with me when I had appointments.

Nashville was more open then. I found Kyle Lehning, Randy Travis's producer, in the phone book. Reading album covers, you learn the names. Get creative, sometimes you get lucky.

When he answered the phone, I explained that I loved the records he'd made.

Kyle said, "Come out to the house. Let's hear what you got."

Pulling up to his door, it hit me. I'm meeting with the man who made "Forever and Ever, Amen."

We talked a bit. He asked what I was trying to do, and I wasn't sure. I played him a couple songs, left my tape. He thanked me for coming, gently told me I wasn't quite ready, but to keep writing.

I got to meet Tom Collins, the producer and legendary music publisher. Personally. I met Cris, his receptionist, too. She loved songs, and we talked about writers we both liked. Cris Lacy became copresident of Warner Nashville.

Tom Collins was a big deal.

"I love some of the records you've made on Milsap," I told him.

"Really?"

"Yes. 'There's No Gettin' Over Me'? The way that melody moves is incredible."

He told me stories, sharing wisdom about hooks and what makes songs work for over an hour. I think he saw how much I wanted it, loved the art of songs and what they do. Old guard guys live for songs, so a kid on fire for songwriting was worth investing an hour or two in.

Big deal though he was, Tom always had time for me. When things weren't working, running into him made me believe there was a place for me.

I met Jeff Gordon, who worked in the A&R department at MCA. He wasn't much older, but he'd listen to my songs, give me feedback. His boss was a woman named Renee Bell, who'd stop by and say "Hello." She didn't need to do that; the biggest songwriters were trying to get her attention as she was the portal for Reba and George Strait.

Jeff knew I had a way to go, but he was encouraging. One trip, he handed me an advance cassette. Back in the day, albums were previewed on high-quality cassette tapes; that was how people heard the music before albums or CDs were ready.

Too Cold at Home was stone Texas country. "Mark Chesnutt" the tape said. A pool of steel guitar spilled into the car; tapping the rim of the high hat, a voice falling a bit behind the beat lamented how hot it was outside, the reality of how frosty things were at the house sending the singer to the bar.

Every song was as good as that first one. There was the promise of "Brother Jukebox" and the far-reaching "Broken Promise Land." Even more rowdy, "Friends in Low Places" rolled out as a buckle-polishing two-stepper looking for its place in the world.

I've got a long way to go, I thought. If country music could be this straight up, talking to a certain kind of listener, I was all in. I couldn't wait to get back to the apartment and play it for Tim.

A few months later, Chesnutt played The Village Barn in Knoxville. Holt and I bought tickets, went to the show, and knew all the words to the songs. That merging with an artist because you not only know, but you feel everything they're singing is powerful. We were the only ones who knew all the songs.

That's when Jack Tottle announced the ETSU Bluegrass Band was going to Russia. That was around the world, another culture, another value system completely. What could they want with a bunch of kids playing Appalachian roots music? I was twenty-two.

We were excited, wholly unprepared for what Russia was in 1990. Mikhail Gorbachev was in power. We landed on a gray summer day and went to a stark dorm outside Moscow. The Cold War may've ended, but you could feel the tension in the air. When we went to eat, we were given cold borscht, cold pasta, and prune juice.

"This is going to be interesting," everybody said at once. Completely unprepared for this experience, our eyes grew wider every day. McDonald's had opened in Red Square; we were so hungry, we waited for over two hours for a Quarter Pounder.

We were there for music, along with students from Italy, Germany, and all over the world. We had two translators, Marsha and Luda, who helped us communicate. We played inside the Kremlin, with its unbelievable acoustics. We toured Lenin's tomb, walked in Red Square, took a group picture in front of St. Basil's Cathedral—places we'd only heard about. We were there.

We'd get on a bus, travel outside Moscow, and play at festivals, that was the big thing. People from all over the world were making music together. A lot of us couldn't understand one another, but we had music.

It was our first taste of traveling and making music, exploring foreign places, and meeting people who had different political and religious beliefs. Everyone grew up differently, but we played the same notes. Music transcended all the differences; that was such a lesson.

When I look out now, I know no matter what football stadium or amphitheater, the teams they love are different, who they voted for isn't the same, where they go to church is all different places. But the songs, that feeling they give us, they connect us.

Coming back from one of those shows outside Moscow, our bus broke down. We were tired and we were stuck. Standing on the side of the road, Marcus Smith looked at Jack Tottle and asked what we were all thinking, "Is this what it's like being out on the road?"

In a small way, it was. We were in school, we had our teacher with us, but we were far from home, making our way to the next place. Things go wrong, but they get fixed. It was the first time I experienced something like that, in a country that had a lot of tension.

And it's funny: When we were leaving the dorm, getting on the bus to go to the airport, we took a group picture. It had only been ten days, but we'd all really connected in spite of our differences because we could pass a guitar back and forth.

THE TURF

Graduation came in December. My grades were good enough to get my diploma. I knew the quadratic formula, the four Ps of marketing—product, price, place, and promotion—and that my destiny lay three hours away.

Fresh out of college, I loaded up my things and hit I-40 West on January 13, 1991, the day the first Gulf War started. I didn't have a plan beyond I had a dream and I was going to chase it. Mom figured I'd get it out of my system, then come home having tried instead of always wondering what might have happened.

Didn't know what I didn't know, but I'd met a few people. That was good enough for me.

When you move to town, you don't know who you're going to meet. Or what roads you're going to go down that you want to keep traveling. I needed to find out, so like a lot of people every day, I moved to Nashville. I got a place in an apartment complex right off Murfreesboro Road. Not much, but I could walk across the street to a country bar called the Wrangler.

The Wrangler was for people to meet up, not listen to music. There was a tree growing in the middle of the dance floor; people would two-step around it. I walked home several nights. As fun as it was, I knew it was a distraction from what I'd come for.

At Gilley's, Nashville's outpost of the famous Texas honkytonk *Urban Cowboy* was based on, I met a guy named David Lowe, who'd been in town a while. We started talking about songwriting. He could see I wanted to learn, write better songs, so we struck up a friendship.

David introduced me to Mack Vickery of all people. I knew he'd written "The Fireman" for George Strait, which was true country greatness.

I looked up to David, who was slightly older. He knew so many legendary songwriters and the way around town. I grew frustrated after a bit, telling him there was nowhere to play. I loved writing, but I loved getting up with my guitar and playing for people.

"I don't get it," I complained. "I need a place to sit on a stool and play. There's gotta be somewhere . . ."

He looked sideways over his beer. "Well, if you can take it, go to the Turf, or Tootsies, down on Lower Broadway."

"Take it?"

"Yeah, it's not for everybody. Some people think it's rough."

"Rough?"

"Yeah, most of the record people won't go down there, but there's real country music."

Lower Broadway then wasn't the party bus, glossed up, bachelorette festival it is now. The neon was old, there was head-in parking, and it was mostly empty. A lot of homeless people, hookers, down-on-their-luck folks; but it felt safe in a crazy way. Everybody kind of knew everybody, left each another alone. Like a small town, this was their world.

It was bars that were forgotten by everyone, except the didn't-quite-make-its, tourists who didn't know better, and street life. Earthy, maybe slightly dangerous, I loved it.

Such a different time. That seediness wasn't like anywhere I'd ever been. It felt magical. You could feel how much of the music's history was in the air. Neither polished nor slick, this was where it started. The Ryman, in rough shape, was being renovated after almost being torn down. She stood there proud, a witness in this abandoned stretch of country's past.

The bars were all dirty, but they had a faded beauty. Years of everything caked in the cracks, the carpet, you'd see signed eight-by-tens of famous people—sometimes before they were famous—taped to the walls. There were pictures of people who'd passed through town, this river of history that moved through these rooms.

Everything was yellow from years of cigarette smoke; some of the older pictures cracking. But mostly guys—sometimes women—would be playing George Jones, Hank Williams, and Hank Jr. songs for tips, sometimes with a story starting, "This is about the time that . . ."

This was the piece of country music kids like me didn't see.

This was Broadway the way Kris and Willie experienced it as broke songwriters, drinking on credit, that Hank did—and all the old Opry stars—sneaking across the alley for a drink between shows at the Ryman. *This* was where Jones had his Possum Holler, a bar with his name on it where he also hung out.

Live music filled the air. Every bar had somebody singing old country songs; a few had bands with streams of the saddest pedal steel guitar rolling into the street. Whether you were a businessman, the bar owner, a hooker, or a veteran with nowhere to go, it felt like every single person knew and cared about music. Strange, but it's what pulled them there.

I played the Turf Club, a fancy name for a rundown bar. There were ceiling fans trying to move the smoke and smell of spilled beer, a jukebox in the left corner for when people weren't playing, and a big cardboard cutout of George Strait in the back.

A basic stage with a six-channel soundboard, it had two big speakers on either side. I learned to set all that up, troubleshoot when it wasn't quite working.

Hardwood floor when you first walked in, the rest was dirty green carpet. The bathroom was covered in signatures, stickers, graffiti, and handbills. You'd almost overload on all of it.

The first shift of music was noon until 4:00 p.m., then it was 4:00 to 8:00 p.m., and the late shift went from 8:00 p.m. to midnight. But if people were drinking, you could stay up there until almost closing time at 1:00 a.m. I started with afternoons. You had to graduate to the later shifts where the people were drinking more and tipping better.

There was a guy named Jewel, long hair, dark mustache. He lived down there in his burnt orange van with his dog named Hussie. Everyone called him the "Jewel of Broadway." He was friends with Tom T. Hall, who was considered a legend. Jewel and Hussie came in every day to listen to me play; we got to be friends. He had a song he'd written called "Come Over by the Window," so I'd call him up to sing a few.

Next door was the Wheel, which always had their door—and sometimes their windows—open. The owner dressed like a star, wearing wild rhinestone-encrusted Nudie suits, with the biggest sideburns. Talk about pictures on the walls. Opry stars, country stars, but also wannabes, people who were never going to make it, like they're all the same, a country music time machine.

Everybody at the Wheel was a character. The ladies had on a lot of makeup, and you could tell they'd been there a long time. People who worked there were almost artists themselves; people came from all over to see them year after year.

My mom came to see me. She'd been to East Tennessee, seen the college bars, but this was much different. She was really scared I'd get stuck there. That never occurred to me. I didn't want to sit still; I wanted to play and get better.

Some people gave me compliments. You knew when they stopped what they were doing and listened, it was working. I'd play "It Ain't Cool to Be Crazy About You," see people looking over their shoulder. I was paying attention, because this was a different dynamic than Chucky's Trading Post.

People came to listen. If I was going to do this, getting past people talking, walking in and out, made me good at my craft. It was a master's degree in how to be a performer. If you want to hold the room, knowing what to say between songs is everything. It was all on me, sustaining the people over four hours, not a song or two.

Every one of those shifts had a different feel. You learned to read the room, to understand what the people were looking for. Knowing the difference between one person's "real country" and someone else's was how you made your tips. If I did it right, I made enough in one night to pay my rent. If I made $200 to $300 with another good shift, that was a month of Taco Bell. I'd have some money in my pocket.

I loved being a part of this long history and tradition. You couldn't imagine it, only be in the middle of it to appreciate the richness of these characters, the different way they lived.

For Johnny Cash, Kris and Willie, Jones, and all those ones who didn't become stars, this was part of the journey. The music was soaked in this culture, and that's what made it special. I couldn't get enough.

Today, the lot where Jewel parked has been paved over; it's the arena now. Ernest Tubb's Record Shop was sold. Having been there, I was in awe of so much of it. To understand why country's drinking or heartbreak, cheating or lust songs have such heat, it was lived on Lower Broadway when nobody was looking.

There's a freedom songwriters cling to. Abstract, but always seeking what's out there. You can't know what you're chasing exactly. When I'd moved to Nashville, I knew no one, really, and that was okay. I was focused on what I needed to do.

WHAT DID I JUST SEE

I'd met a girl in Russia named Svetlana, who was part of the larger group of performers. She danced with one of the folk groups. Very pretty, she didn't speak English, and thought my accent was funny. But there was music, and that's how we connected.

When I came home, a Russian interpreter at school helped me write her some letters.

Writing to someone halfway around the world, from a culture so different from mine, made no sense. I remember the interpreter saying, "Why don't you find a girl here to talk to?"

My answer was simple. "Because I want to talk to this one."

It felt romantic. What was ever going to come of it? She wrote about her life, school; I told her about my songwriting, getting my life started.

When I moved to Nashville, we were still communicating.

One day a letter came. Svetlana was going to Toronto as part of an exchange.

I was mostly broke, but I had my truck. I could have an adventure. Get on the open road and drive to Canada to see Svetlana. Twelve hours, 763 miles. What I would do when I got there, I hadn't thought that far. I didn't tell anyone, not that there was really anyone to tell.

I had two cassettes: The Seldom Scene's *Old Train*, with the blue cover, which I knew from my ETSU Bluegrass Band days, and Mac McAnally's *Simple Life*. I listened to those two tapes over and over, but the more I drove, the more I listened to *Simple Life*.

Mac McAnally's songs spoke to how I grew up. Another storyteller who understood growing up in the South, he embraced small-town values, how church and moonshine are part of the same weekend, believing in love. He wrote about complicated dynamics between people.

Mac was an artist the cool folks knew about. Alabama had a No. 1 with "Old Flame," Shenandoah, too, went No. 1 with "Two Dozen Roses." Nashville stars chased after his songs, and I could hear why. So human and personal, like Jimmy Buffett, his details put you in the moment.

For someone unsure of what he wanted from this trip, "Southbound" and "Down the Road" were perfect songs. Polaroids of a life I knew, a few of where I was trying to go. When I had some success, I recorded "Back Where I Come From," put it in my live show, and realized pretty much everyone understands the life Mac wrote.

I crossed the border in Detroit. While we didn't speak the same language, we had a spark. Maybe this would close the circle of all the correspondence, that quick connection that struck both of us.

Her teachers and chaperones thought she was going to defect.

They were not nice to me, but Svetlana lit up when I got out of the truck. I can't imagine what everyone was thinking: this kid from Tennessee in a pickup with my accent and their beautiful red-headed, blue-eyed student.

They were going to Niagara Falls, so they invited me to come along. I got on the boat with Svetlana—in those blue slickers they make you wear to keep from getting soaked. We were both so curious. Nervous and excited, finally this moment arrived.

Looking at the adults, you saw the hardship of life in their country. There was a weight—beyond suspiciousness about my showing up—to their life, which I saw more clearly in Canada. Their culture was so different.

We spent some time after the boat together, smiling and laughing at mostly nothing.

Not having expectations, you can't be disappointed.

When it was time to go, we hugged. There was too much space between us, too much distance, forget the language barrier. It seemed romantic, and we had to get it out of our system.

Driving back, it was over. I'd had this experience that was fascinating, but I knew we were finished. To be able to experience that at all, maybe that was all it needed to be.

Maybe it's the songwriter piece of me. When you're living life, you observe everything. You don't always know what it means, but you're absorbing it. For me, any time I'm in the moment—whether it's drifting or sitting somewhere reading or being onstage at Gillette Stadium— I'm a pretty happy guy. I try to find the good.

In Nashville, I was making ends meet. There wasn't any extra. I didn't need any extra cash because my energy went to creating. What money I had came from parking cars. I was making friends, and a friend of mine was taking a party bus to see Jimmy Buffett at Starwood Amphitheater outside Nashville.

I was broke, so he gave me a ticket and said, "Come on, it'll do you good."

It rained so hard that night, we were all standing on the lawn. We couldn't sit down, it was so wet. I didn't have a dollar to my name, couldn't buy a beer or a Coke, and I certainly didn't need any water. I was like Roger Miller said, "Fourteen dollars from having 27 cents."

Jimmy comes onstage, and it feels like the only place in the entire world he wants to be. He doesn't care about the weather; he shouted out to the people up on the lawn where we were, a few who were using the wet grass like a slip and slide.

In that horrible weather, he brought so much joy, everybody forgot. Whatever was bringing you down, he melted it with those songs. David Farmer's mother, Frankie, loved *Changes in Latitudes*, and I'd played so many of his songs in bars, I knew the music inside out. But standing there with my jeans and T-shirt soaked, I couldn't turn away.

Fascinated by how he turned the energy, it took my brain somewhere. "Fins" and "Cheeseburger in Paradise" brought the party, but "He Went to Paris" took a kid from East Tennessee somewhere far away. He always showed me it was possible to paint pictures with words, tell stories that held whole lives using melody to carry people away.

I remember going back to that tiny apartment, getting something to eat. My mind was overwhelmed. Not a great song or solo, my mind was consumed with how all the pieces fit together to create this bigger reality that everyone at Starwood was part of.

Lying in bed, I thought, *Wow! What did I just see?*

ACUFF-ROSE

Playing downtown had been a way to play. But I knew that was quicksand. David Lowe and I were writing some songs, making the rounds of people trying to get their feet in the door.

I'd written "The Tin Man" with David and Stacy Slate.

That's what brought me to 65 Music Square West. A steep pitched roof in the front designed to honor the Ryman Auditorium's steeple, Opryland Entertainment had bought Acuff-Rose, the publishing company Roy Acuff and Wesley Rose started. They were the publisher Hank Williams wrote for.

I turned the truck off, put my hands on the wheel. This was it. I'd spent months trying to have a make-a-difference meeting like this.

Clay Bradley, a young man from a country music business dynasty, dealt with new writers at BMI, a publishing rights organization that represents songwriters and publishers. He had been listening to my songs every few months for a year, encouraging me, but never picking up the phone. I was frustrated things weren't moving faster. He told me, "When you're ready, I'm gonna send you out to see some people. But you only make one first impression. Let's make it the right one."

I'd played "The Tin Man" for Clay. I could see it in his eyes. They lit up. A song I started sitting alone in that crummy apartment off Nolensville Pike, watching *The Wizard of Oz* and thinking about how all the characters got what they wanted; but the poor Tin Man didn't realize the heart he was so hungry for would make him hurt in ways he couldn't imagine.

In my song, I wished I was the Tin Man, wished I didn't have a heart.

Clay, who'd sent me to some smaller appointments, said, "Well, Chesney, I guess you're ready."

Like that, everything changed. I somehow knew that song would change my life.

Clay called Troy Tomlinson, a young creative director who'd grown up in a small town the same way I had. He'd been charged with reenergizing the company's roster of songwriters. Clay told him, "He's one of us." A meeting was set. Acuff-Rose had deep roots. I knew that.

A few days later, there I sat.

Ten minutes to ten. I opened the truck door, put my boots on the pavement, and reached for my guitar. Pulling one of the double glass doors open, I was met by a lobby that went two floors up to an open atrium. Pink marble floors. Everything that wasn't glass or marble was brass polished to look gold. Grand, it said everything about what success looked like.

A receptionist named Tandy, super bubbly, greeted me. You could tell she loved being where the songs were. I knew how she felt. I asked for Troy Tomlinson.

A big smile, sandy hair, Troy wasn't much older than I was. An older white-haired man in boat shoes, khakis, and a polo shirt was sitting in his office.

"I'm Kenny," I said, walking across this thick teal carpet. Extending my hand, each man took it—and looked straight into my eyes. They had firm shakes, but not too firm. Solid, not crushing.

"I'm Troy. This is Jim."

Jim Vienneau was a character. I could tell by looking at him, but I had no idea he'd produced important records for Conway Twitty and Roy Orbison. In that moment, he was one more person I needed to make believe in my songs.

The walls held certificates for their BMI Most Played Song Awards. In a glance, there was Hank Williams's "Hey Good Lookin'," "I'm So Lonesome I Could Cry," and "Lost Highway." All in matching black frames.

"You wanna play us a couple?" Troy asked, leaning forward. Not a lot of small talk, but I was there—I hoped—to get a publishing deal.

"Yes, sir," I responded. I didn't want to be too familiar. Respect seemed important, especially here. I slid to the edge of this green couch I'd sat down on. Flipping the clips on my guitar case, I opened it up and took out my acoustic, put the strap over my head.

Troy was looking at something. I looked down, smiled.

"That's an awesome picture," he said, nodding toward an old black-and-white photo. I'd used a hairpin, fastened it through the lining, to remember where I came from, to keep a piece of home with me.

"That's my grandfather JB Grigsby," I explained. "He worked for TVA, back in East Tennessee." Troy nodded. Everyone who grew up in the region knew about the Tennessee Valley Authority and what it meant during the Depression to working people in the Smokies.

I had my pick between my fingers, was finding my way around the strings. I'd tuned my guitar before I'd left the house, but I tinkered, stalling for a few seconds. Now or never was now. I looked down and started "The Tin Man." Written from the heart, it was pure and simple, the kind of truth only a kid can write.

They seemed to like it. Rather than another serious song, I tried a bit of that funny Keith Whitley/John Anderson kind of country. "Someone Else's Hog" was all about living high on somebody else's dime because the girl's got Daddy's money.

They laughed, thought the joke was funny. I relaxed some.

Troy and Jim made real eye contact. I saw it. They weren't going to offer me a deal right there, but I was hopeful. This was somewhere I could grow, take the experience these writers and businessmen had and become better.

I played a few more. I didn't talk much. I wanted to let the songs speak for themselves. When I finished, I thought that was enough. I was right.

Troy was friendly, maybe even invested. Very professional, he said, "We appreciate your time. Your songs are good. We'd love to think about this . . ."

I didn't tell them a couple other people were talking to me about publishing deals. Putting my guitar back in the case, I thanked them for listening. I knew this was where I wanted to be; I'd been studying the credits on records for years. I knew their writers Dean Dillon from his George Strait cuts; Buddy Brock, having success with Aaron Tippin; and Whitey Shafer's name from about everyone's albums.

Two days later, Troy called, asked if I wanted to be an Acuff-Rose writer. You think I'd remember every detail, but the only thing I recall was him asking if I wanted to come in and lay a couple songs down, to see how it sounded.

They say if a song is good, you can strip it down to the bones. I don't know if they were good or not, but we took everything down as basic as it could be.

I was a staff writer at the same company where Hank Williams had written. Making $150 a week to write songs someone else might want to record, I felt rich.

Six hundred dollars a month. I had to figure out where I could afford to live. I'd been parking cars at a place near the bottom of 16th Avenue called Toucan's. It was where people went to be seen. Its upstairs broke into smaller rooms where people could talk business, make deals, or disappear.

Everybody had lunch there: producers, label executives, superstars like Tanya Tucker and Wynonna Judd. MCA Nashville President Tony Brown, who produced Vince Gill, Steve Earle, and Patty Loveless, rolled up one day in a really expensive Mercedes with license plates that said, "BIZZY." Settling into the seat, that leather smelled and felt like success and a lot of money. People who were making it were different.

I decided I needed to quit parking cars. I was in the country music business. I wasn't outside the door, looking in the windows. I was a staff writer at Acuff-Rose.

Years later, Troy told me that he and Jim talked for a few minutes after I left. They agreed they liked the way my brain worked; my imagination and creativity went in unique ways. Troy said he told Jim, "We see a lot of young writers, but we don't often see one with the eye of the tiger. I don't know what will happen, but if we don't sign him, someone else will."

Something about Troy, who was raised in Portland, Tennessee, two counties north of Nashville, felt like home. Jim Vienneau, who didn't need the job but loved being around writers and artists, took an interest in the songwriters as people.

Buddy Brock had come from South Carolina with his friend Aaron Tippin, who was a rising hard country star. He took me under his wing. Like David Lowe, he saw I shared his dream and might need some dots connected.

Buddy helped me find a place. Out in Mount Juliette, down the road from where he and his wife had a house, there were government-assisted apartments. You had to give them proof you were making less than a certain amount of money to qualify. I sure did.

Gray brick, a couple rooms. It was cheap, and I kept it clean. I had a sofa, a small TV, and a bed. I had a folding chair that sat on the slab outside the door, with a cooler I used as a coffee table *and* a place to keep my beverages cold.

I couldn't have been happier. The Brocks would call me up for supper, and I'd go over for a home-cooked meal. Far enough out of town, I didn't go out chasing nightlife, get drunk and wake up hungover. Instead, I stayed home and worked on my writing.

Being the rookie, coming in with ideas was important. Asking more established writers to give you even pretty good ideas wasn't cool. I wanted to show I could bring something to the table.

Staying home had its advantages. I was talking on the phone to old guard songwriter Frank Dycus at 10:30 one night. He asked, "What's someone as young as you doing at home at this hour?"

"Nothing much. Working on a song."

"Well, c'mon out to the house. Let's write one."

Dycus had written George Strait's "Marina Del Ray," plus George Jones's "I Don't Need Your Rockin' Chair," which had every current country star who mattered singing on it. The real thing: He didn't give a damn about much except the songs.

He lived on a mountain in Union Hill, Tennessee, almost forty miles away on the other side of town. I was out the door before he could change his mind. To write with Frank Dycus, especially outside office hours, was a big deal.

I went to Acuff-Rose every day, hoping somebody'd pull me in on a song. Knowing how talented these people were, I realized their scraps and throwaways would teach me.

Acuff-Rose had a blue '50s diner breakroom. Bench seats and booths, a black-and-white checked floor, everyone congregated there before we got down to the day's business of chasing songs, whether looking for melodies, a turn of a phrase, or a No. 1 hook. To see a legend like Whitey Shafer sitting there, blowing on a cup of coffee, thinking about something, was inspiring. They'd take in a sense of you without saying much.

Whitey asked if I wanted to try to write one. He had a house in White House, forty-five minutes out of town. I drove out there excited. He'd written for Haggard and Keith Whitley, songs that examined human behavior. I knew we'd write a song melodically and lyrically that was authentic. Whitey was South Texas and I was East Tennessee, you don't get much more real than those places; "From Midnight to Daylight" nailed lonely people when the bars close.

I got the idea living across from the Wrangler, the working-class honkytonk where blue-collar kids hung out. I'd get up in the morning to get to work when I first got to town, and see all those pickups and small cars left behind as people found someone to spend the night with. When I told Whitey, he knew how many people were living that.

I was learning to trim it down, reach for the unlikely. I started to understand why "Don't bore us, get to the chorus" wasn't a clever line. There's an art to tapping a real feeling, or a moment that cuts into you forever. Brevity helps.

The thing I wanted above all others: to write with Dean Dillon.

"When can I write with Dean?" I'd pester Troy. I knew better than to stalk to the lanky, long-haired writer on my own. Reclusive and elite, he didn't need the likes of me badgering him to write.

With his Old West–looking mustache and way of carrying himself quietly, he seemed like a star. The girls loved him, the men respected him, and I—maybe—wanted to be him. "Unwound," his first real hit and George Strait's first No. 1, was reason enough to covet Dean's talent, but there's "Marina Del Ray," "The Chair" for Strait, plus the David Allan Coe single turned George Jones classic "Tennessee Whiskey."

He'd had an album called *Slick Nickel* that I loved. Back home in East Tennessee, they played it to death on our radio stations. He was our guy.

Dean Dillon was country music. Period. From Lake City, Tennessee, he was also steeped in back home.

"Troy, come on, I'm ready," I'd say. Troy'd laugh. Shake his head.

Tomlinson knew if he asked, I had to hold my own in the room. It wasn't about wasting Dean's time, which was very valuable, but wasting his creative mojo. Still, I kept on.

One day, Troy told me he'd played him "The Tin Man," told him there was something about me. Then he added I was from where he was. Dean actually agreed.

I started counting the days. I have always been early. Respect means not only showing up, but being ready when it's time. That morning, I got up early, humming to myself. I was writing with Dean Dillon, someone who ran on the same roads, drank the same water, watched the same East Tennessee morning television my family and I did.

I hit the highway and rolled into town, mind racing, thinking about a couple ideas I had to get started. Feeling three inches taller than I really am, I bounced out of the truck and into the building.

On the third floor, I headed down the hall for Dean's writer's room. The really successful writers had their own dedicated rooms.

"Hey, Dean . . ." I called as I hit the door. I stopped short, taking in the sight before me.

Cigarette in hand, Dean was staring out the partially open window across Grand Avenue, where Erv Woolsey, George Strait's manager, was pulling into his parking space. Dean was so still and so silent,

I stood there. In starched blue jeans, cowboy hat, his posture was like coming upon a crane in a pond, poised to capture something far beyond this moment.

He took a drag, held it in. Looked a quarter of the way around, as much to acknowledge that he knew I was there as to see me.

I'd pulled my guitar from my case, was clanking around on it nervously. I wanted to get started.

"Chesney, hang on," he said. His tone was quiet, undisturbed.

I didn't say anything, remained suspended in the moment.

"I'm gonna need a minute for my brain to get down on your level."

I didn't know what to do. Nothing seemed to be the answer; the comment was meant to break the tension; I thought it was hilarious. Dean started to laugh. I laughed, too. We stood there at 10:00 a.m. laughing. It was the beginning of an incredible friendship that I've had to this day.

CAPRICORN

After I did my first real demos, Troy and Jim sat me down. Writing my own songs, reworking others, the time I'd spent in all those bars taught me how to connect with a song.

"Kenny," Troy said. "We signed you as a songwriter, but we're thinking we might try to get you a record deal."

"Record deal?"

"If you're in, we'll figure this out," Troy said. "Just want to make sure you're all in."

Nashville's a small town. Almost the entire record business was contained in a four-block-by-three-block area, with a few random satellites in Berry Hill. Everybody mostly knew everybody—the town ran on creativity—and you never knew if the guy coming up to you in a bar was connected or a sleazebag with a line of fast talk.

I had a publishing deal, where I could ask and check people out. I was at a writers' night down on Broadway in a bar that's long gone. I'd played a few songs, drank a couple beers, was talking with the writers.

A guy named Rick Rockhill came up and told me he liked my songs. That felt good when you've got nothing going on. Then he tells me, "I work at a label called Capricorn Records. I want to give your stuff to some of our people."

Capricorn wasn't really in the country business. I'm not even sure I knew they were a real label. I may've told him "I write for Acuff-Rose." He may've handed me his card. I didn't think much about it. A bad record deal, I'd learned, was worse than no record deal at all.

But Nashville being Nashville, it wasn't long until someone got a call. Someone sent somebody at Capricorn a few demos. They might not have been in the country music business like MCA, Polygram, or Sony, but they were respected enough I was told to go over to 120 30th Avenue North.

"Take your guitar. They want you to play a few songs."

Back then, 30th Avenue North could've been Siberia. Near Elliston Place's Rock Block, Vanderbilt University, and Tower Records—and away from Music Row—Capricorn wasn't part of how Music Row business was done.

A brick building with a porch, they'd repurposed a grand Southern home as an office. I trotted up the front steps, guitar in hand, thinking, *Why not?* It wasn't like the big labels were calling, and I was ready to get my dream on.

Turns out so were they. Capricorn was being reborn, still a Southern label. Now run by Phil Walden and his son, they were signing

70 / HEART ♦ LIFE ♦ MUSIC

alternative/jam bands Widespread Panic, Col. Bruce Hampton & the Aquarium Rescue Unit, 311, Gov't Mule.

They'd also signed and were having some success with Hank Williams Jr.

Phil Walden, from Macon, Georgia, was a top-shelf music man. He'd created Capricorn Records, based in Macon, Georgia, as a label for musicians based in the South. He'd managed Otis Redding. He'd started his record company with the Allman Brothers Band, then the Marshall Tucker Band, Delbert McClinton, and Percy Sledge. That was the '70s.

Phil heard this guitar player on a Wilson Pickett record, asked, "Who's that?" When he was told "Duane Allman," he decided to go to Muscle Shoals, Alabama, and meet the long-haired guitarist. Impressed, he helped Duane build the Allman Brothers.

Not quite the same, but in that spirit, he was reinventing his label. Again.

"I'm here to see Don Schmitzerle," I told the woman, looking at pictures and posters of rock bands all over the lobby. Long hair, dark clothes, earthy-looking people. I wasn't sure how I fit, but I trusted Troy and Jim.

A well-dressed man with a lot of gruff energy came out. "Come on," Schmitzerle said, bringing me into an office off the lobby. Phil Walden was sitting behind a desk, wearing a $3,000 Armani jacket, expensive loafers, and the biggest smile.

He'd heard something on the tape. Now he wanted to see what I was made of.

"We'd love to hear you play some," Walden said after some "Where you from?" small talk. Expensive leather sofa, gold and platinum records on the walls, files, CDs, and cassette tapes everywhere.

If you'd asked me back at ETSU how my dream would come true, this would not have registered. Looking at Phil, who played a major role in creating Southern rock, his energy felt bigger than anything I'd seen.

I'd been around country success, but this was something else. Talked slow, thought fast; smooth, able to bring people to his thinking, Walden thrived on creatives, making things happen and creating scenes people wanted to be a part of.

I pulled out my guitar. It was what I'd been doing since Chucky's Trading Post and Jack Tottle's ETSU Bluegrass Band. I had a handful of songs I believed in—I knew Acuff-Rose would help me find some songs that could work. All I had to do was make these two executives believe. In a sea of young male hat acts who weren't appreciably different, I thought I was something more.

Between Rick Rockhill's endorsement, who was their radio mastermind, songs I'd written or cowritten—something most young acts weren't doing in the early '90s—and being comfortable in that room, I could see this legendary executive move from polite to really listening.

I was nervous, because everyone wanted it so bad. Many acts get close, but the deals don't close. Without staring, I could see his brain turning over, thinking about what he knew about country music, deciding whether I was the one worth putting their toe in the water with over some other kid they could sign.

I played "The Tin Man."

"*Saw a man in the movies,*" I sang, "*who didn't have a heart/ How I wish I could give him mine . . .*"

You could feel the attention become a laser. Simple melodies carry the most raw emotion. "The Tin Man" was primed to deliver. Walden tilted his head down, nodding, taking the lyric in.

✦ ✦ ✦

Walden came to the Turf Club. Knowing I'd have to sell myself to America, he wanted to see how I played to people, my ability to deliver live.

Why not show him I could punch it out with the homeless, hookers, rare tourists, and lost souls on their last gasp of the dream?

I don't know if the Turf had *ever* been a fancy place. Those eight-by-tens, signed, some smudged with lipstick kisses, made you think the place had seen better days. If you wanted plain dirt country, this was a good call.

Troy, Jim, and a couple friends were crowded around a table in high spirits. Phil Walden arrived, looking rock and roll without trying,

KENNY CHESNEY

with his wavy hair and subtle but clearly expensive clothes, and a sense of having seen and done it all but looking for more. Clearly, he was not a regular.

With him was Rick Rockhill, the man who'd come up to me a few weeks earlier. Harry Warner, who worked for BMI and was one of

Capricorn Records

June 30, 1993

FOR IMMEDIATE RELEASE

Contact: Mark Pucci
           Marcia Flowers-Simms

Capricorn Records Signs Kenny Chesney

Nashville, Tennessee: Phil Walden, President of Capricorn Records, has announced the signing of singer/songwriter Kenny Chesney to the label's country music roster.

Born in Knoxville and raised in eastern Tennessee, the 25 year-old Chesney got his start playing in clubs while attending East Tennessee State University in Johnson City.

Kenny Chesney will begin recording his Capricorn Records debut album in July at Omnisound Studio in Nashville with Barry Beckett as producer. A Fall release is expected.

As a songwriter, Chesney is signed to the Opryland Music Group and is affiliated with BMI.

"Kenny Chesney's incredible songwriting skill and pure country voice should ensure him a welcome reception at country radio," said Phil Walden. "We feel he has the talent to become one of the brightest new stars in country music," he added.

Walden's best friends, was there, alongside Clay Bradley. Worlds were converging.

If there was a moment when it came together, that was it: In a scrappy bar that'd seen better days. On Lower Broadway that'd been abandoned by all but the most derelict. With my publisher, my friends from BMI, and a man who was rebuilding an iconic Southern record company by once again working outside the lines.

We had a long, long way to go. But we were going.

ROCK IN YOUR SHOE

The way I grew up, I had a lot of women around me. My Grandma Lucy, a woman of deep faith, Kim and all my female cousins, my sister Jennifer, Aunt Missy, who was six days older, and Aunt Sharon, who was mom's twin sister. A lot of them worked at the beauty shop together.

There was a green linoleum floor my mom hated, six or seven chairs, shampoo sinks, a nail station, a lot of light and mirrors, and a reception desk right when you walked in. Styles Etc was a salon, but really a place people came, mostly women and kids, to feel good.

My mother loves people, always has. To her, everybody's got a story to tell, a heart to hug, and a smile that's waiting to happen. When I was in college, it was the first place I'd stop when I came home, to see

Mom. You'd hear all these women venting about life, what was good, bad, crazy; they'd gossip about you know who and you know what.

I spent hours there over the years, catching up or waiting for Mom to close up. I was so proud when she and one of her friends opened their own business. She said she'd gone to beauty school because she knew at some point she'd have to support us. What she did with that education was so much more.

Sitting there, even in high school, there were always *Cosmopolitan* magazines. I read every issue. Women would write in and bitch about everything, especially men and sex.

Part of being a songwriter is to listen, read, hear all the stories, watch the people and make something out of it. Styles Etc was real life, people, and stories in a place where the filters were off and women were telling it like it was to each other. Because—and maybe men don't know this—if there's one safe space where women let it all hang out, it's the beauty shop.

I was learning good songwriting isn't a bunch of silly cliches or phrase turns, packing something so generic together it means nothing. Nothing means nothing, period. The job is to take a slice of life, write all about it, slice it down to what matters, then cut that feeling wide open.

Songwriting was not a nine-to-five job. No matter how successful, all songwriters had cocktail napkins, matchbooks, blank checks some server gave them, or envelopes they might never open covered in a couple lines, a whole verse or chorus, maybe a few chord progressions.

Like a rock in your shoe, ideas are something you feel a little bit all the time. But that doesn't mean you're always on. I watched great writers sit there all morning, get nothing, and be in that diner-looking breakroom complaining.

They'd start talking about getting out of the room, because you never know what you might find. Sometimes that surprise element came from outside your routine. Sometimes that something was me.

Hearing their frustrations and stories, I realized: This is a life path. You can't get frustrated and quit; you get frustrated and get curious. Tinker, go hunt some other path. Don Sampson told me, "Songwriting's like fishing. Some days, you get one, or get on a run and get a whole string. Some days, you get nothing. But, Kenny, even a day sitting on the water catching nothing, especially if you're with your friends, is a pretty damn good day."

You'd see every songwriter in town at Brown's Diner, almost a Quonset hut attached to a double-wide trailer. Gravel parking out back, deep enough for twelve, thirteen cars maybe, they also shared a small paved lot with a convenience store and Friedman's Army Navy on the other side.

Off Music Row a couple blocks, the thick smell of cigarettes almost knocked you over when you opened the door. It was so dark, you'd blink a few times adjusting to the loss of all light, then realize it was plaid all-weather carpeting, rolled wood booths, and cafeteria four-tops. Ronnie Gant, Donnie Kees, Whitey Shafer, and the HoriPro writers hunched over greasy cheeseburgers with grilled onions, Frito chili pies—literally bags of Fritos split open with chili ladled in—*sweet* sweet tea, and coffee *only* in the winter.

A cross between an Elks Lodge and a frat house, there was sports on TV, the occasional french fry lobbed over tables, cowboy hats, ball caps, and a lot of hangovers being cured with cold beer and lunch for breakfast. There were a few lifer waitresses, and a couple young girls who wanted to be songwriters, slinging hush puppies, catfish dinners, and barbecue sandwiches and making friends with someone who might be a mentor and write with them.

Jim would take me to Brown's for lunch. He'd always talk to the servers, ask about their lives, what was going on. That was how I met Aimee Mayo. There weren't a lot of women writers at that time—Matraca Berg, Gretchen Peters, Sharon Rice—and she wanted to join them.

Aimee would write "California" on one of my early records; later "Who You'd Be Today." She'd go on to write "Amazed," which became BMI's Song of the Year in 1999. She ended up BMI's Songwriter of the Year that same year.

But then, she was a dreamer, pouring tea and laughing along at the inside jokes. She was absorbing knowledge like I was and learning that songs are everywhere, if you listen for them.

Brown's was cheap—and an equalizer. You might see an artist

remembering their roots, a big producer avoiding "the scene" at fancy restaurants, Vanderbilt kids, and people doing laundry at the Wishy Washy Laundromat across the street. But here, everyone was the same: hiding out, telling stories, and knowing they might spark something that could be a song.

PUT A SMILE ON IT

Phil Walden and Don Schmitzerle thought Barry Beckett would be a good producer for me. He'd produced Lynyrd Skynyrd for them. More importantly, he'd done *Maverick*, Hank Williams Jr.'s first album for Capricorn and their entrée into country.

Beckett, who came from Muscle Shoals, had also produced records for Bob Dylan, Etta James, Dire Straits, and Bob Seger.

Having done my research, none of it had anything to do with country music. Rick "Rocket" Rockhill told me, "I really trust Barry Beckett." Rick heard something in me I'm not sure anyone else did, so I decided to trust him.

Phil suggested we meet. Barry came over to Acuff-Rose. Things were happening fast, and seeing Beckett made it very real to everybody. Being a new artist, I knew we'd start with my stuff. I played a few things that felt more radio, then I pulled out "The Tin Man." He sat there, shaking his head as he listened.

"Play that again." Beckett listened over and over. "I know *exactly* how that feels."

That moment of knowing someone felt what you wanted them to feel is incredible. But sitting there with Barry Beckett and hearing those words? It was beyond. He looked almost into me.

"I wish we were recording tomorrow," he said. I could tell he meant it.

Beckett was a song man, a piano player, and somebody who knew how to work with musicians. Looking back, I wonder if he thought, *What have I done to deserve this?* He knew I was serious—about songs, recording, everything—but I was as green as they come.

I didn't know who I wanted to be. I was country, look where I grew up? Beyond beer joints and what was happening on country radio, I don't know that I was trying to reach past the obvious. We had a lot of great honkytonk singers—Mark Chesnutt, Joe Diffie, and John Anderson, having a second wave—and big stars who leaned traditional, but progressive—Alan Jackson, Brooks & Dunn, Vince Gill. It wasn't as crazy as it might sound. It was working, and I wanted to work.

We got down to looking at what we would record. We did some meetings with other publishers. Barry Beckett was an icon and you felt it when you walked through the door with him. Even he wasn't going to get some eager kid from East Tennessee "A" songs, not even at Acuff-Rose.

Acuff-Rose did something better. When they decided I might be an artist, they told the writers to start writing with me for my own album. We were trying to write the best songs for me to sing. We had somewhere to start.

"Tin Man" wouldn't be a hit from *In My Wildest Dreams*. It didn't go Top 10 on *All I Need to Know*, either, but Beckett believed in that song enough to carry it over to my second album, which was ultimately released on BNA.

A few consultants said, "If it wasn't a hit the first time, it isn't a hit now," never considering the difference between labels. Conventional wisdom was easier than listening.

Beckett knew. He did one extra-special thing for that song, too. He called Hargus "Pig" Robbins to play piano on it. Pig is in the Country Music Hall of Fame; he's the iconic piano parts you hear on Crystal Gayle's "Don't It Make My Brown Eyes Blue" and George Jones's "White Lightning."

Hearing something in my writing, Beckett seemed to have a sense of who I was: a hungry kid from East Tennessee. Between the writers at Acuff-Rose and myself, I cowrote six songs.

My friend Buddy Brock, who'd helped me find a place to live, and Kim Williams wrote "Whatever It Takes," my first single, which died at No. 59. Buddy also brought me a song—"In My Wildest Dreams"— he'd written with Aaron Tippin, who was having success.

But that almost wasn't the point: I was making records. Coming out of the Turf, I didn't really understand how sensitive those vocal mics were. I came over the top of them so hot, my country twang really emphasized.

I listen now and cringe. Putting my whole heart in there, you can hear it. That feeling you get, when you're singing with master

Who knew this was a glimpse into my future?
Christmas morning, me, my mom, and that plastic guitar.

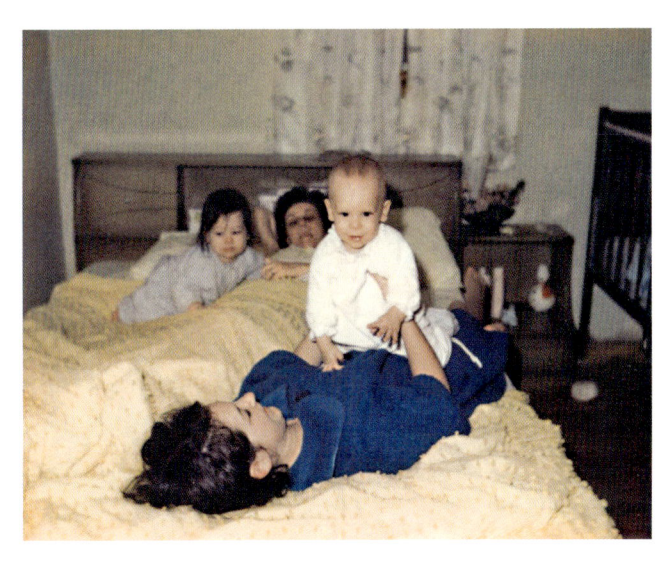

There was so much love in Grandma's house.
Aunt Missy, Grandma Lucy, me, and Mom.

I was always ready to go.

Myrtle Beach was my happy place.

"The Boys of Fall" started here.
Running through the Gibbs Eagles sign and taking the field.

Norris Lake. The Farmers' houseboat was fishing, family, water skiing, and growing up.

Gibbs High School graduation day.

The ETSU Bluegrass Band in front of St. Basil's Cathedral in Red Square, Moscow. *Front*: Lynn Becker, Stephanie Fletcher *Back*: me, Marcus Smith, Jack Tottle, Mike Carter

Acoustic Sunday at Quarterbacks. I had a gig and the very beginning of a dream coming together.

Fan Fair Week '94. With my friend Buddy Brock.

Passing time, waiting for the bus to get fixed in "Nowhere, Colorado."

Back where I come from. Press Conference at Neyland Stadium in Knoxville, Tennessee, to announce our homecoming party. *Left to right:* Dale Morris, Kate McMahon, me, Louis Messina, David Farmer, Clint Higham.

Neyland Stadium. My first stadium show.
I kept looking up at Jim Cogdill's box, thinking about all those Saturdays . . .
and feeling the energy on that stage.

Well past what the fire marshal would allow.
The *Keg in the Closet Tour* was one bus, one van, one small truck,
and three-plus hours of every song we could think of.
Gainesville, Florida.

musicians—especially when they're playing for Beckett—is its own kind of pressure, because you want to meet the moment. But you also are so excited, because it feels good.

"Put a smile on it," Barry would say every time I'd get in the vocal booth. "Make sure people can feel that smile . . ."

Barry made an even bigger contribution to my career outside the studio. Things were starting to come together, and I had nobody to help me beyond Acuff-Rose. Barry and I had been spending a lot of time together and he saw how much I wanted this, that I'd do whatever was required.

"You need a manager, Kenny."

I didn't know how to get someone who could make a difference. I knew I had no clout.

Even if Capricorn wasn't a major Music Row label, Mark Pucci, who'd broken all those Southern rock acts, was doing publicity, and media loved him. Marcia Beverly was my product manager; she was already thinking of ideas to make *In My Wildest Dreams* happen—and we didn't have a record yet.

And I knew Rick Rockhill would fight for me.

"You should really consider Dale Morris," Barry said.

"Dale Morris?!" I was stunned. I *knew* who Dale Morris was. He had the blueprint from Alabama, who defied every notion and rule Nashville ever had. He was so far beyond all of it.

"Yes."

"Barry, this man created Alabama's success . . ."

"Yes. And I can get you a meeting."

Then it hit me. If he could do all that with them, he might be able to really help me.

"Please. Get me that meeting."

DALE

By the time I came into Dale Morris's orbit, he'd been to the top of the mountain with Alabama and redefined what was possible in country music. Alabama not only won *all* the awards, sold millions of albums, had iconic hit after iconic hit, they'd created a new mainstream country star who actually looked like their audience.

They'd spent time in bars playing other artists' songs for people seeking a good time. Like me, they wanted their own music to matter. Alabama was high energy, the drums were rock and roll; Jeff Cook played fancy guitars and Randy Owen's voice had this believability.

Barry played Dale some music. He made Dale really listen to "The Tin Man," told him what he thought about the song. Dale told me that, half-joking, then got dead serious.

"Son, I love that song. That's good writing, really hits your heart."

When Alabama landed at Red Gate, there had been a fifth person. A man with white hair, I figured might have been someone's father. Over time, I realized their manager had been the one to see around corners, didn't do business the way everyone else did, made a space for a band who'd shown up looking like their fans. He didn't care about anything but getting the music to the fans—and that was me, standing in a field, waiting for Alabama to arrive.

This is one more example, I believe, that it's all written down—there are guardian angels pushing us together. When you move to Nashville, you don't know who you're going to meet. So many people meet "advocates" who are dead ends, and that's the end of their dream.

I met David Lowe, Clay Bradley, Troy Tomlinson, Rick Rockhill, Phil Walden, Barry Beckett. Each led me to the next. And now Dale.

Dale, sitting there in an expensive jacket the way most people wear a T-shirt, leaned across the table, asked me about my dream. He wanted to know what it looked like. What a question. Nobody'd ever asked me that.

He also asked hard questions, really digging in on what it took. He wasn't fearless, but forthright. This wasn't a game. He didn't need me, obviously.

"How hard are you willing to work?"

"How far will you go when it's so hard and it's not happening?"

I would have said anything to get Dale Morris to manage me.

I literally craved work. That was where we would connect. It wasn't saying what he wanted to hear, it was owning what I'd give to make music happen.

We talked about country music. Even more than Alabama, how songs and charisma were such a part of it, that spoke to country people.

DALE / 87

He told me his story. The similarities emerged. He was from South Carolina, another small Southern town with heart and people who all knew one another. He worked hard, to build a life, to create something more. He'd been a salesman, and he had that used car salesman thing where he could slap you on the back, be a good ole boy like your best friend.

He loved music, made friends, some people thought he could be a manager. He started with Billy "Crash" Craddock, doing booking, picking up Jerry Lee Lewis. Successful, but he wanted something more. He'd seen a band in Myrtle Beach, who'd put out an independent record. They needed help.

Dale applied himself. Once he and Alabama got going, they were in it together. When he realized arenas weren't paying country acts like the rock bands, he took his band to the fields. Literally, set up a stage, charged a fair price for the fans, and tripled their money. Red Gate was one of those shows.

I sat there mesmerized.

He talked about rewriting the rules, expectations, the game. He did have the blueprint. Here was this polished, seasoned man who not only didn't need me, he didn't need *anything*.

Classy, grateful, and humble, he knew how to make deals and close. I had a friend who called him "Make a Deal Dale."

He was raw, too. No airs, just unfiltered honesty about how rough it could be. He had relationships with everybody: labels, radio stations, big promoters, TV people, and publishers, but also the fair buyers, the country bar owners, the folks out in America who held careers together. We were gonna need them even more.

I didn't bother meeting with another manager.

Dale loved the game, and he loved coming up with new ways to do it. If I was willing to work as hard as I said, maybe I was the kid who'd let him do it all over again.

He didn't believe in contracts. Didn't have one with Alabama, didn't need one with me.

He said, "Let's do it."

WILDEST DREAMS

Rick Rockhill was head of promotion. That also meant he was the promotion team, with backup from a woman named Tammy Brumfield. He had Hank Williams Jr. and me; that was "the Country Division."

He'd spent decades in pop promotion. They called him "Rocket" because he'd had a hand in breaking Elton John's "Rocket Man." Before moving to Nashville, he'd gotten out of the business. Phil Walden got him back in.

Since Capricorn didn't have a country promotion department, Rick hired six indie promotion companies and turned a dozen indie promo people loose. To get everyone to feel invested in this unknown kid, when I signed my deal, Rick and his wife, Buffy, had all of them, plus the Capricorn staff, over to their ranch house in Green Hills. He created a belief: "Together, we can do this." Even though the odds were against us.

"Rocket" and I would hit the road, visiting radio stations where nobody cared, trying to make them like us. We knew no one, but we made some friends as we went. People didn't care we were there, but we connected.

Many days I'd go to the office, where Rick, Tammy, and I worked the phones. If they got lucky and someone would talk to me, I'd jump on their call, say "Hello," tell them why I loved country music, talk about the legendary Barry Beckett, ask about their families or what was going on at the station.

I didn't understand what an independent label meant, so it was confusing.

Les Acree, at Knoxville's WIVK, played the hell out of *In My Wildest Dreams*.

Lara Starling in Macon, where Capricorn started, was great to us. Bob Sterling at WUSY in Chattanooga, another East Tennessee powerhouse, gave us real airplay. Completely random, Debbie Turpin, at a station in Salt Lake, played the almost gospel country "Somebody's Callin'" like it was the new Alan Jackson record. Every scrap or nibble meant the world; so many stations never listened.

It was so rough that Capricorn publicity head Mark Pucci sent a press release: "Kenny Chesney Cracks the Top 75." Pucci was a music guy; I'd hear him talking to writers about a guitar solo on one track, how Beckett felt about "The Tin Man."

Mark swore we got some good press. Tower Records' *Pulse* magazine raved about *In My Wildest Dreams*. But I wanted to hear my records on the radio. I wanted to have hits like a lot of other new acts were having.

Dale and I would go to lunch after lunch, and I'd vent about what wasn't happening. Dale'd remind me it was about the build, a step at a time—and those steps matching where we actually were. We'd sit in the stucco Granite Falls in midtown, the entire industry swirling around us, and he'd stay so focused. People would come by, ask about business; he'd crack a big grin, say, "Business is great."

They'd leave. He'd return to what he was saying, reinforcing the idea things may be given to some, but that's not what we were doing.

"Kenny," he'd say, taking my scowl in, "those things don't last. They're not built on anything. You can't ask people to care if there's nothing to care about. That's why we build it."

Almost three years out of college, all I could think was, *Why isn't it happening?*

Having played sports that were hard, I understood putting everything in, getting beat up, the physical pain of striving. There's a psychology to being tough enough to stay in. This felt like something else.

Thanks to Les Acree in Knoxville, people back home believed I had something going on. He played every one of my singles as if they were the hottest records in the country. My family and friends heard "Whatever It Takes," "The Tin Man," and "Somebody's Callin'" as if they were actual hits. They'd call me, excited, saying, "I heard you on the radio. You're taking off."

I didn't have the heart to tell them.

Mom knew. She always did. I was home, visiting. We were talking in the kitchen. She was concerned. She'd seen me play in Johnson City, where people talked while they ate their enchiladas. She'd listened to my stories—chasing a publishing deal, the characters at the Turf, songs I was writing. She probably wondered when I finally told her I was being paid $150 a week by Acuff-Rose. But she also felt my joy.

She felt my frustration over these months, hoped more things would be happening.

"Kenny, are you sure? You know you can always come home."

I looked at her. Who loves you like that?

"Mom, I can't. I *am* going to do this. Whatever it takes, however hard I have to work. It's maybe not happening as fast as I want, but Dale says the things that take time to build are the ones that last. I want to be in this for the long haul."

I could feel water in my eyes. I was tired. I was learning the deck was stacked against us.

"You sure?"

"I am," I said, blinking back tears.

"Then, Kenny, we will never talk about it again. I promise."

Before we had enough work to have a bus, I got booked to open for Patty Loveless at Knoxville's Tennessee Theatre. An artist's artist with

WILDEST DREAMS / 93

great song sense, she wasn't flashy, didn't play the sexy female game, though she was damn sexy.

Built in 1928, the Tennessee Theatre is a beautiful National Registry of Historic Places building. Pulling up in a loaner bus, almost looking "the part," I was a jumble of emotions. Thrilled to open for an artist I respected in this historic theater. Excited to play a real show with an actual band in front of my hometown. But also sad, because I wanted do this every day; I wanted my name on the marquee.

We didn't have much to unload in front of all Loveless's gear. We set up quickly. For some reason, we sound checked first. It was fine; I don't think any of us knew enough to know any better.

When Patty came out, she and her band were serious about levels, how each sound was processed. She had a fiddle, a steel guitar, the whole deal—and a voice straight out of the Smoky Mountains. Me and the band looked at one another.

We had a ways to go, but man, we were here. I soaked up her whole sound check. Someone brought me onstage to say hi, which is always odd and awkward. Artists are working, their minds are usually somewhere else. Patty, with her red hair and kind smile, had had a scrappy career. She knew all the bumps ahead of us. When she looked at me, I could tell she saw a kid with a dream, and she knew that could go a lot of ways.

In the hallway after sound check, her acoustic guitarist was standing there. He'd sung like a bluegrasser. I walked up, complimented his Martin guitar. He held out his hand, "I'm Tim Hensley." We talked a bit.

Seven years later, I'd hire Tim to be part of my band.

Because WIVK had been so good to us, people knew a few songs. We got up and played our set. We hadn't been together long enough to even be good, but we were fine. Mostly, it was a rush, a blur, telling the radio station "thank you" for their support. The people who came to see Patty Loveless appreciated we were a true country act. All in all, a fine way to debut.

After the set, I went out to the lobby. Capricorn had sent some twelve-by-twelves, what was called "a flat," a thin cardboard of an album cover record stores used for displays. We had some black-and-white pictures, too. I sat and signed, visited with everyone who came through after Patty played.

We had just enough airplay, and there were enough chain clubs as well as iconic bars, including Denver's Grizzly Rose, Chattanooga's Governor's Lounge, and Fort Worth's Billy Bob's, we could work. They needed acts at a reasonable price, so we could play them once, twice a year.

WILDEST DREAMS / 95

Mark Chesnutt, who'd had success with "Bubba Shot the Jukebox" and "Too Cold at Home," had become a really successful honkytonk star. I can't tell you how many times we'd pull up and see "Kenny Chesnutt" or "Mark Chesney" on the marquee. It made me crazy, because I was Kenny CHESNEY. I didn't realize then the club owners might be nervous and hoped people wouldn't know the difference and trick another hundred into buying tickets, so they could sell more beer.

Around that time, a kid going to Belmont University, who wanted to be a manager, was also looking for his shot. Colleges offering music business degrees weren't common. Smart kids knew the value was interning at the actual companies.

Clint Higham had been chasing his dream since he was eleven years old. Stalking artist managers for Tammy Wynette and Barbara Mandrell at local Northern California hotels, he asked everything about what they did. He knew he wanted a career handling talent.

Dale recognized that desire in the sandy-haired college student. He gave Clint a shot as an assistant around the booking agency.

One day, Dale introduced us; said, "This is your guy."

I didn't know what that meant. Dale was my guy. Clint went to work immediately, getting me all kinds of bookings. Without meaningful hits, that wasn't easy. We played a lot of smoky strip mall honkytonks, now long gone; did a lot of county fairs—sometimes using flatbed truck beds as the stage.

Clint would batch-sell our shows to Rich Mishell and Bob Romeo, who promoted country festivals. George Moffatt, whose Variety Attractions bought the talent for communities and smaller fairs, worked practically wholesale. "Buy nineteen shows, twentieth is free."

Catering, usually flat meat and a promise of "the gals cooked up something real good in the crockpot," didn't get more down-home. George understood the kind of people my family back in Tennessee were because those were his kind of people, too. We played a lot of shows for him in campgrounds, fields, and tiny outdoor arenas in those years.

By then, I had found "the Iron Lung," a black Prevost tour bus so old, it pumped diesel fumes into the back lounge. We had twelve bunks, fourteen people, and a tiny trailer. When we pulled up, nobody cared. But we did. We were making music, pranking one another, and learning how to travel on the road and play for people.

We had fun, no matter what. No satellite TV, no PlayStation. VHS movies, a lot of music being played, smack being talked. Like a submarine, it was our world cut off from everyone else as we rolled down the highway to the next show.

Sometimes, the next show was the only show. One of Clint's first bookings was a 4-H fair in Plentywood, Montana. It was 1,547 miles away, almost a twenty-four-hour drive if everything went well.

Months away, Clint could come up with some "routing" gigs along the way to even out the cost of the run. It was an unlikely choice for an isolated date. A small town of less than 2,000 with a small high school, they had an AM radio station that played country music. It was a lot like where I grew up. There was plenty of time to book a fill-in show or two. Sure, let's do it.

Suddenly, a month out, and there's nothing. No club gig, no fair date.

A week away, still nothing.

Before getting on the bus, I walked into Clint's office. Annoyed, I said, "Okay, I'm going to Montana."

We took a picture, Clint and I holding up the deal memo before I left. I was upset about it, but the truth was: no one would have us. Looking back, that was the best it was going to be. Clint did everything he could with what he was given at the time. But nobody wanted us.

I drove all the way to Plentywood, Montana—up 94 West, across Minnesota, North Dakota, almost to the Canadian border—to play seventy-five minutes, pack up, and go home. We made $1,500. It probably cost me with fuel, show pay, per diems, and the bus, close to $4,000. And almost four days of travel.

Morale wasn't great. Frustrated because I'd thought—and I laugh now—you put a record out, people played it. Learning how the game worked and how hard it is was tough. Accepting there was only so much I could do, but showing up anyway meant I was still in the game.

We'd had a gig somewhere in Rhode Island with a day off before another show in Maine. I asked the driver, "If we swing through Boston, could you make that work?" He nodded.

I'd met Ginny Brophy, of WKLB, at an industry event. I'd kept her card. It was a long shot, but I called her from a truck stop as we were heading her way. No label, no indie promo guy, just me, my guitar, and, of course, my tour bus.

"You think I could stop by?" I asked when she picked up the phone.

She started laughing, "Where *are* you?"

"About thirty minutes out . . ."

"And you want to come by?"

"Yes, ma'am. If I can."

"Well, come on."

My driver pulled up to the front door. I went down three steps and hit the sidewalk. Ginny was waiting on the curb with a big smile on her face. Clearly, she thought I was crazy, but she respected the fact I'd picked up the phone and called.

I went up to her office, stacked with CDs and cassette tapes of records that weren't even out yet, pictures and award plaques from Trisha Yearwood, Brooks & Dunn, and Alan Jackson. She showed me to a chair, and we talked about music, our families, who she thought was coming on strong, the Red Sox. She may've been in Boston, as urban a city as there is, and I was from a rural town in East Tennessee, but we loved what was in the music.

She put me on the air, talking to the morning drive disc jockey for a bit. They played a few songs off my album. It might've been a couple hours, but it made me feel like—whether she added my songs or not—there was a place for me.

More rejection ahead. Indifference in some ways is worse than being hated. At least with hatred, you get something back. Dale drilled into me: You quit and you're done. This isn't about now, it's the long run that matters.

The band and I kept pushing. When I was out with Alabama, I'd sit and sign pictures and T-shirts after playing my thirty minutes. If people came up, I'd have a moment of real interaction; they'd remember, tell their friends. It wasn't a swarm, it was thirty, thirty-five, maybe fifty people a night, but the numbers add up. If they tell a friend, or two . . . Next time, it's better.

On a good night, we might sell enough merch—whether T-shirts, CDs, or pictures—to pick up a thousand dollars. I was going in the hole, and tired of being broke. Some nights, that extra thousand dollars is what put gas in the tank to get down the road.

And then there was Fan Fair, nothing like CMA Fest today. Held at the fairgrounds, artists set up booths in the livestock barns—posing for pictures and signing autographs. Tower Records set up a record store in one of the buildings so people could get CDs and cassettes for their favorite artists to sign.

Tower also put a stage in their parking lot and used artists as bait to lure the fans into their store. The fans came because they could hear music and get close to the artists playing.

While Capricorn wasn't "a major," the label was practically across from Tower Records' exit. Having a lot of bands college kids liked, they knew the staff; they got me one of those very coveted slots. I could show people how much fun music can be. "Whatever It Takes" was my new single; these people understood that thinking.

When I got done, I made a line to where I could sign people's records outside the building. I didn't want anybody leaving for something else. People lined up! They were buying copies of *In My Wildest Dreams*, walking up and asking me to sign it.

Looking each person in the eye, thanking them for supporting my music, I sat there over an hour and a half. The other acts were done, darkness was falling. I looked around, not quite sure what had happened.

Tim Holt, who'd come over from Knoxville to help my then-assistant Cheryl Bevis with my very basic booth, couldn't believe it, either. I don't know if they ran out, but Tim seemed to think they'd sold over a hundred CDs. What made that powerful, the people in the parking lot weren't from Nashville, but all over the country. If they liked my music, they'd go home and spread the word.

A week, maybe ten days later, I received a typewritten letter from Martha Sharpe, the head of A&R at Warner Brothers Nashville. She was the woman who'd signed Randy Travis, one of the most respected executives in town. Between that parking lot show, our booth, and the buzz, I'd ended up one of the biggest record sellers at Fan Fair—and she wanted to acknowledge everything I was doing for country music, and wished me luck.

I wish I still had that letter.

I was proud of that record Barry Beckett made on me; there were some great songs. We were swimming upstream. I wouldn't take it back because it molded me. Taught me to work, not for the outcome, but the music and people you played for.

It was hard work getting mostly nowhere. But that discipline and work ethic was ingrained in me from my family, my mom—as a beautician running her business—and my father, as a coach.

It wasn't an epiphany, but no matter what happened, I couldn't give up, only show up—and pay attention.

Growing up, like all kids in the South, Lynyrd Skynyrd was a big deal. More than "Freebird" and "Sweet Home Alabama," songs like "Simple

Man," "Tuesday's Gone," "Curtis Lowe" were etched into my soul. It's honestly why the drums and the guitars are what they are now in my music.

Frustrated after many months, we were booked into a small theater in Jacksonville, Florida. I bet the place held 2,000, maybe even 2,500. We'd sold maybe 1,000 tickets, which meant playing to a pretty empty house. You try not to focus on all those open seats and really give it to the people who cared and came out.

This was Skynyrd's hometown, and they were on my label. One day while I was making radio calls, I'd seen a poster in Phil's office for their *Endangered Species*. I'd asked if I could have it.

"No, you can't," he said. "Not until I have all the guys sign it for you."

That was Phil Walden, always wanting to do something kind. He did, too. Had it signed, framed, and gave it to me a month later. It still hangs in my house.

So me and the band are in Skynyrd's hometown, and it's another one of those nights. David Farmer, my childhood friend who'd left life as vice president at a credit union to run away with the circus, walks on the bus as we're trying to psych ourselves up.

"You're not going to believe this . . ."

It couldn't get any worse. There was no airplay, no story in the paper.

"Gary Rossington, Johnny Van Zant, and Artimus Pyle are on their way down here."

Everybody's jaw dropped.

"You're kidding," I said. Phil knew we were mentally hanging on by a thread.

Lynyrd Skynyrd cut into our lives; David and I weren't that far removed from seeing them at the Knoxville Coliseum, one of the first concerts we went to without our parents. They were heroes to us. Their songs hit hard, but told stories about our lives.

They were headed our way.

They came, watched the show, looked like rock stars, high-fived us all. Gary Rossington, especially, told all kinds of stories about starting out, touring when they were scraping by and crammed in a station wagon. It wasn't very different from what we were doing. Although they'd become one of the most iconic bands of the '70s and '80s, maybe ever.

That visit inspired us to keep working.

Those dreaming-with-Dale lunches—how it would be, what it would take—eventually turned to a hard truth. As much as I respected Phil Walden and what he'd done, it wasn't going to happen on Capricorn Records.

Dale told me he was going to talk to Phil.

I convinced Dale to let me do it. Phil had believed in my songs; I felt I owed it to him to look him in the eye. I also felt confident I could ask in a way he'd understand.

Phil knew we weren't competing. I think he was a little uneasy and disappointed, too, in what was happening when I asked, "Can I come see you?"

Less than two years after walking out of that office with the Lynyrd Skynyrd poster on the wall, I was walking in to say, "Let me go." Sad, but deep down, I had to be honest with myself—and him.

Phil was nervously moving papers around his desk when I walked in. Looking up, he said, "Tell me what's up. What's going on, Kenny?"

"Not much," but we both knew better.

"Tell me something good," he volleyed back.

It was football season. It was a Thursday, and Tennessee had a game that weekend. "The Vols play Saturday, that's good."

He laughed. Moments like these are hard, but inevitable. He had a clock I swear I could hear ticking.

"Phil, you and I both know we're not competing like we want to. Your guys are working so hard, really bringing it. But . . ."

I paused. Get to the point.

"I'd be grateful if you'd release me."

I doubt he was surprised, but I know he was disappointed. When Phil Walden believed, he believed deeply.

It was the longest ten seconds of my life.

He pressed his lips together, leaned forward a bit over all those papers on his desk. He wasn't doing drama, but weighing the moment.

"Kenny, I signed you because I believed in you. I'm letting you go because I really believe in you."

Gratitude flooded my body.

There was a moment when he collected his thoughts. Then he said, "Have Dale call me. We'll have the lawyers work out the details."

TURNING THE TIDE

Dale had a plan. Joe Galante, who'd signed Dave Matthews to RCA New York, was returning to RCA Nashville. They'd turned Alabama into the biggest thing in country, and Joe trusted Dale to be a partner. Dale sent Joe *In My Wildest Dreams*, hoping he'd sign me—and give us a chance in the marketplace.

I'd been working hard. Kim Williams, Buddy Brock, and I had written "Fall in Love." Upbeat and hopeful, it packed the innocence first true relationships should be wrapped in. We had "All I Need to Know," too. They would go Top 5, then "When I Close My Eyes" hit No. 1.

It's not as simple as change labels, be a star. But it proved how important infrastructure and those relationships are.

I told Joe I wanted to be on RCA, because of the dog and the gramophone—and Elvis. But they put me on BNA Records, which had fewer artists. John Anderson, on his third or fourth label, was there, having the biggest success of his career.

Joe knew it would come down to music, and my ability to more than make the radio executives believe in me. Too many twentysomething guys were releasing "young love" songs, which were working. Galante wanted acts who'd still be stars when the trend dried up.

Once "Fall in Love" was chosen as the single, the label went to work. I'd never seen anything like the integration and synchronization of regional reps, sales teams, promotion vice presidents, and the other departments that support all this.

Rick Rockhill and I had made some calls and driven to a few stations, but this was another level. Armed with an AT&T calling card—in those days before flip phones, maybe even BlackBerries—I was sent on a radio tour that sometimes meant four stations in a single day. Always on the lookout for a pay phone, I was charged with making believers.

Getting off the plane in Little Rock, I'd been told to find Scott Michaels. Not a big airport, but that was all I had. We'd never met; I had zero clue what he looked like.

In this time when people could go to the gate, there was no one waiting. I walked around, lost and unsure, hoping he'd see me with the guitar. After a couple minutes, I called Britta Davis, Joe's longtime assistant, and admitted I wasn't sure what to do.

"Go to baggage claim. You'll find each other."

I picked up my guitar. Over the airport's loudspeaker, I heard, "Would Kenny Chesney please report to Baggage Claim B."

Nobody knew my name, face, or music. This wasn't a good sign.

I see this guy walking toward me in a pair of Wrangler jeans, a Mo Betta shirt—which was really "in" back then—and these boots that screamed "I'm somebody." He was about five nine, had a cowboy hat with all this ragged rust-colored hair flying out the back of it. Stopped me in my tracks.

"You Chesney?" he barked, walking straight to me. I felt overwhelmed.

"Yeah."

"Get in the car," he ordered, turning and moving toward the curb. "We're late."

Stomp, stomp, stomp. "And I'm not carrying your guitar, either."

Inside, I went, "This is what I'm in for?" That attitude and intensity was something I hadn't experienced. We swung by a local donut shop, grabbed a dozen, and headed straight to the station; me with my guitar, Scott armed with donuts for the staff.

He was somebody who wanted to work; we were going to *work*. Matter-of-fact, this-is-how-it's-done: We're late, get moving!

We hit both Little Rock radio stations. He wasn't playing. We walked in, people were ready to see him, hear what he had to say, listen to his records. Cracking open the guitar case, I knew they were listening because of Scott, but I made sure they heard me.

I can't tell you over all the years—and Scott Michaels remains part of my radio team today—how many in-person radio visits we did. Scott would bring donuts, have pizza parties at the stations. I'd sit in offices playing my upcoming album, or in conference rooms singing my songs, sometimes with local listeners, too.

Any chance to meet decision-makers, create connections, I was there. Two, three, four stations a day, sometimes two different cities—often by car. We did that nonstop for three, four months. Whether they wanted to see us or not, we were coming. Scott and I built a real rapport with those people, so my singles weren't just one more record on the stack.

We'd talk about the business, how it worked, how it *really* worked. Promotion is a tough job; some people do it by math and the research, some by whatever the story is. Scott did it with every cell in his body, all heart, all fierce passion. Even when he didn't always agree with what was chosen, he'd fight to the death for my records.

Thanks to Dale, I opened entire tours for Randy, Teddy, and Jeff—those cousins from Fort Payne, Alabama—and Mark, their drummer, before I had anything really going on.

I'd done a lot of one-offs and clubs, festivals—and would make my band stay long after we were done so I could study the headliners. I didn't care who it was; every act had something to teach me.

Touring with Alabama sent a message to radio, because everyone wanted to open their shows. Radio programmers were also being confronted by BNA's promo staff, who'd remind the stations that Alabama represented the heart of their listenership.

That was the beauty of Alabama. Dressed in their T-shirts and jeans, they hit the stage hard. Ready to play, really lift that crowd up; they understood how people worked hard, and they wanted to give those fans the night of their lives.

When Randy Owen sang "Dixieland Delight" or "Mountain Music," he'd get fans stomping, clapping his hands over his head, but when he sang "Feels So Right" or "Love in the First Degree" in that solid baritone, you felt the women's knees buckle.

Introspective, I didn't know if he liked me for the longest time.

Jeff Cook, with all his guitars, fiddle, and playing that Stratocaster behind his neck, was the opposite. Quick with a joke, a slap on the back, a look that said, "Of course you're here," life was an adventure. Knowing they were a bar band with great songs no one saw coming, he savored every moment.

In the middle was Teddy Gentry, the bass player who looked more like Randy. After I'd been out on the road with them, doing their weekends or Thursday/Friday/Saturday runs, filling in with my own dates and any radio anything the label had asked for, we had this moment.

I was twenty-six, feeling my oats, but also zigzagging in and out of time zones. How many mornings was I making a 6:00 a.m. flight, to do a morning show, then drop by a retail account? There were sound checks, interviews, anything else that might help. It'll wear you down.

One afternoon, we were playing a parking lot in Reno with Alabama. In the hours between sound check, dinner, and meet and greet, I was watching the guys fine-tuning a song. Teddy came off the stage, walked up, and asked, "What's wrong with you?"

"I'm tired," I said, being honest.

He looked at me like I'd lost my mind. "Wait 'til you've been out here twenty-five years. *Then* you can be tired."

I got the news I had the opening slot on the George Jones/Tammy Wynette reunion tour. Was it Norro Wilson, who knew them? The Morris Agency? Slightly more true traditional than some of the new acts, I was picked to open for two Country Music Hall of Famers, who'd once been one of country's stormiest couples.

Those two legends didn't need me to sell tickets, but I would get to watch two of the country's greatest vocalists every night. My peers were blowing by me, but they weren't doing this.

That first show, I got off the stage, put my guitar up, and went back to find a place side-stage. I didn't want to be in the way, but be as close as possible to watch the mighty Jones. My whole family loved that charge in his voice; I knew I was taking a deep dive into greatness.

To be that close to a legend while they work is intense. You're sucked in, and you don't have any sense of time or place. I was consumed by every vocal lick, bent note, and vowel. "He Stopped Loving Her Today," as well as "White Lightning," thrilled me.

As Jones was doing his growl and tilting his acoustic guitar neck into the air on "The Corvette Song," a dark-headed woman with a pixie haircut tapped my shoulder. Intently watching, I was startled. Realizing it was Mrs. George Jones, I worried I'd done something wrong.

Smiling, she asked, "Kenny, are you going home?"

"Yes, ma'am," I answered. "Me and the boys wanted to stay so I could watch George sing."

"Back to Nashville?" she confirmed. I nodded.

"Would you like to fly home with us?"

This was not happening. I was being invited to fly home with George and Nancy Jones.

"Yes, ma'am," I said, hoping I didn't jump out of my skin.

"Okay, as soon he's done, we're running for the airport. If you need to bring anything, you better go get it."

"No, I'm good."

"Be by the back door and ready to go. We'll get you home."

I'd never been on a private plane, never even really talked to Jones. So many thoughts rushed through my mind, including, *Please, Kenny, don't embarrass yourself.*

We hustled into the car, straight to the airport. I didn't have to talk much as Nancy, who managed her husband, talked about the show, what worked, some business that was coming up. When we got to the airstrip, I looked around. This was a whole other world.

"You have fun tonight?" the legend asked, as we headed to the small plane.

"I sure did," I replied.

They both laughed. We walked up the stairs, settled into the seats. The pilots told us how long the flight was, and I acted like it was another day. I knew my band—on the bus—was several hours behind me. But they all high-fived when they realized what was going on.

"You're a good country singer, son," Jones told me. Talk about a compliment.

He asked me where I was from. I told him about East Tennessee, that Thanksgiving concert. Mostly I went on and on about how much my Grandma Lucy loved him, about how she'd die if she knew where I was. He chuckled. "Well, don't tell her then! She sounds like the kind of lady you need to keep around."

I didn't want to be so starstruck they made jokes about me. It happens when young acts have no sense of what's appropriate. I wanted to do this again, to take in as much of the Joneses as I could.

Maybe my being so excited made them laugh. Maybe they could tell how much I cared about the music. I don't know. But anytime I was going home on those weekend runs, they took me on the plane.

Me, the kid from nowhere, on a private jet with George Jones. Sure, why not?

8 SECONDS

Things picked up. Beckett leaned into that "young traditional" country that was working, and suddenly, I had a pair of Top 5 hits: "Fall in Love," which I cowrote with my friend Buddy Brock and Kim Williams, and "All I Need to Know."

The success wasn't substantially greater, but now, there were people who specialized in sales, marketing, radio. Country music, every day. Whether I was having a Top 5 or a stiff, they were out there working.

I opened for anyone who would have me. Alabama kept me working; that remained a major talking point for BNA, because they were one of RCA's major acts. Country was booming; bars were plentiful. We were on the Iron Lung, crisscrossing America and deploying our thirty, forty-five, and sometimes sixty minutes with the two hits three, four, five nights a week.

Bob Crout, my longtime accountant, came to me. He saw the reality before I did.

"You need your own bus," he began. "Instead of paying somebody to use their bus, you should own your own. There's different ways of looking at it, but for you, buy a bus."

I didn't have two nickels to rub together. I owned the pickup I'd moved to Nashville in and my guitar. But if I owned my bus, we could keep bringing the music to people.

Something about "owning" my bus felt like a tangible commitment to this dream. Talk about sending the universe a message.

Somehow, Bob went to the Bank of America and talked them into loaning me $250,000 to buy a bus. This is 1996 dollars, mind you. I didn't own a house, nothing. I saw it as an investment in myself. When they said yes, I went for it.

To this day, I don't know why they loaned me that amount of money.

I found a used white Silver Eagle with tan interior. We named it Moby after the great white whale in *Moby-Dick*. It was another twelve-bunk, fourteen-person situation. Like Jackson Browne's *Running on Empty*, where "The Load Out" talks about all the country and western on the bus, R&B, disco, 8-tracks, cassettes—that was us. We played it all: from bluegrass to rock, sometimes taking out our guitars.

I didn't know I was investing in a piece of my heart—Moby's been everywhere with us, washouts, my first real arena show, Virginia Beach rigging our own slip and slide on the lawn for a makeshift hurricane party during Hurricane Charley, sliding into a ditch while pulling our merch trailer—as much as transportation. When it got rough, I knew we could play shows because I owned my bus.

In 2015, rolling out of St. Louis on I-64 West to Des Moines, the odometer rolled over. Right past Exit 24, those six nines turned to zeros. Moby had traveled one million miles. Smooth as could be, keep the oil checked and the tire pressure good, that ride remains the same. Moby's seen an awful lot of dreams come true. Moby's been a crew bus, home to No Shoes Radio, but more importantly, a physical reminder of how far we've come.

"If This Bus Could Talk" became a song I wrote with Tom Douglas. I got to joking about how it's good Moby can't talk—or we'd all be in trouble. You don't know when you're signing away your life as a scared kid, what you're buying is so much more than wheels.

All I Need to Know had dropped June 13, 1995; *Me and You* arrived fifty-one weeks later.

I'd been working so much, I hadn't written anything strong enough to make the album. The title track—like "The Tin Man" from *Wildest Dreams*—not only migrated to my second BNA release, it became a secret weapon.

I was glad we recut the quiet, piano-driven "Me and You." Based on "Tin Man," I didn't think it would be anything more than an album cut.

I wasn't prepared for "Back in My Arms," our first single, never making the Top 40. "Back in My Arms" stiffed. It's one thing to have a last single stall, but a stillborn first single? Was this my second strike? Was the problem more than an indie label that couldn't compete?

"Me and You," though, was a song everyone believed in. We carried it over; made it the title track. There wasn't much to the arrangement, but maybe that sincerity would work. Maybe there was something believable enough in my vocal that people would respond.

We'd done crazier things. We put it out. It couldn't do any worse. We weren't selling, the singles weren't getting played, and I still didn't know who I was as an artist. Everyone knew how badly I wanted it, how hard I worked—and how I tried to have a good attitude about all of it. Britta Davis, who kept all the executives on track, called me, very matter-of-factly. "Joe wants to talk to you."

I'm not gonna lie, I was nervous. Galante was a finance guy; he understands cutting losses. Maybe he got to thinking about it. All I could think was, *Well, this is it. He's going to drop me.*

I forgot where we were headed, but when we got there, I went straight to a pay phone. I nervously punched in the numbers of my AT&T calling card. When Galante picked up, it felt like a jolt of electrical current.

Without missing a beat, the head of my label goes, "I've got some news."

I'll bet you do, I thought.

"Your album sold three thousand units last week."

When you've been selling, maybe, ten records, all I could say was, "Wow . . ."

"We see a little movement with this song, 'Me and You.' We're watching your album. A couple more weeks of this, we're gonna kick in."

The next week, he calls, and it's 7,500 pieces. Then it was 20,000. The song died at No. 2, but it didn't matter. It was having an impact.

A couple weeks into the song, we were set to play at 8 Seconds in Orlando.

We pulled in several hours before showtime, and there were people lined up all the way around the club. Cars parked everywhere, people trying to figure out how to cut the line—and you could feel the buzz.

This had never happened before. I was used to pulling up to a club hoping the staff was there. The people had heard this song and they'd connected. They were coming to see me, not anybody I was opening for. This was *my* audience.

So excited, I called Dale and almost couldn't speak. I called Joe, thanked him for being patient.

When I walked onstage, I felt like Alabama. I got what they felt. These were my people.

After the show, I called Dale again, raving.

"Well, buddy, I told you if you were patient, it was only a matter of time." He was clearly delighted by how blown away I was.

A couple years before, I'd called Dale after a show in Greenville, South Carolina. I'd played a club and nobody came. I told him, "I'm never playing Greenville again. Never."

Greenville is where Dale is from. He knew deep inside if I connected with those people, they'd be with me a long time. But Dale is smart; he didn't argue or tell me how wrong people were. He waited.

A few nights after that show in Orlando, we played Greenville. The club was packed so full, we knew we'd never play there again. Next trip would be the arena. Funny thing about Greenville: I can't tell you how many incredible nights we've had at the BI-LO Center since then.

That was how everything changed the first time. In a parking lot in Orlando, Florida.

Nobody was looking, most of all me, and the people showed up. That's the one thing you can't fake.

Radio, as I was learning, didn't always care. After the two Top 5s right off the bat, we hit a slick spot. Maybe "Me and You" went to No. 2, but that's not No. 1; country radio knew a culture of turntable hits may ring the bell, but no one cares long-term.

I knew enough to know we weren't out of the woods.

Chart numbers don't matter in the long run, but when you're starting, especially when people think you're one more act, they're life and death. I was a long way from being accepted at country radio, so there was real urgency on that front.

Joe ramped up the pressure in the field. I could tell I was becoming a priority. I could feel the energy, the difference when I went to radio stations. It wasn't something done because the rep said so, they wanted me stopping by.

One thing about Galante: He wasn't going to let me waste his team's efforts. I'd have to think about changing producers. My records were going to have to sound, well, more something.

I'd seen Buddy Cannon, who was running Polygram's A&R, coming to Acuff-Rose looking for songs. He wrote with Dean Dillon, too, and Dean said he was a real song guy. That's how I found out he'd produced Vern Gosdin, as well as cowriting his "Set 'Em Up, Joe," a massive classic.

I needed to meet him.

Across the street at Mercury Records, their receptionist was Mollie. She was cute, so pretty much every day I'd go flirt with her. With Buddy coming in and out of his office building, I could strike up a conversation. Multitasking, but one had a real purpose.

Troy knew I was going to have to make the change, too. He loved the idea of Buddy and Norro Wilson, who'd written "The Grand Tour," because everything they did, songs were the starting point.

Dean had recently written "I've Come to Expect It from You," a No. 1 for George Strait, with Buddy. We were writing, talking about what I was going to do, knowing I needed to figure it out. That's when Dean started connecting the dots: Buddy played bass with Mel Tillis; he was a true musician, but he also came out of the rhythm section and understood the power of groove. He knew songs, he wrote classics. Dean spent a lot of time with Buddy, loved his vibe.

"Kenny, add it up for me. Vern Gosdin, Hank Cochran, Bill Anderson, all these great songwriters. Isn't that the energy you want?"

As a songwriter, I loved everything about that idea.

And Norro? I'd met him with Jerry Bradley, who ran Acuff-Rose. He was a character, funny and elegant. I loved the guy. I knew Norro before I even moved to Nashville, because I'd read his name on a Con Hunley record.

One day, flirting with Mollie, Buddy walked into the lobby.

"My name's Kenny Chesney," I said.

"I know who you are."

We started talking about music.

Meanwhile, there were shows to play, station visits to do. Back when Walmart and Target had music sections, there were in-store appearances to sign records. There were photo shoots, videos to make, just getting from one place to another. In a lot of ways, it was a blur.

I let Barry know I was making a change. I was grateful for everything he taught me; knew his lessons would continue to serve me.

I spent every free moment in town with Buddy and Norro, listening to songs; they wanted to hear everything I was writing, anything that caught my ear. Because of whom they produced, they heard the top-shelf songs saved for superstars whose records were automatic adds. That airplay added up; the bigger the hit, the bigger the BMI and ASCAP check for the writers and publishers.

Suddenly, I was hearing songs I *knew* were hits. This wasn't Acuff-Rose throwing us a bone, these were competitive, right-out-of-the-gate hits. Craig Wiseman had been coming on strong as a writer; in the pile was "She's Got It All," which felt good and seemed like exactly what we needed.

We put it on hold, cut it shortly thereafter. I wanted *I Will Stand* to mean something, but I didn't know what. We cut "That's Why I'm Here," a song about attending AA meetings, Dean Dillon's "A Chance," and Tony Joe White's funky "Steamy Windows," which Tina Turner had put out. I got to record with George Jones, too; "From Hillbilly Heaven to Honky Tonk Hell" wasn't going to be a single, but hearing that voice over big studio speakers? Bucket list, 100 percent.

We were in Puerto Rico, doing the photo shoot for the *I Will Stand* cover. Someone said, "Give Les Acree a call." He'd been a hometown supporter, so it was always good catching up.

On a pay phone in Mayaguez, Puerto Rico, I made the call. Hearing his familiar voice, I asked, "What's going on?"

"Not much," he said. "But I got a question . . ."

Before I could ask, he dropped the ultimate dime, "How does it feel to have a No. 1 record?"

WHAT? "When I Close My Eyes" hit No. 1. Only on *Radio & Records*, but for country music, that was the dominant chart.

"You're kidding me . . ."

After everything, all of it, I finally had a No. 1.

You'd think I'd feel a rush of elation, and I did. But I felt an even greater surge of relief.

It would take "She's Got It All," that Craig Wiseman song, to top both charts. Otherwise, *I Will Stand*, which arrived thirteen months after *Me and You*, didn't turn me into a bankable star at radio. But I joined the club: artist with a *Billboard* chart-topper.

Did the money go up? Probably some. Clint was good at getting people to see my worth. Like Dale, he believed "underprice and over-deliver." That makes the promoters want you back—and with my slick spots at radio, the ability to be the artist who gets the gig when three people want it mattered.

I couldn't tell you how things changed. We were all on one bus, but we traded the merch trailer for a truck that we wrapped with the album cover. I had a house outside of town, because Bob Crout told me I should buy something to put the money into. So, I did.

I was a priority to the label. You could tell they were going into battle to get my records up the charts. When the music's not dialed in, that organized attack makes a difference.

When some artists had a few hits, they added buses and layers of people between them; they started saying no and acting important. I lay awake at night, wondering, *What else?* Writing in my journal, creating scraps of songs when a phrase caught my ear. Calling Dean and my songwriter friends, asking what they were working on, seeing if they had any time to write: It was all part of it.

I had a couple relationships, but they always fell apart. Any girlfriend, no matter how much I cared, was going to finish third or fourth, maybe even fifth. First, there was how music consumed me. Second, there was songwriting, followed by the fans, my career, and what that required. Then, there was my team, the people who'd thrown their dreams in with mine, as well as my island family.

Always gone, always leaving. People say it's a sacrifice, but if all you want is to make music that gives people the soundtrack for their life, how can that be anything but a blessing?

SEXY TRACTOR

Renee Bell called me, laughing. Paul Overstreet, who'd written Randy Travis's massive "Forever and Ever, Amen" and "Deeper Than the Holler," had enjoyed a very long lunch—as songwriters and A&R people sometimes did—and played her this new song.

When Renee got excited, the light brunette had a way of extending not just her long Georgia vowels, but really sitting on the last consonant. "You have to come heeearrrrrrrr this song! It's kill*errrrrrr!*" she trilled. And when Renee Bell trilled, you knew she had something because Renee Bell knew songs. "It's a big ole hit!"

In the background, I could hear Paul Overstreet laughing. Renee continued, reeling me in like a fish. "A big ole hit, or it'll kill your career. Either way, it'll make an impression."

Their enthusiasm was contagious. "I'm on my way . . ."

Over the years, I'd pulled up outside RCA Records, so Renee could jump in my truck—or me into her car—and listen to songs loud enough to rattle the windows. It's like being in lust, you can't wait to get into the house.

When I pulled up, her bangs were falling across her eyes and her smile was double wide. "You're gonna *LOVE* this," she said, as she opened the door and slid into the passenger seat. She put the demo on. The funkiest rhythm started pouring into my pickup. Seesawing, almost lurching, an almost too country melody dropped into farm work, hot sun, and a girl who thinks that's sexy.

BOOM! The picture matched by the melody; the choppy beat had a ground-tilling feel to it. I looked at Renee, who was looking at me. By the time we hit the chorus about a girl who wasn't into cars or pickup trucks, but found farm equipment arousing, I knew Renee had done it again.

The song was a slice of pure 4-H delight, wrapped in a tale of farm kids having their own special mating ritual. She thinks my tractor's sexy? Indeed. *"Right?!"* she asked rhetorically. Knowing I knew an earworm when I heard one, she was betting I'd recognize the power of how the riff, groove, visual cues, and melody created a song that turned the hook into something far larger than a mere hit record.

"Yeah," I agreed, head nodding in time. She was right. It could kill my career, but it could also blow it up—putting me into a whole other orbit. There was no denying the potency "She Thinks My Tractor's Sexy" packed, and I needed to break out of the pack.

"I want it," I announced.

Simple as that. Magic, lightning, and monster hit songs all strike fast. You know instantly.

Of course, you have to hook the track in the studio. But Buddy, Norro, and I were zeroing in on something more aggressive: real country, but almost on steroids.

When I played it for them, they both smiled. They knew a crazy smash when they heard one.

We were at the Music Mill at the corner of 18th and Roy Acuff. The dark wood building that looked like a giant log cabin was where Alabama had cut all their biggest records. Capable of cutting sixty-four tracks, it was cutting-edge and down-home all at once.

Sessions players hear it all. They work hard at showing nothing, because they're not hired to have opinions. But you can always tell when they're amused. When we played the demo, some actually laughed out loud as they sat scattered on the control room couches.

Eddie Bayers, the only drummer in the Country Music Hall of Fame, had his head down, really absorbing the groove. His eyes were glittering. You could see he had a notion from across the room.

Sometimes a random moment sparks everything. Accidents you don't see coming set the session in motion, and that's what happened. As the musicians were settling in the studio, Rob Hajacos was trying to get his fiddle tuned up; sawing away on this lick that slithered back and forth, the pattern he was riffing jumped out.

Buddy, who was sitting in the control room, looked at me through the glass. He could tell I thought I heard something. Nodding, he said to Rob, "I don't know what this is, but I know nobody's got anything that sounds like it."

Before the moment stiffened, Buddy said to the players, "Okay, boys, let's try one. Let's let Rob kinda lead with that lick . . . Eddie, you do what you do, and the rest of you fall in around it."

Just like that, a single that would change my life was born.

✦ ✦ ✦

Everywhere We Go was my fifth record. I'd been having Top 10s, even No. 1s, but wasn't standing out. A lot of guys looked like George Strait, sang a certain kind of young man's love song; it worked. It was working for me. I was playing as many shows as I wanted. But I was one more of many.

Something needed to happen. "Forever" felt good. That's the first rule. The second: What kind of hook have you got? Beyond a song about happily ever, "How Forever Feels" may be the only song that invokes Richard Petty *and* Jimmy Buffett.

Even wilder, the semitropical, semi-honkytonk rhythm stayed at No. 1 on country radio for eight weeks, half the time I spent on *George Strait's 1999 Country Festival Tour*, playing stadiums on a bill that included the (Dixie) Chicks and Tim McGraw. Booked to play third, it was blazing daylight. Except the humble support act had the summer's biggest hit—and people were showing up early.

I'd had momentum and lost it before. I knew what it was like to stall. I also knew sometimes you should do the unthinkable. When Renee played me "Sexy Tractor," I knew it wasn't for everybody; I also knew five boys I grew up with who'd fall out when they heard it.

I never feared "Tractor." It might be a work record. But we'd had work records before. Work didn't scare me, being lost in the pack did. Some people didn't get it; some people made fun of it.

We doubled down. Taking it literally, we shot the video with me on a tractor and the performance portion in a barn singing all alone with a vintage microphone. But we juxtaposed it with the girl, who shows up in the field in a tiny black dress, swinging her high heels and dancing like it was a disco.

At one point on the next summer's Strait tour, where I was still on in broad daylight, but closer to sundown, George Strait came up.

With a smile, he leaned over and said, "I'm hearing everybody talking about how much they like your song."

This was pre-internet, when people fed on the buzz they picked up from their friends. I was on the biggest tour of the summer, and the man on the top of the bill was hearing about it. We could feel it when we were onstage, the rush of energy had hit a whole other velocity.

Now that meant something.

Everywhere We Go certified double platinum. The singles were working. "Tractor" had, indeed, broken me out of the pack. If I'd wanted a basic country star career, I was set. Only I didn't want to do what everyone else was doing.

We now had two buses, one for the band and one for the crew, an 18-wheeler half-filled with gear, half-filled with merchandise to sell at the shows; it was wrapped with the *Everywhere We Go* album artwork, a rolling advertisement flying down the highway. Eight years in, all the trappings suggested I was happening.

Playing those Strait shows showed me what was possible. People were clearly getting there early to see us; they knew the songs, even if many people had no idea who I was.

The energy when we played tempo hits, especially "Tractor" even before it was a single, was electric. Rolling down the highway after that final 2000 Strait show, I was thinking, *I don't know how to get there. But why would I want anything less?*

I understood "Tractor" was a novelty. Though when some kids sent a VHS tape to the management office that showed a pack of them dressed in their tuxes and fancy dresses riding to prom on a bunch of John Deeres while their jam box blared "She Thinks My Tractor's Sexy" full blast, that was a moment of knowing you'd connected hard.

I needed to find songs that would ignite that same passion without the novelty. Write or find songs people burned to hear. My job: figure out what that meant. Surely, message and moment can meet.

Because we'd had all these songs on the charts, it was time for a *Greatest Hits*. We pulled songs that never had a moment like "Baptism," a live version of Mac McAnally's "Back Where I Come From" recorded in Dallas, as well as a few new songs that could go to radio. It would buy time.

All my singles were consolidated in one place. Maybe now people would connect some of the music to the man making it.

THE ISLANDS

In early 1998, I was in Puerto Rico for a photo shoot with Peter Nash and the label's creative team of Mary Hamilton and Susan Eaddy. They saw how much I loved being in Puerto Rico and working in that environment, how it brought out a different calm and joy in me.

At dinner Susan said to me, randomly, "I just got back from the Virgin Islands. If you like Puerto Rico, which isn't very far from there, you should go check it out. If you love this, you're gonna really love that."

I went, "Great," but knew there was no time to go anywhere. We had dates booked; life moves on, and I was chasing the dream, even if it wasn't chasing me back.

Several months later, we went to St. Thomas to shoot the video for "How Forever Feels."

A big-budget, multiple-day shoot with Martin Kahan, who I'd worked with on "Tractor."

Being December, we ran into bad weather. When they pushed the shoot a day, I decided this was my chance. I got on the ferry at Red Hook, settled in for a twenty-minute ride across the water. Gray, downcast, but I didn't care. What Susan Eaddy had said stuck with me.

Landing at Cruz Bay, I found a charming local town. The buildings, both cement and wood, were painted bright colors; chickens ran through the narrow streets. There was an energy there that was local, not tourist-driven.

I walked straight off the ramp and up the path to where a few public buildings were lined up. The trees seemed ancient, bent and with thick leaves. There was an earthiness that was exactly as it should be.

Heading up the street, I heard a familiar voice.

Looking to my left, there was a bar called Woody's. Drifting out of its open door, George Jones's voice poured into the street. In the Caribbean, I'd come to find out, country music is a big part of the culture. For whatever reason, several classic country songs are as ingrained as reggae, calypso, and other forms of island music.

I walked through the door, into this small room with a counter on one side, a cooler and a lot of bottles behind it. Two young men from Missouri were tending bar. Todd and Chad Beaty, two brothers from the middle of America, decided to go to the Virgin Islands and try to make a go of their own bar.

"Are you Kenny Chesney?" one asked.

I was stunned they knew who I was. This was before "Tractor," before things had kicked in. But they were country kids, and they loved music. Hell, they were playing George Jones in the middle of the day.

"I sure am."

They looked at each other. Then they asked me, "What'll you have?"

I ordered a beer, sat there and talked about life on the island. I wanted to know what it was like leaving what you know behind to live somewhere so far away, but so magical. They asked me about what I was doing there, and I told them about the video we weren't shooting.

We talked about sports, music, whatever else. We were killing a few beers on a slow afternoon when nothing much was happening. No big deal, just a moment. That was all I saw of St. John that day.

I got back on the ferry, went to Red Hook, checked in with the label folks. But I knew settling into my room that night I had been somewhere that was going to be part of my life. I didn't know how or even when I'd get back there, but I knew.

Next year, I went down with my dad.

I'd toured hard, so I rented a house when it was done. We met a lot of locals, some who'd become my best friends.

Sharon and Ed Metz, who I'd rented the house from, showed us around the island. We'd gone to a restaurant called Morgan's Mango.

The hostess was this cute dark-headed young woman named Emily. My dad started asking her, "Do you know who Kenny Chesney is?" She did not.

But my dad wouldn't let up, so she finally came over to say hello to the table.

Emily, who's bright and welcoming, and her husband, Ben Bourassa, who also worked at Morgan's, were super-friendly. We all immediately became friends. They introduced me to all of the people who worked in the restaurant, all of their friends—and suddenly, I was part of the scene. We had a blast.

Whether we were out on a boat, hanging in Morgan's, Woody's, or one of the bars they went to after work, I had an instant friend group. I was dialed in to all the gossip, all the who's doing what with whom. It felt like home, but it was so much more.

If it wasn't happening for me yet, they didn't care. It didn't matter to them what I did.

We had an almost coconut telegraph. Be at the Beach Bar at 11:00 a.m., ready to go. If you wanted to get out on the water, show up. Bob Shinners was from Milwaukee and liked to say, "It's complicated." Like so many people, he came to the islands and decided not to go back. He ran Low-Key Watersports, doing charter sails and dives for paying customers—or the local kids who worked in the bars.

How many trips did we make on a boat called the *Hey Now*? Going to Jost Van Dyke, the Willy T, an anchored boat with a bar where we'd get naked and jump off the top or simply float somewhere and watch the sun move across the sky.

It made perfect sense and no sense all at once.

It became a refuge, for the people as much as the water and the native beauty, that pulled me to it. When I wasn't working, I was there not working.

After a while, I bought a boat and hired Ben from Morgan's to be my boat captain. We were running buddies, so it was a logical move. I'd rent houses, too—places I could have family and friends stay with me. But when I'd go down for a few days, I'd live on the boat and exhale, let my mind unwind and let the songs come in.

There, I could let go of all the things that came with trying to make it happen. More than the stress, forgetting the expectations and deadlines, what everybody thought. To get my guitar and sit on the bow of the boat, listening to music or playing a few chords, looking up at the stars, awestruck at everything that had happened, was a freedom that allowed me the sort of balance you can't find when you're on the road or in the studio.

In those hours of drifting, I asked myself a lot of questions about what I wanted and was willing to do. I was meeting unique characters who fed my soul. The Ghost from Jost, whose real name was Curtney Chinnery, was one. He embodied the spirit of the island, free with his poetry and songs, he was always ready for a conversation.

We would talk about life, how he saw the world, and I took it in. It fed my mind and it fed my music in ways I didn't understand at first.

My friends were bartenders, boaties, builders, waitresses. They worked on charters, in real estate offices. They cleaned houses, were dishwashers, cooks, anything you could imagine a person in their twenties doing, especially when they were living somewhere because they loved being there.

It opened my mind to many different kinds of people, ways of life and living, thinking, and experiencing the world. There were people from all over living there, as well as the West Indians whose families had been in the islands for generations. That's what made it paradise for me.

The more people I met, the more I realized: My songs needed to work for *all* of them. It wasn't about the stereotype, it was for anyone who worked hard at whatever they did. Because all my friends in the islands worked—and played—hard.

I was in my thirties, but we were all on the brink of becoming who we were supposed to be. We were alive to life, in awe of how much we all loved one another and what we shared. It wasn't about status, what you had or what you were seeking, it was about being together.

It's also where the New England connection began. Nine out of every ten people was from somewhere in New England. You'd ask, "Where you from?" You'd hear "Vermont," "Maine," "Rhode Island," or "Anywhere, Massachusetts."

I'd never been anywhere much beyond Key West. Now I was hanging on an island that was protected by the National Park Service. There are wild donkeys, abandoned sugarcane factories, small churches, and an innocence that showed me what I needed was to be who I was.

As things picked up, as life started to take on a momentum I couldn't have imagined, the island remained a place I could disappear. Before cell phone cameras and social media, we had the ability to run wild, laugh, and drink, carry on and get carried away.

It's why every time I got off the road, even if it was three or four days between shows, I would fly down and Ben and Bob picked me up in the boat. Sometimes, depending on the weather and time of day, we'd make a quick stop at Molly Malone's, an Irish pub right by the docks. There was nothing like a quick breakfast or lunch and a spicy Bloody Mary before walking down C Dock where my boat was tied up and waiting.

Making our way across Pillsbury Sound, we'd talk about what was going on, laugh about road life, and catch up on island gossip. It was like I'd never left.

As soon as we tied to the mooring that our friend Chuckles let us borrow, we'd take the dinghy into Cruz Bay and tie up to the dinghy dock. We'd head straight for a bar that's no longer there called the Quiet Mon. Also an Irish pub, there in the middle of town, no matter when or why I was coming, my entire island family would meet me at the top of the steps with a drink and a "Welcome home."

To feel so safe, so accepted, you can face anything. It's how I was able to figure out without quite knowing what the next phase of my life was going to require. It was there I learned to be as you are.

SEA CHANGE

In 2001, we decided to do the Tim McGraw tour. He was a headliner, and a friend. I also knew it might be the last time he and I would be able to tour together.

I could sell 2,000, even 3,000 tickets in a lot of places. That's not a real "headlining tour," just dates in small halls. We'd done a lot of "compassionate business," as my friend Shep Gordon, who manages Alice Cooper, likes to say, with the fair buyers. They'd been great to us.

But I needed to sell "hard tickets." We needed to be smart, because if you go too early and don't do good business, you handicap your growth. After two years on the Strait tour together, our bands and crews knew and liked one another.

That summer, we played a lot of basketball, smack-talked, and went out there for our hour to do what an opening act is supposed to: play so hard the audience is blazing when the headliner takes the stage. That hour was full of hits. Even if people didn't realize I was the guy who sang them, they knew every word; more than the choruses, but the verses, too. Our sets flew by. The crowd was dancing, waving their arms and lighters with the songs.

In Albuquerque, New Mexico, halfway through the tour, we were having a pool party. Everyone loved the sun, water, and unwinding that goes with it.

Clint and Louis Messina, who'd promoted those Strait stadium tours, were headed straight for me. These are not beach people. Clint looked like a business guy and Louis looked like a rock and roll promoter who'd not only done tons of dates with the Rolling Stones, but he'd created the legendary Texxas Jam.

They were sweating a little, so I hid my smile.

"What's up?" I asked, sitting up on the chaise lounge where I'd been working on my tan.

"We've been talking," Clint said. Clint was as voracious about being a manager as I was being an artist.

"You're going to headline next summer," Louis said, directly. Whippet thin, not overly tall, his nervous energy pulsed through his skin. Louis wasn't playing.

"Uh . . ." I figured they'd come to tell me about a big tour for 2002. Those things usually book a year, eighteen months in advance. Headlining?

"I saw your merch numbers jump on that second Strait tour," Louis continued, matter-of-factly. "They've jumped again out here. T-shirts! That's how we measure passion. That really says something."

The sun was out, I had a hand up over my eyes and was squinting.

I couldn't read Clint's face, but it didn't matter. He wouldn't suggest this to fail.

Did I believe in myself in that moment enough to say yes?

A lot of indicators were in play. I'd had seventeen hit singles, two years with George Strait, and strong dates on my own. Plenty of acts decide they're big deals, get out there as headliners, and implode.

The sweat was starting to bead up on the guys. I figured, "Trust your people."

Exhaling, I responded, "If you really think we should do it . . . Okay, let's do it."

Buddy and I had a major come-to-Jesus talk where I explained everything *had* to go up several notches. Beyond dialing in the man I was becoming, we had to be more.

"The instruments need to hit harder," I told him.

"I want songs that talk about what I value, what I've lived," I explained. "Not a truck and a girl, but really saying something about being young, alive."

He nodded. He'd written enough classics, he knew the difference.

"And fun, Buddy. I want to be real, but let's create some fun."

Like Bruce Springsteen said in his Broadway show: "I had a magic trick, a secret that nobody knew."

I didn't believe we could sell hard tickets in bigger arenas and amphitheaters. But I knew the music was coming into focus.

The last show with McGraw was at Starwood Amphitheater outside Nashville. It felt right to close the tour out in our hometown. There was a big tent beyond the backstage. Everybody was partying and saying all those things you say when a tour or a school year is over. Business as usual. Sort of.

I now had not one, but two magic tricks, two secrets nobody saw coming: the music no one expected and a headlining tour.

My soul was changing. All the time I'd spent in the islands, I was seeing and feeling things differently. My voice was changing, maturing and deepening. More than finding out how to get the most of the studio mics, I was understanding how to show people my world and bring how I actually felt into the vocal booth.

These new songs were authentic expressions of my spirit. I realized that being me was the most honest thing I could do. Would people want to hear it?

I was thirty-one when my *Greatest Hits* came out. I was thirty-three when we were getting ready to release what became *No Shoes, No Shirt, No Problems*. Even more than making a record that was more coherent from top to bottom, I'd realized a lot of things about where I'd been, how I'd made decisions that weren't as focused as I'd believed.

When you're making money on the road, it's easy to believe you've got it under control. But that wasn't the case. I realized I'd allowed people to make decisions for me, taste-wise especially, because I didn't know the difference. So many of those videos made me cringe. I did what Martin Kahan, the director, and the label people said, because I didn't know any better. They were experts. I should listen.

I didn't know what it meant to be an artist, but I was starting to understand.

I wanted to find out. I felt like that kid in the backyard again. If I didn't know what was out there, I trusted it was coming. I wanted to explore. I listened to a lot of songs, exhaled into the moment and got closer. I wasn't unsure in my own skin. I wasn't wearing a big belt buckle trying to be George Strait. I was dressing the way I actually dressed.

Once I agreed to the *No Shoes, No Shirt, No Problems Tour*, I changed a lot about my life. I'd been working out in Nashville with Matt Royka, a very motivating trainer. I knew I needed more focus. I wanted someone on the road with me to work out daily and get my body into serious shape.

Even when I was a boy, I'd dance with that plastic guitar when a record was on. Music was something I physically felt. When I made the move to headliner, I intended to use that urge to cover the entire stage. Some artists stand at the mic, and they're awesome. But I wanted something physical, where every inch of that stage was mine.

I met a young guy named Daniel Meng, who'd been a baseball player in college. He'd moved to Nashville from Indiana to do sales but realized his passion was helping people get healthy. He was twenty-four, the perfect age to run away with the circus.

We named him "Burns" because of his sideburns. Daily workouts became as much mental as physical for me; as I was building my strength to do the show I imagined, the training also rewired my brain for endurance. Committing to how hard these workouts could be gave me focus for everything else in front of me.

Whether it was the Wheel of Death, a tiny bicycle wheel that I would use to do twenty-five-yard forward and back walking planks, running three to five miles three times a week, working up to 300 push-ups in ten minutes, it was about making my body strong enough to be able to get onstage and give it all away. I wanted to throw all the energy and joy I felt inside the music into the crowd, to get them to feel the way I did up there.

Daniel knew I'd changed how I was eating. He asked, "You wanna get really serious?"

Everything in this window was real serious.

"We can measure everything you eat. Be super specific. Anything going into your body has a purpose. Nothing else. If there's not a reason, you don't go there."

My life became egg whites with vegetables and salsa for breakfast; a turkey sub on dry whole wheat with lettuce, tomato, and jalapeños for lunch; and a skinless chicken breast or broiled salmon with vegetables for dinner. Oh, and coconut rum with sugar-free Red Bull when it was time to get the party on.

Knowing I'd been so normal and common, ten other acts could do what I did, we were leaping with "Young." Written by Craig Wiseman, who'd write *No Shoes*'s biggest hit "The Good Stuff," "Young" took rock guitars and the slamming drumbeat I'd loved and lashed them to a song where the fiddle had as much swerve— and the lyrics spoke to who we were when we were kids jacked up on life, lust, Friday night football, and dreams you couldn't tell us wouldn't come true. You have no idea what it takes, and that's the beauty of it.

If that record summarized my life to that moment, I wasn't alone. Partially, the sound. Partially, the groove. Both were insistent, forward, almost the centrifugal force of youth.

A celebration of how alive you can feel, especially sharing it with your friends.

We mixed it hot, knowing the recording had a spark that wasn't on country radio. When "Young" played on my rough mixes, I turned it up without thinking.

Nobody saw this song coming. Eight years, I'd been on the road, making money and putting it all back into my career. I had a reasonable house and a hunter green Four-Runner. Nobody thought anything about us.

I'd spent so many nights driving home, wanting things to speed it up; frustrated about not knowing how to make it happen.

Suddenly, I knew. We had the song—and the album.

The title track was a brazen, island undertowed, cast-it-all-off fiddle-driven song. Not forgetting my roots, I also recorded a half-sung, half-recitation recounting of all the regrets over a life by my old friends Dean Dillon and Bill Anderson called "A Lot of Things Different."

Maybe most personal, there was "Dreams," a ballad I cowrote with Skip Ewing. Inspired by a late-night call with my mom, who said, "Men my age all want someone younger," it was a truth bomb. Talk about a song that cuts open a moment and an emotion: really good women who deserve to be loved and cherished in a society that seemingly only values the youngest and prettiest.

That willingness to be real—as well as playful—emerged with *No Shoes*. It's not that it was "a grown-up record." There's no shame in loving being alive, but I also wanted to tackle things that were complex.

Bruce Springsteen's "One Step Up" was that. A gut punch of how we betray ourselves. I'd arrived at a place where I'd had enough relationships blow up that I had the experience required to sing it.

If Bruce was more forward in his version, I was a guy lost at the bar, shaking his head. But I found that same self-examination that made this song so powerful. That line about the girl across the bar, burning a hole into you, when you're at your most frustrated? Two steps back for sure.

As we were finishing the album, my publicist, a Cleveland girl raised on Bruce, challenged me to send Springsteen the cut with a note. "Own it," she said. "He's going to hear it. You should explain your reasons and stand by your work."

Louis Messina, who'd promoted countless Springsteen shows, got the address of his studio. A CD of my recording of "One Step Up" and a note explaining how the song had haunted me was sent off. I felt strange but knew it was the right thing to do.

Two weeks later, a FedEx arrived from New Jersey. I looked at the return address. I knew who it was from even before I opened the envelope. It was a moment of truth I wasn't sure I was ready for.

"I always believed *Tunnel of Love* had a country soul," said the half-print/half-script handwriting. The words talked about what the song meant to him, believing in me as someone to sing his song. "You brought a lot of sensitivity to the lyric of 'One Step Up.' Thanks for the care." I stood there, looking at a notecard with Bruce Springsteen's name printed across the top, frozen. He was so humble.

The hours I'd spent listening to this man whose world looked nothing like mine, whose reality was rock and roll, urban, industrial, and hard charging. He showed me how characters drove songs—the more specific you drew them and their emotions, the more people related. Unfailingly honest, especially outsiders or people no one sees, you remember them.

Walking back into the control room, I looked at Buddy and shook my head.

"Hey, man, what's going on?" he asked, curious.

"I got a letter." I held it out. Buddy's seen and done so much with so many artists, he takes things in stride. He saw the signature and his eyebrows went up. Looking closer, he read the note.

"You know there aren't many of those around," he finally said. All I had was, "I imagine not."

We worked hard on getting the sequence right, creating a flow that takes listeners somewhere. Ballads, album cuts, were meant to be as powerful as what was pumping.

Right before the first single dropped, Rick Moxley, one of the regional promo reps, came to the house. I played "Young" for him, said it was going to be the first single. He listened, grinned, responded, "It fucking better be."

Until then, it wasn't intentional, because I had no intentions. It was a watershed moment. Growing meant making decisions, hard ones.

I told Joe Galante all this one night at a Grammy event in New York. He gave me the "Yeah, kid, okay" look, because he knew artists. Most aren't willing to do the tough things. It's easy to talk, but doing? That's a whole different deal, especially when it involves people who you care about.

I'd spent a lot of time soul-searching. I could sense where the music was going: harder, brighter, more about the thrill than the country-leaning stuff. Joe told me if this was what I wanted, I needed to look at my band. Beyond Dave Matthews, he'd signed ZZ Top in the '90s.

I changed my band, and it killed me. Those guys who'd been out there on the build weren't the right musicians for what was coming. I needed players with the same influences who could rock. Not only Conway and Jones, but Tom Petty, Van Halen, Bruce, and Steve Miller.

When Joe heard, he called. "I can't believe you did it."

"I'm serious. It's not easy, but it's about the music."

"Well, Chesney, you may just get there."

Where it was going to lead me, no one knew. Uncertain, excited, it felt good because it was truly me up there. All the ups, downs, disappointments, growing pains, and frustrations had led to this moment.

Anxious, but never have I felt more alive.

IT'S ALL HAPPENING

"Young" officially dropped on the last day of 2001.

Nobody expected the video to show me eyes blazing, looking into the camera, daring everyone who'd ever felt that way to come along.

That video *was* my journey, my destiny. Me singing into that camera in my actual Gibbs High School varsity jacket and the home movies of me banging away on that guitar and little drum said everything. One more kid amusing the grown-ups, pretending. A boy in a football jersey, sitting up so proud. Even flirting with the cheerleaders, that was us.

Maybe I didn't have a garage band, but those boys on the trestle, they were younger versions of Tim Holt, David, and me. All the small-town trouble we'd gotten into, all the laughter and big talk about one day . . . Everybody does and feels that. But when the teenagers walk out of rehearsal, turn into three grown men, and walk up on what really was my tour bus, that *was* what our life became.

Whether you were young and in the middle of it, in college or starting out or established, you could crawl into "Young" and find your own wild spark. It didn't hurt that claps and drum cracks, as well as that guitar, evoked John Mellencamp's own youthful rebellion from the heart of the country.

But for country radio, in that moment, it was a very clean record with bold presence. It punched out of the car speakers with velocity. People felt the joy of it. This wasn't novelty, this was truth. How I lived, we lived—radio was betting a lot of other people lived, too.

I'd felt things ramping up in the fall. Before the single dropped, the video was shot, things were shifting. We soft-headlined smaller arenas, including the Nutter Center in Dayton, Ohio, and the Greensboro Coliseum in North Carolina.

It was my stage, my sound, my name on the ticket—and my show to do. With a *Greatest Hits* heading for its third million, people were realizing "I *know* that song." Now they needed to know that singer.

Every weekend, we'd been gone for three, four shows. It was like cramming for a test. We knew the tour, the real tour that was major venues promoted by Louis Messina, would be here in a few months. We were learning about pacing, but even more, I was seeing how much they craved—like I did—those guitar solos that sliced through everything.

These were young people—teens, twenties, early thirties—like me—who were as ready to live as I was. We weren't invisible, but we hadn't registered in a pop culture sense.

I'd sold a couple double platinum records, had hits, but even the people listening to country radio didn't realize who I was. In this moment, I could tell they were figuring it out. Looking into their faces, they saw me. That was better than any drug—something I've never done—you could take.

I'd return to Nashville, having thrown everything I had into the audience, spent. They would roar, match my energy, and send it back. It was crazy how real that connection was, and I was still figuring out how to maximize that stage and the people.

When we'd arrive at the bus lot, where my green SUV was parked, it was often right before sunup. Those are the hours the day is yours. Always an early riser, I'd be awake; looking at Danny Tucker, my driver, I'd say, "See you Wednesday . . ."

Getting on the road, I'd shake my head. The highway would be wide open and Nashville lay quiet before me. Heading into the I-40/24/65 merger, I'd roll down the window. Sometimes it was Marley, *Running on Empty*, or Jones, mingling with the mist of that early hour.

After so many years of wanting it all to be faster, I wanted to slow it down.

Selling out the arena dates, you could feel the excitement when we'd be walking through the halls to the stage. I'd been challenged to rethink how we did press, which had always been more fan magazines. I was told, "It's a different way of addressing your music, but if you're making a change, it's good for people to understand what you're trying to do."

Press had always been one more thing. *Critical darling* was a tag that never applied to me. I'd been a punching bag in town. I knew what people said behind our backs, knew some of the people who made fun of me.

Some was the taste factor. Those videos? I didn't know enough to say no, let alone understand I had the power to refuse. We're talking label executives, directors who'd work with massive rock and pop acts. Sometimes I didn't even know: There was a live special for *Greatest Hits* where, without telling me, Jon Small, the director, rolled a mirrored tractor out as we were going into the song and a woman jumped up and started dancing. I had no idea. But there she was, four bars into the band's introduction. That's the moment, as an artist, I became a control freak.

Dancing girls coming off salsa bottle labels, girls who look like dancing mermaids, the cocktail dress in the cornfield? Nobody thought how those things might impact how writers at big magazines or music critics at daily papers saw the music. I could feel it deep down, but I hadn't had the power to say no.

"How can you expect people to take your music seriously if you don't?"

The question stopped me in my tracks. I did take my music seriously, more seriously than anything in my life. I had put every spare dollar, every extra moment, every experience I'd had that could be turned into a song back into the music I was making.

"Well, people don't realize that" was the response.

Challenged, I changed how I thought about media. It wasn't that everything was deadly serious, but I realized people need to know why and how. In that early fall, I got a call about an interview. Steve Morse, the longtime critic at the *Boston Globe*, was willing to talk to me.

Willing, because I'd been pitched to the man who'd championed U2, Bruce Springsteen, and countless legends, as being the voice of the flyover. Talking to a country artist wasn't on his top fifteen things—unless maybe they were a critical favorite.

"He looks at what connects people to artists and music. He's been sent a few songs from the next record—including 'One Step Up'—and he's intrigued. He realizes growing up in the Rust Belt, the Farm Belt, the South is different."

New England had always been good to me. Beyond Boston, those young people are no different than anywhere else.

It was a completely different experience. This man was thoughtful about the songs, the writers, who the music was for. He was listening with his heart; he said that "Young" felt like a classic Mellencamp or Springsteen song.

Our freewheeling spirit was more than a whisper. The shows were selling out when we put them on sale. When we'd pull into a city, there were people waiting for the buses. People would honk at our merch truck when it rolled down the highway.

Momentum was picking up. Having always loved being onstage, there was a lot more time to really build to a climax. We were more than coming into our own, we were carving a lane for something we were in the process of defining.

As the bus rolled into the night, hoarse and spent, someone prodded me to play a new song, one that wasn't on *No Shoes*. "Be as You Are" was very different, quiet and sorting my life in the islands. I knew the label wasn't going to want an album of that music out, but I also knew—playing for my friends on the bus—that was the truest picture of my soul in that moment.

Almost forty shows later, we were at Nashville's downtown arena.

It was New Year's Eve. The Gaylord Arena, as it was called then, held over 18,000 people the way we set the stage up. Who'd want to ring in the new year with us? Turns out a lot more people than we'd thought.

This was what I'd dreamed long ago. Standing with the band, Bobby Lowe, Melvin Fults, James "Catfish" Wingate, Terry Fox, and "Side Phil" Robinson, as we turned up the guitars, played Van Halen's "Ice Cream Man" at sound check, I smiled. In spite of it all, here we were—and it was our name on the ticket.

Eating PF Chang's on the bus before the show, *Almost Famous*, the film about running off with a rock band, on the TV, I didn't feel any different. I realized a decade ago, I was playing at the Turf, talking to the ladies in too much makeup, the tourists wanting to hear Haggard and Jones, Jewel and his dog Hussie; it was less than a hundred feet from where I now sat with a few songwriter friends and my mom.

I was about to ring in 2002 in the city where I'd built this dream. Last year, I had partied in the islands with my friends, an incredible day on the water, laughing, watching dolphins jump alongside our boat, swimming with the ones who jumped off. We listened to music, talked about what we wanted our year to bring—and I drank enough coconut rum and Diet Coke, I actually passed out in a weathered blue wicker rocking chair out on the beach of the house I'd rented.

The sun woke me up, hitting my face as it came over the hill and into Peter Bay. I was covered in mosquito bites, more annoyed than anything, head not pounding nearly as bad as it should have. I knew in a matter of hours, we'd do it again. I'd smiled.

Waiting to get on that stage, I smiled again. How fast things can change.

WHO THE F IS
KENNY CHESNEY?

West Palm Beach was the perfect place to start the tour. Big country market, South Florida's filled with people who work. It felt like the man I was becoming. Coral Sky Amphitheatre, as it was called, was far enough outside of town, it wasn't meant to be a big fancy place to go to shows.

A classic pavilion with 8,000 seats under the cover and a half circle of grass that could hold another 12,000, it was a good place to start a tour. Also, to kick off the next phase of a career that almost felt like a new beginning.

We arrived a few days early, to load in and rehearse. I wanted the band to feel confident in owning that stage. It's easy when you're playing air guitar to think you know how to do it. It's another thing when there's cables and speakers, risers and what have you everywhere.

After a fall of small arenas to get ready, I was leaving nothing to chance. Enough people in Nashville were sure we couldn't pull it off, I wasn't going to give them any reason to be right. Plus, we loved being onstage, playing these songs.

January in West Palm Beach was warm enough, not humid, with a hint of salt in the air. Every night when we went onstage for rehearsal in our T-shirts and shorts, I'd mentally measure the distance to the back of the lawn. Clayton Mitchell, my guitarist; Wyatt Beard, on keyboards; and Nick Hoffman, with his fiddle, were determined to play with a showmanship that matched their musicianship.

I had a rock-solid foundation to work from. Sean Paddock on drums, Steve Marshall on bass, Tim Hensley on acoustic guitar, and Jim Bob Garrett on steel played country music for all it's worth.

We'd have dinner, jacked up on the spirit of what was about to happen. Everyone talking in catering about ideas they had, something that sounded extra good.

As the day's heat broke and the sun went down, we'd get onstage to run the entire show. We were learning the momentum, how one song built and broke into the next. There's a rhythm to a great set list, a way it builds, ebbs, rises again, and pushes you over the top. We were looking for maximum delight.

Finally, January 31 arrived.

We did a long sound check in the afternoon, taking our time. That jagged guitar sound from "Live Those Songs Again" floating into the hot South Florida afternoon; it felt so right. Maybe people weren't doing that, but I knew our fans—like me—would love it.

Out on the lawn, a single woman was dancing. Whether she was an usher, a box office person, or caterer on break, I never knew. But I can see still her hands in the air, hips twisting—figuring that said everything.

Before the show, there was the usual rushing around. Opening acts getting road cases in dressing rooms, gear onstage, asking for meal tickets, receiving their laminates. Security people checking in with the ushers, someone setting up an area for meet and greet.

How many shows had I been grateful just to be on the bill?

Wanting to mark the moment, I gathered everyone who'd played a part into this tiny greenroom for a picture. Louis Messina; Rome and Kate McMahon who routed, settled, and marketed the dates; Joe Galante; Tom Baldricca and his whole radio promotion team, Tony Morreale and Jean Williams; Dale Morris; Clint Higham, who'd worked with Louis to make it happen; and the band! We were a gang of music, moving into a space no one expected.

There was a full moon hanging beyond the lawn. Palm trees stood in silhouette against it. So did all the people on the lawn who got up to dance, throw their arms around one another, and sing these songs with us.

Why not be bold? I thought.

We opened with "Young," announcing unequivocally this is how our future will sound. We were a month into the single. Though the album wouldn't be coming until May, "Young" landed like an established hit, people screaming the chorus as if they were declaring their soul to the universe

We didn't sell out, but close to 12,000 people packed the pavilion and filled out the lawn. Toward the end, the general admission folks surged toward the stage. We told security to let them come.

Maybe because it was my audience, that energy was breaking over us in wave after wave. Untamed and loud, it kept rolling. Trying to not get so excited we threw the songs into tempos way too fast to recognize, it was a sustained rush. In a space where music was the ultimate way of letting go, the band, fans, and people working were caught up in the music together.

Coming offstage, I hugged everyone in the wings, then bolted back out onto the stage with a force I don't think I recognized. We came to play, and man, had we.

The Southern swagger of "Keep Your Hands to Yourself" has its own velocity. Grabbing the mic, throwing my boot onto the monitor, I tore into that opening line and kept going. We had delivered our first true headlining show. And people loved it.

Loved it so much I could see them pointing, cheering, laughing. We had the Georgia Satellites, followed by John Mellencamp's "Jack and Diane," a perfect benediction for all of us kids nobody saw coming.

So caught up in the moment, I didn't realize one small thing: When I leaned into that first line with my foot on the monitor, I literally busted my inseam. The entire space where the seams come together had torn open, and all of West Palm Beach got a look at what I was packing.

The night was so inspiring, I didn't care. I laughed. Truly, opening night, I had left it all onstage.

After the pictures were taken, the last handshake and hug was given, and the memory of all those cheers died off, I went back to the state room on my bus to take it all in. Rather than obsess about the seam of my jeans tearing, all I thought about were the surges of energy that kept slamming into us—the way people screamed and sang along, the bliss on their faces.

They were so passionate. Everything I'd believed about "Young," this shift I had wanted, manifested right there. I'd seen it. This sound, the tropical rhythms that were coming, but especially the rock energy changed the way people absorbed country music. Making something passive into an active force of life.

Overwhelmed, I took in the stillness.

I wrote a contract with my soul that night. Sitting alone in the back of my bus, idling in the parking lot, I made a commitment. No matter what it took, demanded, or required, I was going to give everything to this. I was going to push the limits but never lose sight of who the people living inside these songs were. For me, giving them anthems they could put their lives inside, feel seen and understood, was a big piece of it. But even more, when they came to—literally—live those songs together, I wanted to absolutely deliver them with complete immediacy.

I wasn't going to give a lot. No, it was more. I wasn't going to save anything for myself. Whatever it took, however I had to deliver it, I would give it all. That was my mission.

I knew what music meant to me. I wanted this music to mean that to them.

Word began to spread about our shows. Radio stations in the markets we played clamored for give-away tickets, talked about what they saw on the air. It was more than a buzz, it was a witness. I was determined to live up to all of it.

Seeing's believing, so Clint, Dale, and Joe started bringing people to the shows, which were selling out. By the time we hit towns, there were no tickets, and scalpers would be on the side of the road trying to buy even single tickets if they could get them.

With military precision, the setup for *No Shoes* went into overdrive. Marketing meetings became deep strategy sessions: How many cities could we hit street week? What was the best routing to get three, four stations in a day? What media should we do?

It was a long way from that first *No Shoes* meeting at the end of December, where someone projected we could sell between 135 and 142,000 pieces in the first week. What you need to remember in those days before streaming, people got in a car and drove somewhere to purchase the new record. It was a commitment; many albums were impulse buys at Target or Walmart, but to create something people came into the store for? That was a big deal.

Walking out of that first meeting, I got on the elevator concerned.

"We can do more than that," I told my team.

"That's a lot of records," someone said.

"No, I can feel it," I said. "We can do more. I promise."

"Well, son," Dale offered, "there's still time for setup."

"Yes, but they can't buy records that aren't in the store."

◆ ◆ ◆

Were we now on track for more? I didn't care about the number as much as I cared about every fan who went to buy a record being able to get a copy. The more shows I played, the more excitement I felt. These songs really were something the fans were living and breathing.

I was in the best shape of my life. Anticipation was my middle name.

"You ready?" Galante asked, as we headed to the airport.

All the years to get here had prepared me. I was feeling things—those shows kept getting louder and bigger—I'd never imagined, but I'd done the work. I knew we were hitting another gear, and I couldn't wait.

There's a momentum when the record company actually leases a plane to maximize the amount of ground covered: on the jet, off the jet, get in the car, hit the station or stations, maybe grab a bite with someone important, or eat a Subway turkey sub as you're rolling; moving at the speed of sound, you tell the story, take the pictures, share the smiles, say thank you as many ways as you can think—and move on.

You know all the faces and places, old friends, new people. It's very specific in the blur; but the time and order smears, the days get out of sequence when you look back. The best way to do it is lean forward, pick up your feet, and throw your hands in the air. As long as you embrace the great moments, there's an energy that propels you.

New York. Boston. Atlanta. Chicago. Dallas. Houston. Minneapolis. DC. Los Angeles. Baltimore. Kansas City. Knoxville, then Bristol/Johnson City. Chattanooga. Salt Lake City. San Francisco. Pittsburgh. Philadelphia.

It was a rush, a scramble, a lot of energy. Then it was over.

When the chart printed on May 29, 2002, *No Shoes, No Shirt, No Problems* sat at No. 1 on *Billboard*'s Top 200 Albums chart. We'd sold over 235,000 copies of our album, not quite double the initial projection.

Everyone knew we'd top the Country Albums chart. I'd done that.

But the Top 200 was everything: rock, pop, hip-hop, alternative, and Black music.

Suddenly, the guy nobody knew sang those songs was on top of the biggest chart of all.

"Who the fuck is Kenny Chesney?" was the question of the week.

They were about to find out.

LIVING IN FAST FORWARD

All those people who had no idea who I was, what I sounded like, were trying to figure out how they hadn't seen me coming. Country music existed in its own world; that's why nobody in the pop world expected us to hit so hard. But plenty of Nashville people were equally shocked.

The shows were turning into frenzied experiences; tickets gone long before we got there, the party often started hours before doors opened. In the afternoons, we'd play basketball and hear the tailgating.

Car stereos blasting *Greatest Hits* or *No Shoes*, Aerosmith, or Dave Matthews Band as everybody pregamed. Some people grilled, others filled metal tubs with ice and beer. No matter who you were or who you came with, people were making new friends and talking about the show.

I wanted to be out there so bad, I'd get Ed Wannebo, my production manager who brings me my margarita every night during our show, to mix up a couple pitchers of margaritas, and then Farmer, Burns, myself, and a few people would climb onto a green John Deere gator. Zooming through the parking lots, we'd pour margaritas for the surprised fans. Jay Cooper, who shoots and directs our live video, sometimes filmed it. Swooping down on a group of tailgaters was awesome.

In Charlotte, North Carolina, the show was beyond sold out; a bunch of creative fans took wire cutters to the chain link fence around the PNC Music Pavilion to get on the lawn. If there was anything that defined this moment, it was all the fun people were having. Whether you were in the crew, on the lawn, or listening to the records, there was a real sense of finding people who, like you, worked hard, played hard, and engaged life completely.

Seeing all those faces—some with their eyes closed, some with their eyes wide open—swaying and leaning with their whole being, I realized these songs connected their worlds as much as mine. Some nights the crowds were so loud we could hardly hear onstage.

No Shoes was platinum in a matter of weeks; the stories about our tickets blowing out were everywhere. I'd try to remember: "Focus on what you can control. Think about the fans coming to the shows, singing those songs at the top of their lungs. They love you; that's who matters."

Jim Pitt booked me—a mainstream artist who made no sense—on *Late Night with Conan O'Brien*. An alternative-leaning, super-late-night show, commercial country music was *not* what they did. Rather than play "The Good Stuff," our single, we played "No Shoes, No Shirt, No Problems," a song for being chill and taking it as it comes. The college kids, restaurant workers, and night owls loved it.

◆ ◆ ◆

Those first few years felt slightly *Wayne's World*. We had a day off in Columbus, Ohio, where Van Halen was playing the Schottenstein Center at Ohio State the night before us. Louis set it up for me and some of the guys to go.

Walking down the hall, there's Sammy Hagar in turquoise pants, all that yellow hair everywhere. He lights up like he's seen Elvis, shouts, "Kenny Chesney!" as if I was somebody. Holy shit! Sammy Hagar, the voice of Montrose, "I Can't Drive 55" and "Eagles Fly," plus all the modern Van Halen hits. Animated, he's heading our way.

We'd meet Eddie and Alex Van Halen that night, along with Michael Anthony. But it was Sammy who stood out, because he made us feel welcome. For Farmer and me, who'd devoured "Bad Motor Scooter" and "Rock Candy," it was outer body. This was a hero, and he seemed excited meeting us.

Our heroes were often cooler than we could've even imagined. With a day off in Salt Lake City, we were hanging at the pool, getting some sun and some stillness. Unplugging sometimes does as much for the engine as running six or seven miles.

Across the water, I saw him first.

"Farmer, you're not going to believe this . . . Look over there."

"Whoa . . ."

"Joe Walsh."

The Eagles were in town for a show that night. Joe Walsh, whose solo career created some of the greatest rock songs where the guitar parts were as iconic as the vocals, was doing the very same thing we were. When the speed of touring seems too fast, there's a reset in something as simple as sitting in the sun.

We walked over, introduced ourselves, asked about "Rocky

Mountain Way" and "Funk #49." He couldn't have been more genuine; he didn't mind talking about those James Gang records; he seemed to appreciate our asking.

Farmer, Holt, Hobby, and I decided to buy tickets and see the Eagles that night. Those songs were everywhere when we were teens. Why not slide into the building and experience a concert the same way people were experiencing us?

Hearing Joe's solo on "Life in the Fast Lane" was crazy. We looked at one another like teenagers, playing air guitar solos.

A mutual friend from Palm Beach decided it was time to meet Jimmy Buffett. People thought I'd been chasing him musically, but other than loving how he drew characters and put them in stories, I knew there was only one Buffett. I loved the ocean, no doubt, but I came at it—and island living—from the place of a small-town kid raised in the Smoky Mountains.

We were in Vegas playing Mandalay Bay. Jimmy was headlining the larger MGM Grand. We walked over to the Four Seasons. There, sitting in the sun with a couple of his friends, was Jimmy. Reading the *New York Times*, and talking sports with his buddies as we walked up.

"Hey, Jimmy . . ."

In a cabana at the Four Seasons, I was shaking hands with a hero. Small talk was easy. Jimmy'd been a *Billboard* reporter in Nashville; working the folkie circuit, Jerry Jeff Walker took him to Key West. He knew about shifting longitudes, attitudes, realities.

We talked about Music Row, the publishers, the Exit/In, Don Gant, and Don Light, who were all part of his early years. We talked about Mac McAnally, who was a Coral Reefer Band member off and on. I told him about how hard Mac's "Back Where I Come From" hit with my audience.

He understood everything about where I'd been; he seemed to like talking about a Music Row that was almost gone. Having been at Acuff-Rose and the Turf, I understood his Nashville. That creative core, if you get steeped in it, never leaves you.

We visited fifteen, twenty minutes, then I figured it was time. He didn't need me hanging around, but I wanted to let him know how much I respected him.

"Thanks for coming by," he said. He seemed to mean it.

We both smiled. Jimmy got back to his friends and his paper; I headed to the Pink Taco with Farmer and a friend. What stands out, even now, is how similar our paths were, how much we both loved characters and creative people. And yes, the ocean.

I met a hero at the pool. I had no idea he would—like Joe, Sammy, the Van Halens—become such a good friend.

The shows kept stacking up, sold out, louder, brighter. "The Good Stuff" was flying up the chart. A meandering ballad about what really matters in a world of pride and ego, no one expected it to spend seven weeks at No. 1. By the time the year was over, it was *Billboard*'s No. 1 Country Song of 2002.

Any chance I could, I'd escape to the islands. A couple nights on the boat, the generator hum would finally start to cross fade into the sound of waves hitting the hull. Seagulls in the morning and the smell of the sea replaced diesel fumes and the sound of forklifts moving gear.

Always listening to songs, I'd take stacks of demos and hear the joy of songwriters' imaginations at work. We might not need an album for another year, but with *No Shoes* being a breakthrough, I wanted to keep pushing what was possible.

I wrote some: in my journal and on my guitar. Dean Dillon, now a good friend, would come down. We'd philosophize about life, love, or the lack thereof. Marvel in that resigned way about how life works; we both understood fairy tales aren't real—whether you're a romantic dreamer or a stoic realist.

Over the last year, I saw songs change lives. People who found courage—for hard things, but also shooting their shot, taking that crazy chance—by turning up the volume.

Long before the tour was over, we were talking 2003.

From left field, Clint brought up something I'd said as a joke.

"Why not Neyland Stadium?"

"Nobody's played there since the Jackson 5."

"But if we could figure it out? A homecoming show . . ."

"You want *me* . . . to play . . . *Neyland Stadium*."

"Yeah. I think it could be great. Take you back home, let you headline the stadium. You're not the Jacksons, you're a local guy makes good."

"I think this is crazy."

"If I can get this done, though, you're in."

The tour rolled on. Isolated shows, six-date runs, zigzagging across the country.

We were now moving to four, then five buses—one for me, the band, two for the crew. When you get your own bus, it's a big deal; but even with Farmer, Holt, and Hobby, it felt different, quiet. Where did all the people go?

We passed time with marathon College Football PlayStation battles. All the smack talk of high school sports, the bragging rights, threaded through those trips and hours between my 4:30 supper, meet and greet, and the show. I was a grown man, turned back into a kid.

I have held shows for two, three, even ten minutes trying to finish a game, determined not to let Hobby beat me. Competitive to a fault, I once threw an entire console out the window, flying down the highway because I lost to Wyatt Beard over a really stupid play.

We were coming into the fall; decisions needed to be made.

For every girl—who ever had a dream—there was only one next single choice. "Big Star" had come up in every meet and greet, radio station visit, and internet message board. Written by Stephony Smith, it told the story of a girl who wanted to sing, who got up there and did it, doubled down, and kept going. It talked about petty gossip, jealousy, and how those who are afraid to try cut you down.

I wanted a song that gave that empowerment back to the fans. Raised around women, I loved the idea of a young girl turning into a superstar. It wasn't a boys' club, or shouldn't be. "Big Star" made that point wide open, and then some.

Everywhere the story's been told about how we had Taylor Swift booked to open for us. She may've been young, but she was a good songwriter, had that fearless look in her eye that said, "World, here I am . . ."

She was everything that song was about. I couldn't have been prouder to book her to open our shows, or more disappointed the beer company sponsor said we couldn't have someone underage as a support act. When I explained what happened and why, I sent her a check for the lost dates; would she get another summer tour? I hoped so.

But I wanted to see her win, so it seemed like the right thing to do.

She said it was the most money she'd ever seen, used it to pay off her bus and give her band bonuses. To see a young artist with so much spark and knowing I'd done the right thing was a good feeling. More than paying it forward, it's knowing you're empowering a great artist.

❖ ❖ ❖

I agreed to another New Year's Eve at the Nashville arena, ringing in another New Year in Music City. I had Montgomery Gentry, who knew how to stomp and rile up the crowd, and Keith Urban, who was starting to have real hits, open.

How much had changed in a year. I was grateful because this was what I'd wanted without understanding exactly what it was. So much had happened—heroes met, songs written, a confidence that wasn't faith, but baked in.

When midnight hit, the confetti flew, and we sang "Auld Lang Syne." For me, it wasn't about saying goodbye to 2002, but looking ahead to my hopes for the years to come.

BACK WHERE I COME FROM

Neyland Stadium was on. It had been almost two decades since the University of Tennessee had allowed someone on their hallowed field; the Jacksons' *Victory Tour* was in 1984. Given that, I can't stress enough how sacred that space is; the idea we were going to play there still hits me in the heart.

Coach Phillip Fulmer, who'd won the National Championship in 1998, had let me watch from the sidelines during my rise in country music. Again, he was supportive. When we announced the show, he joined us for the formal announcement. Dad was there, too, making it a true meeting of the sports and musical forces in my life.

Billed as the *Back Where I Come From Party*, I was very much a local boy. All those Saturdays listening to John Ward call games on the radio? Neyland Stadium was part of East Tennessee's essential being.

The anticipation around this show was more than "This is gonna be big." I wanted it to be special. Brooks & Dunn agreed to play; they were about as industrial strength honkytonk as it got.

I'd met Bobbie Ritchie playing Pine Knob, outside Detroit; ended up at an all-night party at his place that was greater parts music to mayhem. Given what this show was shaping up to be, having Kid Rock show up and do "Cowboy" was exactly right.

He agreed.

I called Bobbie back. Uncle Kracker had recently spun off his Twisted Brown Trucker Band, dropping an album and having a massive hit with "Follow Me." Soulful, melodic, driving in a groove-forward way, Kracker might be the left turn I needed.

"Call him yourself," he said. "Here's his number."

Uncle Kracker was trying to create his own identity, but Matt Shafer was game. "Sure, I'll do it."

For a kid who'd wanted to play sports when he grew up, then stopped growing and left any chance of college athletics behind, I was about to play Neyland Stadium. I had two of rock and pop's biggest stars as guests; I had Brooks & Dunn as loud and proud as real country got.

Talk about coming home.

It was chilly, even into the afternoon. People were swirling around backstage.

Walking to the lift under the stage, I looked around, thinking about that kid seeing the Vols beat Notre Dame.

Stepping onto the platform, preshow tape rolling, I stood taller. Over 60,000 teens, young families, and a lot of East Tennessee had turned out for this show. They loved—and lived in—the songs, but even more, I was theirs. I grew up, went out into the world, and came back.

If I could, why couldn't they?

That was the beauty of the night.

My heart pumped harder, almost in time to the backbeat. If walking out to 20,000 was starting to feel normal, this was a packed-out crowd of 61,780; there was a physical wall of sound and love that hit me.

Walking down the riser and onto the stage, those faces were fresh, so alive and happy. I stood there taking it in. Massive spotlights were whirling out on the field, the Goodyear Blimp was in the sky. Everyone in my world was over the top.

What was a high-energy show was also an emotional conversation. I dropped out during "Young," to let the crowd sing, and heard the chorus delivered more like a revival witness than a sing-along. It happened again and again.

All night, I kept looking at a spot where I'd spent so many Saturdays with my dad. Looking up, there was Jim Cogdill's box—Section KK, Row 1—in the upper deck, where the three of us experienced the thrill of seeing Reggie White, Willie Gault, or Alan Cockrell and the rest of the Vols play throughout my childhood.

When the band kicked into Edgar Winter's "Frankenstein," signaling the end of the show, my guests came out of the wings to wave and sign autographs with me. In that moment of jubilation, Kid Rock took a mic, prowling the stage, and began exhorting the fans to cheer, "KAY . . . CEE . . . from TENN-e-SEE . . . KAY . . . CEE . . . from TENN-e-SEE."

And that was how the party ended.

I GO BACK

I woke up the next morning, got on the plane, and went straight to the Caribbean.

I wrote all the time, grabbing songs from everyday conversations. I needed to be still, though, for those moments to come through; to take something like Mark Tamburino saying, "Whenever I hear 'Sweet Home Alabama,' I go back to that bar, Willie T's . . ." and realize that was the story of my life.

"I Go Back" was born in that eye of the roar. Invoking church and the chicken dinners after, graduation trips to Myrtle Beach, trying to impress girls, raspberry wine, two-tone cars, frat parties, my school friend Lance Wilson who was killed in a car wreck at seventeen, and pulling them through the needle's eye of John Mellencamp's "Jack and Diane," Steve Miller's "Rockin' Me," Billy Joel's "Only the Good Die

Young," that cloud of church organ in the final chorus, it arrived in blue ink on yellow paper.

We all have a song that somehow stamped our life / Takes us to another place and time was a truth for all of us.

That April, I found myself at the Beacon Theater on the Upper West Side of New York City. Willie Nelson was turning seventy, and someone decided to do a TV special. Few people can bring as many different kinds of artists together.

Eric Clapton. Ray Charles. Sheryl Crow. Lyle Lovett. Wyclef Jean. Everywhere you turned, there was someone more famous than the next coming together for the love of Willie Nelson.

I'd been booked to duet on "Last Thing I Needed (First Thing This Morning)," one of those philosophical gut punches Willie does so well. A bunch of the musicians who played on my records were the house band, so rehearsal was easy.

Kris Kristofferson, somewhere in his sixties, saw us coming out of the maze of one-on-one interviews. He reached out. "Hey, man, I love what you and your guys are doing."

We talked for a few seconds. He had a publicist pushing him to get going; I understood. When you've got a schedule, that many artists, you keep moving.

"Let's get out of here," I said to Clint and a friend.

It was brisk, rainy. Out the side door, down the block—not wanting to get too far away—we found a neighborhood Mexican restaurant. Seemed appropriate before a concert honoring Willie, who defined Texas for the world.

"You ever think you'd be here?" the woman asked.

"No, never," I said. "Even dreaming about success . . ."

"You don't dream these kind of details," Clint explained.

"It's kind of surreal." But also totally cool.

Mark Rothbaum, Willie's longtime manager, met us when we checked back in after dinner. He wanted to say "thank you," as if the pleasure wasn't all mine.

Watching the performances on a monitor in the greenroom, I saw the power of a career created on one's own terms. Willie battled the Nashville system, went to Texas, and made country music his way. People didn't understand, and he didn't care. He knew what he wanted to do. Whether it was singing with Julio Iglesias, making an album of reggae songs or *Stardust*, his take on the classic American songbook, he'd become a compass for other artists with their own vision.

WHEN THE SUN GOES DOWN

In the downtime at Neyland Stadium, I'd played "When the Sun Goes Down" for Kracker.

I thought it would make a good duet, something a couple friends looking forward to chasing the night might sing. Kracker, in the front lounge of my bus, head bowed, bounced in time as he listened. About the second chorus, he picked his head up.

"That's fresh. I'm in."

Several weeks later, Kracker rolled into a studio in South Nashville, bag full of Krystal hamburgers in his hand; his wingman Shifty driving. As Detroit hip as they came, Uncle Kracker was covered in tattoos, sporting a gold tooth and wearing a mechanic's shirt.

Raspy, but warm, Kracker's voice drew you in. Its tone felt like talking to an old running buddy.

I knew "When the Sun Goes Down" was a hit when I'd heard it. Adding Uncle Kracker, it expanded the camaraderie, taking it from party song to anthem.

He got on the mic, and that voice poured out. If I was friendly, he was chill; if I was solid, he was danger. He was also one of the funniest human beings I've ever met.

When we told him to have fun vamping on the song's fade, he put his hand up to his headphones. Next thing we know, the "Sexy Tractor" ad libs "She thinks Kracker's sexy" and "Uncle Kenny's hotter when the sun goes down" were born.

CNN was in town and wanted to cover the collaboration. We talked to Denise Quan about what we had in common, Neyland Stadium, maybe touring together next year. It all felt so open and free. Anything is possible if you start from the music. As I was learning, common ground came from the soul, how you lived and what you listened to. Not how you were marketed.

Uncle Kracker knew as much about George Jones as I did. Soulful though he was, he got that working-class reality that gave country its spine.

Uncle Kracker, who'd spun out of Kid Rock's orbit, was an unexpected future member of my road family. With the jokes and his knowledge about artists and songwriters, he fit before we realized we'd adopted him.

In that moment, he wasn't a guy coming to sing on a song he liked. He'd enjoyed the hang in Knoxville. He was willing to get on a plane, venture into country music before mass media thought it was cool.

Like us, Kracker had no idea when he headed to the airport he'd sung on one of the most iconic summer songs of the decade. You can't know stuff like that. We knew our vocal chemistry was strong, the track felt good, and the sentiment gave people permission.

When the Sun Goes Down was *Shoes* on steroids. I wanted to say more, mean more, rock more. I wanted songs that took a bite out of life, showed the world who people in Detroit, East Tennessee, New England, and Tampa, Florida, were. The throttling tale of my—and so many other people's—college days, "Keg in the Closet" was a handful of Polaroids of us partying.

Sun also took a spare country turn. A song I wrote with Skip Ewing, "Being Drunk's a Lot Like Loving You," used a metaphor to draw a raw sort of pain.

Whether I'd lived it or not, the songs on *Sun* reflected the lives of people I knew. We needed to get a first single out while finishing mixes. Rather than positive up tempo, the decision was a ballad that takes what seems a shattering moment for a kid on the verge of starting his life and flips the script. That mistake turns out to be the best thing, then the baby grows up, drives off with her future ahead.

"There Goes My Life" didn't happen to me. But I knew a couple people who experienced it. Over the years at Acuff-Rose, signing autographs after shows, talking to radio people and fans, I'd learned real life—*real* real life—trumps everything else. People want to hear their lives, especially the seemingly difficult patches, delivered with empathy, even a happy ending they can't see. More than truth, it's hope—and something people need as much as a raging guitar solo.

"There Goes My Life" hit a nerve.

What that moment of time felt like:
a boat, a guitar,
nowhere to go, and
all the ocean I could see.

Maiden voyage on the *Hey Now*: 01-01-01.

A lot of life was lived, a lot of songs were written on my first boat, *Sixth Gear*.

Boat Captain Ben Bourassa, me, and Low Key Bob Shinners heading out for adventure.

After the storm.
We flew the Love for Love City flag
at what was left of my house after Hurricane Irma.
Knowing the spirit of the USVI,
they defined the power of hope in those years of rebuilding.

The last night at the Quiet Mon, thinking about all of the laughs, beers, and friends made.

Dale Morris believed in a couple kids who had pretty strong dreams. Celebrating with my managers Clint Higham and Dale.

The night everything changed.
Later that night at Coral Sky Amphitheater in West Palm Beach, Florida, I'd sign a contract with my soul.

A rock star, a free spirit, an inspiration—but especially, Grace Potter is my friend. Even before I knew her, her voice felt like coming home.

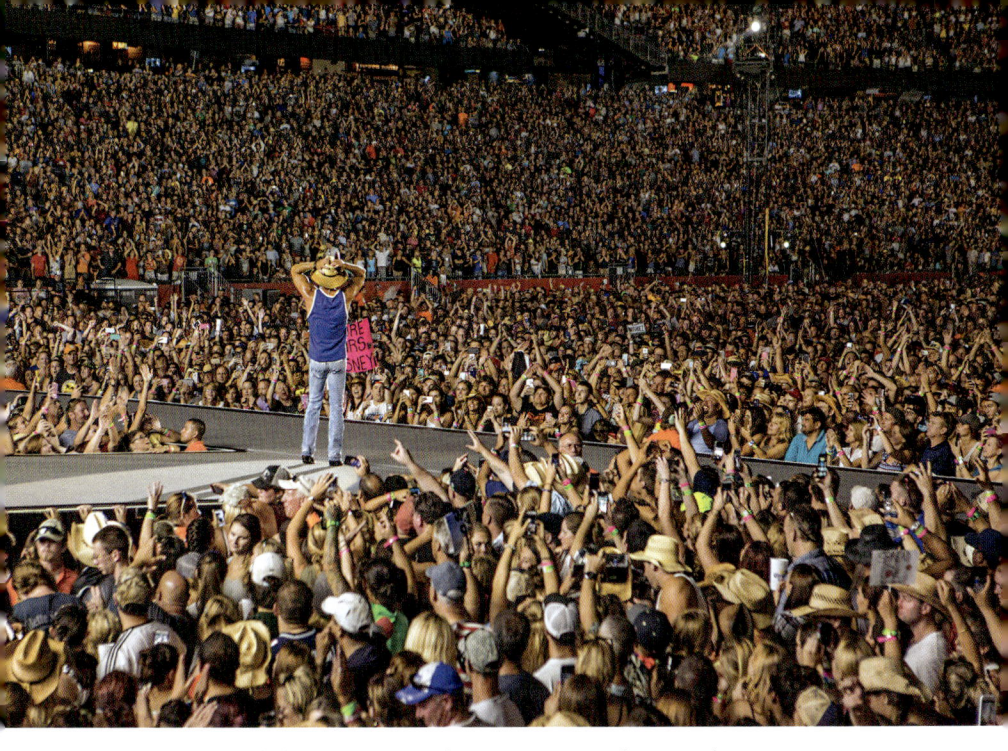

Feeling all that energy and emotion, it's a lot to take in.
Gillette Stadium in Foxboro, Massachusetts.

Every stadium, from the beginning, I go up to the very top and sit there for a while. I measure the distance from that seat to the stage, because I know that person in the nosebleeds is the one I most want to reach.
Heinz Field, Pittsburgh, Pennsylvania.

With my friend Uncle Kracker, who was such a part of what happened.
And look—no phones!

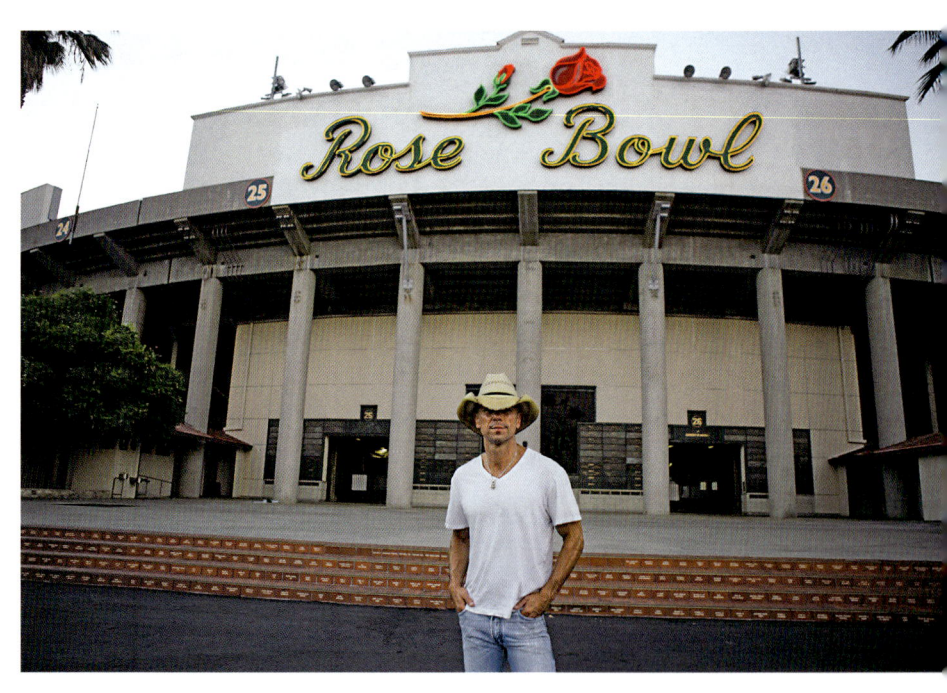

Rose Bowl. Pasadena, California. *The Big Revival Tour*, 2015.

This moment of connection
I look forward to every night.

Arrowhead Stadium,
Kansas City, Missouri.

She stole my clothes,
my hat, and she rode
a child's tractor
like she stole it, too.
Megan Moroney
pulled the ultimate prank
in Foxboro, Massachusetts.

For my Christmas present, Megan Moroney wrote a song about her journey—and asked me to sing on it. This is my favorite moment from the video.

KEG IN THE CLOSET, KENNY IN THE KEYS

All the characters, challenges, even moments playing shows on the back of a flatbed truck, or being told, "You've done more with less talent than anyone I've ever seen" by Jimmy Carter, a syndicated TV reporter, made the trip worth taking.

The beauty of everything that happened was finding a road family who were as up for adventure as I was. It's the reason this circus carries a giant marlin I reeled in in the Virgin Islands' North Drop named Marley in its very own road case; rolling him up onstage and plopping a giant sombrero on him keeps us all from taking things too seriously.

♦ ♦ ♦

"Keg in the Closet" was its own force.

The single and video for "Sun" and "Keg" tours converged. The single dropped the day the album came out; the surprise college tour was part of ramping up for the year ahead.

It's easy to be jaded when you've got five or six buses, trucks carrying sound, lights, staging, and instruments. It's big business. When you're playing for over 20,000 every night, it's easy to get swept up in a "we're so massive" mindset. We'd done shows for over a million people each of the previous two years. I was up there with U2, Dave Matthews, Springsteen, and the Rolling Stones.

Unthinkable. But before we got carried away, I wanted to get back to our roots. Almost making Kate and Rome McMahon, who do tour marketing and routing, want to shoot themselves, I decided this would be an excellent time to do unannounced shows at college bars. Tickets were available the day of show. I'm pretty sure they were free. We'll see you at the War Eagle Supper Club in Auburn, Alabama; the 40 Watt Club in Athens, Georgia; Floyd's Music Store in Tallahassee, Florida; New Amsterdam's in Knoxville, Tennessee; and the Jupiter Bar & Grille in Tuscaloosa, Alabama.

Barnstorming, really. One bus, one van, one small truck, and the thrill of being onstage in an overcrowded club, no video, no light show, a bunch of covers, a few hits, and bars filled well past what the fire marshal would allow.

When you've got the audience almost toe-to-toe with you, there's a different urgency. Loose, loaded with energy, there's no escape. But why would you want to? Those shows went for three, sometimes almost four hours, because we were having too much fun to stop.

Into that righteous mayhem, Uncle Kracker appeared. He'd come down to Florida to shoot the video for "When the Sun Goes Down" on a beach in Coconut Grove, camping out and literally rocking knee-high in the water with a group of hula girls dancing on the water behind us. Beyond the opening, where I bang on a vintage VW van's side door to roust my pal for a gig and am met by a squad of girls in grass skirts emerging, we hung out, played guitars, and belly laughed like you never do on a day of shoot, stop, shoot over.

When Shaun Silva, the director, suggested we take the grass skirts and leis to Athens and the 40 Watt, Kracker was all in. We only needed one night, but Matt, his assistant and his tour manager, got on our bus—and kept going. That part—all of us telling jokes from our bunks, trying to top each other—was like summer camp with guitars.

Kracker would do his hits with us, but he was as much about what else could we sing? Coconut rum and sugar-free Red Bull were definitely involved. But my decision to go crowd-surfing some nights, especially in Gainesville, Florida, didn't require any liquid courage. We were inside the curve of the moment, shooting the curl and feeling the fans' buzz.

Once again, our street week was fierce. All the cities, the morning television, crisscrossing America. The label knew what we had and intended to go hard. Everybody else seemed to know it, too. We could feel people watching, seeing if we were for real.

When the final sales were tallied, *Sun* was over 635,000—certified gold out the door, platinum a few weeks later. "When the Sun Goes Down" was flying up the radio and video charts. A few more weeks, Kracker and I parked at No. 1 for a six-week run. For Brett James, the songwriter who'd originally been signed as an artist but gave us his song, he became a go-to songwriting force.

Over the years, Brett and I would write or share so many songs. The day after Christmas one year, we jumped on a plane, went to the islands, went out raging. The next afternoon, when I emerged at the pool around 2:30 p.m., I announced through my hangover, "Well, we went out last night."

We both cracked beers, grabbed guitars. Three hours later, "Out Last Night" *and* "Reality" were finished. Top-to-bottom, what you hear. We headed back into town to do it all over again.

There were photo shoots for *Sports Illustrated* with Swimsuit-issue models, taking your friends to see the Rolling Stones, singing at the White House the night Saddam Hussein was captured, stuff you wouldn't know to dream.

As we were shutting down "the machine" for the holidays, I got a call. From Jimmy Buffett. He had a couple songs he wanted me to listen to, see if maybe I'd want to come sing one.

"License to Chill" felt like everything people think he and I were about. I wouldn't have cared what we sang, but singing a song written by Jimmy, Mac, and Al Anderson seemed like an excellent idea.

Key West, a few days later. I'd flown in the night before the session. I figured we'd go to a nice dinner before the studio. My phone rang.

"Kenny, it's Jimmy. You got plans?"

"Going to dinner."

"Meet me at La Trattoria on Duval Street. It's the old part of town. Let me take you to dinner, 524 Duval. You'll love this place. See you there."

Painted white with big picture windows, you could easily walk by it. Classic old Key West, La Trattoria's been around for years. When we walked in, Jimmy and Sunshine Smith, the co-owner and creator of Margaritaville, were already there. He got up, introductions were made, hugs all around. To the untrained eye, he was one more guy of a certain age in a ball cap; but if you listened to his stories about the Key West he found in the early '70s, long before the cruise ships arrived, who else could it be? Even his speaking voice sounds like the records.

Listening to Jimmy tell stories about Tennessee Williams, Hemingway's writing, Captain Tony's, Shel Silverstein, as well as the characters who lived, fished, dreamed, and smuggled there, time dissolved and the mythic Key West came to life. More than the chickens running in the streets, three-toed cats near Truman's Southern White House; you felt the action and recognized the shadows falling on the street.

It was the Conch Republic, the southernmost city in the United States. All the history and legends became real hearing his asides and details. Like an outlaw hideout, it was where outliers could find their own kind. Navy personnel, Cubans, hippies, fishermen, folksingers, pirates, painters, famous authors, he'd seen them all. Generous with his memories, it was an immersion course in the currency of things you cannot buy.

We were in the middle of dinner when Jimmy tapped my collarbone, leaned over, and whispered, "Come on. I want to show you something."

As we'd ordered our meal, the annual Key West Christmas Parade had begun. Walking outside, we were in the midst of it. All the crazy pomp, colorful costumes, the drill teams and marching bands flowed down the street. It was brilliant, buoyant, free.

What a special way to be introduced to the local soul of Key West. In all these people churning with the music pouring from the clubs, I felt the spirit of what was. I've never been so grateful to see through someone's eyes.

A couple hours later, the pasta and gelato were gone. We got up from the table and spilled into the night. The idea Jimmy cared enough to show me that part of his original Key West was a gift.

The next morning, I reported to Shrimp Boat Sound, the studio Jimmy built in the corner of its Historic Seaport. Blink and you'd miss it. But with its Neve soundboard meant for analog tape, where you move the faders with real hands, his control room was a sacred space.

Record-release promo materials shared wall space with a massive blowup of Jimmy's high school yearbook picture.

"Kenny, come sit at this board," Jimmy directed. "It's a '69. I bought it from Gordon Lightfoot, who was very particular about sound."

Sitting there, you knew incredible, historic music had passed through that console. Levels were set, distortion rolled off. This felt so natural, as if hanging around the studio with Jimmy Buffett was no big deal. I thought about that night at Starwood Amphitheater, where I couldn't afford a Coke.

DIVER DOWN

Running errands around Nashville, Irving Azoff, the LA supermanager, calls. He lets me know I'm going to be getting a call. That's all he says. Okay, great. Whatever Irving needs.

A few minutes later, the phone rings. No caller ID. Here we go.

"Hello," I say to the void.

"Hey, Kenny . . ."

It's Eddie Van Halen. Even before he tells me, I know who it is. That voice is almost as recognizable as the way he plays guitar. Irving had told him about me and the guys coming to see them in Columbus, he said.

If you take half a beat and exhale, you'd be shocked how easy and normal the conversations are. The secret is to not torque up, fall to your knees, and start muttering, "We are not worthy . . ." Or more realistically, "I'm such a fan."

I told him about seeing the band at Knoxville's arena; how we were in high school, and they blew our minds, that I was dying to hear what they did to "Hot for Teacher" live, "Running with the Devil." He took it in.

Tim Holt, Matt and Lance Wilson, and I listened to *Diver Down* nonstop when it came out. *1984*, too, while shooting baskets all day in the summer scrimmaging with friends. I was digesting those lyrics, the layered guitars and loud drums. Van Halen changed how we heard rock and roll; so clean, it cut right into you and shook your frame.

We talked about how the road's changed. I told him my guitar player Clayton was one of those kids who'd locked himself in his bedroom, learned to play every single riff, lick, and solo from their records.

The conversation made him happy. All artists want their music to strike people in a meaningful way, to inspire them. Telling him about my guys, he knew that his music inspired us to make country music hit harder.

After that, Eddie and I talked sporadically. Check in, catch up about the road, our families, what was going on. He was always interested. When we played the professional soccer stadium outside Los Angeles, Irving called: "Eddie wants to come see you guys play."

Like that, Eddie and Alex Van Halen were on the parking list.

When two of the most iconic rockers of all time walk down the hall at your show and you realize they're there to see you and your band, everybody's heart beats faster. Not to show off, but to show up and show your heroes how strong their impact was.

Van Halen took the arena-rock model and supersized it long before MTV. Who was bigger than Van Halen? Louder? Knew the power of a great hook? The way melody threaded through the pounding of Alex's drums pulled people in.

When Eddie and Alex told us they wanted to play, I thought Clayton was going to die. It was Santa saying, "Double Christmas this year!"

One of the best things about what I do for a living is making don't-dare-to-dream fantasies happen. Every member of my crew was at attention on the side of the stage.

Eddie, whip thin, shirt open, and cowboy hat perched on his head, rolled out onstage with that iconic red-and-white Frankenstein guitar. He looked over at Clayton, nodded, and Alex, who'd jumped on our drummer's kit, kicked into "You Really Got Me," then "Jump."

The stadium went nuts; even without knowing, the fans understood what a meeting of forces this was.

BEER IN MEXICO

And there was Sammy Hagar. One of the greatest rock singers of all time, he's a box of fireworks all going off at once. No one lives the rock star life more robustly than Sammy.

He loves seeing young acts coming on strong. That night in Columbus, I had no idea he'd become a dear friend. I knew we'd have a good time, anytime we saw him, but someone who's part of my life?

Sammy's unbridled love of a party, that *What else can we throw at it?* is one thing. But what makes Sammy special is he understands how much people who enjoy his music *want* to party with him.

When Sammy asked if I'd come play his birthday bash at Cabo Wabo, no thought was required. Play *for* Sammy? In *Cabo*? At his bar? No problem. My guys, even Tim Hensley, the bluegrasser who'd played with Ricky Skaggs and Patty Loveless, loved Van Halen, loved Montrose, loved Sammy.

"Come on down. I'll get you a house. Set you up. We'll have fun."

There's fun, and there's fun the Red Rocker way. Nothing prepares you for the hurricane of hospitality that is Sammy. He makes going to the DMV an adventure, so hosting a birthday party in Mexico?

Clearing customs, we were road-burned and jet-lagged. Walking out of immigration, there was Sammy. He'd met us with a mariachi band and two trays of margaritas.

"Welcome to Cabo!" he cheered, raising a glass as we circled around him. "Here's to my birthday weekend. And you guys for being a big part of it!"

Three days of nonstop fun, music, and tequila. If this was work, somebody forgot to tell us. We were in the most amazing villa, filled with all the food and booze we could consume; we had a pool, we were on a hill with a killer view across a not-so-developed Cabo San Lucas, down to the sea.

Walking into Cabo Wabo, a stucco pueblo building on the outside, a festival of neon on the inside, the energy buzzed. For Sammy's birthday, they sell 500 tickets. That's it, and people are packed in, so that energy feeds on itself.

"Is there anything you want us to play?" I asked.

"Have fun, man. Play what you want. This is gonna be great."

"Sammy, we're gonna crush this," I wanted to say. Really, I wanted to show, not tell.

That stage was so loud, so alive, we dug in. Two hours turned to three with another frat party–dive bar set. I was looking at Clayton, who was looking at Sean, who was counting off songs almost before the last one was over. Our set was like a bobsled of every rock, reggae, country staple you've ever heard, all played at peak velocity.

It was so insane having Sammy onstage with us to sing "Finish What You Started," then Michael Anthony joining us for a few songs, too.

At one point, I caught Farmer's eye, gave him a *Can you believe this?* look. With a big grin, he shook his head. When he left his vice president job at the credit union—*Lost his mind*, people thought—he couldn't have imagined this.

We'd been onstage for three hours and forty minutes when someone finally called it. They say, to this day, that's the longest anyone's ever played at one of Sammy's birthday bashes. Looking back, it still doesn't feel all that long.

Not that coming offstage slowed us down any! Sammy was turning fifty-seven, but he rocked like he was twenty-five. Leaving the party, we figured we should keep rocking, too. Shaun Silva, Boat Captain Ben Bourassa, Farmer, the band, and I headed to a place called El Squid Roe, a colorful local bar built in a warehouse.

Tequila Jell-O shots were plentiful, the music turned up loud. An attitude of "This is how it's done" permeated our postshow glow. While everyone partied, something was pressing inside.

Remember when I said songs are like rocks in your shoe? They make themselves present, often in annoying ways. I didn't know what it was, only that I needed to go home and sort it out.

Walking into the house, I got my guitar, found a notepad, and went out to the pool. Sitting there, watching the stars in the sky, I began scratching out lines for a song.

I was thirty-six years old. My career had kicked in, a lot of dreams had been realized, as well. What happened at Sammy's bar was something I'd have never thought was even possible.

I'd hit that age where you're supposed to grow up. I understood how life worked. I even knew why it mattered. I'd realized music was my master; songs and ways to enhance my tours drove every decision I made. How to be better? Connect harder? Deliver music that hits the state of someone's life?

I'd left so much on that cantina stage playing for Sammy, there was a stillness inside me. Sitting alone in the quiet, I had a talk with myself; took an inventory of who I was deep down. That glimpse inside my soul let me see where I was.

As it did, it hit me.

Seeing my friend Sammy blowing it up, rocking so hard made me question what was expected. Humming this melody line, which kept swirling around my brain with an urgency, I had something. What it was I didn't know, but it was coming in fast.

I wrote it all out, the things I was supposed to do, the obligations and expectations. It was a song, but so much more.

Why did I have to decide anything right now? Who said I had to figure out all the answers? What reason was there to decide when or how I was going to grow up? Why couldn't I simply enjoy being in Cabo with Sammy Hagar and my friends?

I kept writing.

That's how you write songs that matter, you live them.

By the time everyone got back, "Beer in Mexico" was about done.

BE AS YOU ARE

There was a moment in 2003 or 2004 when I'd come home for the holidays. Every year, it's the same. Cedar Ford Baptist Church, then my grandmother's house to eat her peanut butter fudge, all those vegetables she'd slow-cooked, the biscuits, ham. My Aunt Missy, by then, had learned how to do the chicken and dumplings.

Everything felt like always, and we were us. We'd laugh at all the same jokes, tease each other. Nothing hurtful, just enough to show you were loved.

Mom, though, looked at me with concern. She was happy for me, proud. But *No Shoes* went from chasing-a-dream busy to warp speed. Finally, she pulled me aside and said, "I feel like I can't reach you anymore . . ."

I knew what she meant. I was gone, mentally as much as physically. I gave her a hug, acknowledging what she said, but I couldn't change it. Nothing was going to slow down; I knew that.

I don't think any of us expected how you get pinned by the momentum of how quickly so much needs to be done. I now say it's "being in the business of being Kenny Chesney," that goes beyond making the music I love.

I didn't care about being a celebrity. I didn't care about award shows or magazine covers. The things people chase weren't that important to me.

Creativity carried me. I lived a lot of life, especially in the islands, that fueled the songs that defined me, as well as No Shoes Nation.

I didn't have a phone, a watch, anything down there. There was a small white church in the middle of town; I'd hear the bells ring every hour on the hour. I could measure the passage of time by how many times they'd rung.

The antithesis of my life in the States, I could disappear.

Nothing knocked the road dust off faster.

I was invisible. Sitting in the corner of the Quiet Mon, with their dial-up internet, I'd check my email every day or two. Even my best friends on the islands didn't understand my life on the mainland.

One night ramped up on too much of grandpa's cough syrup, I decided I was going to be the bartender. Quiet Mon Kelly, Quiet Mon Kenny, Van, and Quiet Mon April actually let me. At Woody's, I'd sometimes short-order cook, answer the phone, and DJ behind the bar. I had no experience, but it was a blast.

Quiet Mon Kelly even had business cards printed up for me. To this day, they're the only business cards I've ever had.

At Woody's, on a slow afternoon, a girl named Jocelyn came in with her father. She was looking for a job. I'd had a few, and Chad let me do the interview. I can't imagine what Dad thought, but she got the job.

It was very much if you weren't here, it didn't happen. That freedom gave me balance. It also started to give me songs, sometimes pieces scratched out on paper, journal entries.

"Sherry" was actually the first song. From the very first trip with Nick, Clayton, and Tambo, as we called Mark Tamburino. We were raging at night, getting a tan during the day—and catching songs in all of it.

We'd gone to lunch at this beach bar, and a very pretty, blond-haired girl who was full of energy was our server. Clearly an island girl, you could feel she was part of this community of people with their roots in the air. Nick and Clayton were trying to talk to her. I won't say hit on her, but they weren't opposed to the idea, either.

Every single thing they said was probably what every tourist says to her. I was making fun of them, because that's what friends do. She liked I wasn't up in all of that.

"What do you do?" she asked.

"I'm a songwriter."

Her look said it all. Clearly didn't believe me, but she would indulge me.

"Tell you what," I said. "We're down here for seven, maybe ten days. Before I leave, I'm going to write a song about you. I'm going to come back, pull you out of this restaurant, sit you down on the curb out there, and play it for you."

She laughed like I was crazy.

"Deal?"

"Deal."

I asked her questions about her life, how she got here. She said she'd grown up in Southern California; like a lot of young people down there, she'd come to the Virgin Islands to start a life. She wanted something different; she wanted the ocean. I understood all of it.

We paid the bill, left, and I started thinking. It took me a couple days, but I wrote until I had a legitimately good song.

Once it felt finished, I got my guitar, put it in the Jeep, and drove into town. I parked across from Panini Beach, where she was working. When she saw me, the shock hit her face like a splash of cold water. She laughed, shook her head, as I came in.

"Come out here. I want to play you something."

Sherry followed me outside, sat down on the curb, and I played "Sherry's Living in Paradise." Basically her life story, it was also many people on the island's tale. She couldn't believe it.

"Okay," she allowed when she stopped laughing. "I believe you now. You really are a songwriter."

She stood up, hugged me like she meant it.

We've been amazing friends ever since. Sherry and her husband, Jessup, still come to shows.

After that, I went back to the house, thinking, "Maybe I should write more of these 'journal entries' about my life down here. These aren't songs for country radio, the career, or anything else, only the moment."

A journal entry of my life, her life.

That was the thought process that started it. Several songs started even before "Old Blue Chair." I had a way to bring all of this to life, take my friends with me. Even if nobody would ever hear it.

Starting in 1998, it seemed eight out of every ten girls I met in the Virgin Islands were from New England. Whether in the bars, in restaurants, or on boats, those accents you can't miss.

Having some local friends, I could hang out and run into someone I knew.

I kept seeing this one bartender. She wore a Red Sox cap backward, and you could see she had these baby dreadlocks peeking out from under it. Didn't matter when or where I saw her, she always had that Boston cap on.

You never know why something strikes you. Someone's spark, a random detail catches your imagination.

I was in the middle of writing the *Be as You Are* album, though I didn't know it yet.

I had these songs that didn't have a place on my commercial records, but they were talking to one another. More authentically me than anything I'd ever done, I kept writing.

All that was whirling around my head one night when Mark Tamburino started playing this guitar part. It had a real groove, with a melody inside it that felt good. I was in my bunk thinking about that bartender, about a lot of stories I'd heard from a lot of my friends down there. That groove started circling around my head, the beats dropping just so . . .

She wears a Red Sox cap . . . to hide her . . . baby . . . dreads . . .

In a bunk on a bus rolling down the highway, "Boston" started to take shape.

I had no idea how far that song would travel. I only knew it was an authentic truth about that bartender, but so many other people in the islands as well.

Writing these songs, the people came with me.

Even when I wasn't there, the islands colored my writing. Scheduled to play the University of Texas's Frank Erwin Center in 2003, a freak ice storm canceled our show. Trapped, because the roads were too icy to travel, Tim, Daryl, and I were stuck.

"Somewhere in the Sun" fell out of that frozen—literally and metaphorically—moment in time. Trapped in a Holiday Inn parking lot, on our buses and in these old hotel rooms, songs emerged. I started describing where we were: the bad room service, the TV with only *Andy Griffith* and *Barney* because the cable was knocked out.

Whatever channel we could get, there was an ad for Cancún that kept airing. I could feel the melody as I was writing it all down. Danny Tucker, my bus driver at the time, threw out the toast that became the bridge, so he was a cowriter on the song, too.

A love letter to the people and places I was discovering, you can hear the pull of this other life. Some people thought I was recharging, but it was more opening up and letting go. There's a quiet you need to hear your soul, something you can't do when there's a bunch of buses and trucks, people needing answers.

The answers I needed were found in hidden bars only the locals and sailors knew.

When I was beyond exhausted, Ben and Emily dropped me off at a campground in the British Virgin Islands. They left me with a cooler filled with beer and water, another with bread, mustard, bologna, and tomatoes.

They understood what my soul needed. They knew where I could find it.

We were all so close, I trusted them without question. I got on the boat, didn't even ask where they were taking me. I smiled when we pulled up to a driftwood building at a rustic open-air campground.

I slept in my clothes because the mosquitoes were so thick. I'd wake in the middle of the night, wander down the path to the edge of the water, and look up. There was no light pollution, only stars and the sound of the waves.

Ivan's Stress Free Bar was from a time forgotten. You'd wake up, go to Ivan Chinnery's bar on the beach where they made eggs and some bacon each morning. Anyone staying there would meet at the counter. We'd have some orange juice and visit. The pace was slow.

Ivan Chinnery started the place as an honor system bar for the campers. It felt that way, even though now he was behind the bar opening local beers and making drinks.

I might go back to my room, with the two coolers outside the door, write in my journal, and listen to the waves. Sometimes Ivan and I would swap songs, passing the guitar between us. He loved music, jazz and blues especially, as much as I did. He had a passion for the sake of playing.

Ivan and Seddy helped me relax when I didn't even realize how badly I needed it.

Seddy Callwood owned the One Love Bar and Grill. He'd hold court, pull you in with his good vibes and card tricks. When he'd see me coming, he'd have a cola and coconut rum ready before I got to the bar.

Like Ivan, he knew things about people. Sitting under all those flags with friends, I'd talk philosophy, laugh at how crazy the world was.

· · ·

Ben, Emily, Rob, KJ, Will, Missy, Kristi, Janine, Todd, Chad, Janna, Dan, Jordan, Jamis, Hedy, and Low Key Bob were all part of an extended crew. Different people with the same dream: chase the sun, enjoy the ocean. People came for a vacation, lived there twenty years.

> ~~Bruh,~~ ~~Bruh~~
>
> I've been down island now for a while but today I finally felt it. A certain sense of freedom you get when you feel your soul exhale. When you feel your mind and body let go of stress, timelines, expectations, and anything that can weigh your life down. Sometimes it takes a while for me to feel that down here! There have been times I've never felt it due ~~to running~~ to all the different frequencies running through my head. But today as I was washing the boat getting rid of all the salt, it happened!!! ~~Somewhere between~~ ~~maybe it was the~~ ~~memory of the acid~~
>
> ~~The sun was shining on like a stereo~~
>
> Maybe it was Marley on the stereo, ~~the sun on~~ ~~the way~~ the way the sun was hitting my shoulders, the peace and sense of community I feel here, or maybe I finally washed ~~off the acid memory~~ the memory of someone away with rum last night. Maybe it's all those things combined! But for the first time in a while I felt still, content, and HAPPY!!! I'll drink and toast to that! Which is what Boat Capt. Ben, myself ~~and~~ Bob, Chad, Kristi, and several other friends are getting ready to do! Cheers, K.C.
>
> (P.S. might try Power Hour!)
>
> Stress is the enemy
>
> 9:20 P.M
> Nov 12 U.S.V.I

Everyone had a story. Even as my life was changing, they were steadfast, supportive, the anchors I needed. People left me alone then.

When people started to realize I was there, my friends were protective. They created my "office." We called it the Executive Suite. You could only get to it through the kitchen. We'd sit on a white plastic table in the gravel by the big coolers and the refrigerator. There were giant propane tanks nearby. Glamorous, that became "drinking downtown."

Countless rum punches, chicken sandwiches and pasta salads, and too many orders of shark bites were consumed back there. That space became such a part of my life, I was doing 60 *Minutes* and they asked for something "authentic."

Not just authentic, but uniquely, completely me. I had the spot.

Anderson Cooper looked shocked. Maybe he thought it was a prank.

"This is it?"

I'd had a few rum punches at dinner, decided I should take him to my spot. Once he knew this was real, he had a different impression of me. He'd been on the other side of fame and the media, been in society. Looking around the scattered crates and plastic chairs, the bustle in the kitchen behind us, he recognized how normal—even unpretentious—we all were.

Every day was a new day. We lived it for what it was. No two alike, show up or you miss it. I still didn't recognize an album was brewing. Every trip was a postcard or two set to music. I may journal, but my truest expression is usually songs.

How we lived was threaded into a collection of songs that didn't sound like Kenny Chesney. At least what people heard on the radio. I didn't care.

More personal than anything I'd released, they spoke to this place. Early on, I would sleep on Ben and Emily's couch for a couple days. Before I had my boat, *Sixth Gear*, we'd go out on other people's boats. I was drawn here.

Literally walking offstage at Neyland Stadium in Knoxville, I went to the airport and flew through the night, so I could see the sun come up with my friends. After a night like that, there was only one thing left.

Five or six years passed. Carefree, spur of the moment. Take over a commuter ferry in St. Thomas and lead a Christmas carol sing-along. When Nick Hoffman's then girlfriend Kimmer faced a battle with cancer and he couldn't make it, we all dyed our hair his same white blond so he was with us in spirit. I had to go to a funeral for Scotty Brown, one of my bus drivers; most of my road family didn't recognize me.

The islands were Kacey at Willy T's calling us "those redneck boys," as a term of affection; playing "Sweet Home Alabama" when he saw us coming. It was Seddy sending us home with two live lobsters to cook after a long afternoon at One Love, as well as Party Gears that ranged from First Gear—"had a few, feeling good"—to Sixth Gear—"wide open, might not remember."

Listening to the songs, I decided: These songs aren't merely songs. They're an album, a series of songs that connect and reveal pieces of me that show you my soul. This person dreamed beyond the spotlight. Sometimes pensive, there was an introspective piece.

But there was also Bobby Crouton, capable of raging with his friends, running wild and creating mayhem. My alter ego, Crouton was the life of the party, always ready to hit the bar or spend the day anchored somewhere, loving life for all it's worth.

If the fans were as invested as they felt, why wouldn't I explore this?

◆ ◆ ◆

People at the label didn't understand. I'd had so much success with *No Shoes* and *Sun*, they couldn't say no. Indulging me, very little marketing happened. A CMT special where I played several of the songs, a few network TV appearances, no singles was how we sold it.

It still debuted at No. 1 on *Billboard*'s all-genre Top 200 Albums chart—and sold over a million copies quickly.

What I knew—that they didn't—was how many people craved what I found. They wanted that exhale as much as I did, songs that let your mind drift, slow down.

What mattered more to me was sharing the people I'd met with my friends who loved the music. "Island Boy" was Boat Captain Ben, but he was every other young man hitting pause on their life for a few years.

"Be as You Are" was written on my boat with Dean Dillon. He knew the power that watching the sun move across the water held. A blessing, a benediction, it was an invitation for everyone in what would become No Shoes Nation to inhabit their truest self.

DRAFTED

Coming from outside Knoxville, sports was everything growing up watching the Vols. We didn't have pro teams, but it didn't matter; the Tennessee Vols and even our high school teams were a point of real pride. As a fan, that passion was real.

Over the years, I've become friends with a lot of pro athletes and coaches. In 2002, as things were starting to move faster than we thought possible, our friends in training camps kept us sane. We'd drop by, visit, talk about the upcoming season. We'd share tickets—if they didn't have curfew—to the show.

But you don't always see great friends coming.

A few months into the *No Shoes Tour*, we were playing Albany. Kerry Collins, the New York Giants' quarterback, invited us to preseason practice. The Giants' quarterback coach was Sean Payton. Nice guy, we exchanged pleasantries.

We invited the whole team to come to the show. You never know who's a fan, so throw it wide open.

We had a big Giants turnout. They were having a massive time, and I remember thinking, *They've got to be close to curfew.* Nobody left. They were rocking; nobody wanted to go home.

Sean Payton wasn't there, but we made an impression. The next morning, he got a call from the Giants' head coach Jim Fassel. "Sean, we have a problem."

"We do?" he replied.

"Sixteen players missed bed check last night."

In training camp, they might have two or three misses for the entire preseason. Sixteen in a single night? Sean started making calls. Someone gives him the list of everyone who missed curfew.

It had to be that concert, he thought. At least, that's what he told me later.

Dan Campbell, now head coach of the Detroit Lions, finally told Sean, "Jeremy Shockey gathered everyone together, and said, 'This is too good a time. We're staying. I'll pay everyone's fine.'"

It was $1,480. Each. Shockey, a new player from Ada, Oklahoma, loved country music. He didn't care about the money, he was having too much fun. He wanted to spread the love on a night he wouldn't forget.

Sean Payton, getting the call about *sixteen* players smashing curfew, wasn't going to forget, either.

It wasn't until 2006 we really clicked. In the wake of Katrina, which did such terrible things to New Orleans, Sean was hired as the Saints' head coach. When we played the Cajundome that April, a forty-minute drive from where he was living, Sean wanted to come to the show.

He jokes about our Vibe Rooms back then; says it was a jar of salsa, some tortilla chips, a veggie tray, a couple beanbag chairs, and a table with bottles. Back then, country artists having a private space solely for their friends wasn't done, so a room set aside was revolutionary. He forgets that now, but swears he'll never forget that night, even though he doesn't remember most of it.

Everyone loved Sean by then. He was always ready to enjoy the music. He got in the Vibe with everybody, telling stories, having a ball. He came to the side of the stage, hanging with Uncle Kracker—and decided he might want to have a puff of Kracker's cigarette. Sure, why not?

Onstage, I'm so focused on the crowd, I don't know what's happening in the wings. Everyone looked like they were having a blast. Nothing out of the ordinary.

Somehow, there's a picture of Sean passed out in the median between the Cajundome and the Holiday Inn, literally two football fields across the street, with a caption from General Manager Loomis, "After a long, exhaustive search, Tom Benson, Mickey Loomis, and the Saints have found their head coach . . ."

Sean laughed at himself the same way we did. Once that happened, we were brothers.

A year later, we hit Riverbend Music Center on the Ohio River for our *Flip-Flop Summer Tour*. Sean was in Cincinnati for a preseason game against the Bengals. By now, Sean and the team practically expected us.

At the practice facility, the media room is right next to the Saints' locker room—and Sean has this great idea. He didn't know who was *in* the media center, but he puts the word out: He's calling a press conference. He played it to the hilt, saying something about a receiver "we're taking a look at today."

Twenty-eight people were on the other side of the door when he walked out. It was a full-on press conference: cameras on sticks, rows of reporters. Sean didn't flinch, played it straight right to the end. "Young player, walk-on. Has some raw talent. We're signing him today."

Then Sean introduces the player, me wearing a white Saints jersey. I walk to the podium. You could feel the reporters' annoyance. A few laughed, thought it was as funny as we did. Sean takes what he does seriously, but that doesn't mean you shouldn't do things for fun and morale.

I go to practice, do some more interviews. Joe Vitt, Sean's assistant head coach, was against it, thought the team needed to be serious. Sean believes you can laugh while you're busting your ass.

Sean has another bright idea: putting me and my No. 7 jersey into practice. It was fun catching passes from Drew Brees—it's everyone who watches the game's fantasy.

That's when Sean pulls his next trick.

"Tell you what," he announced to his team, "let's really put Kenny out there. He's worked out with all of you, done the drills, gone hard all day. Here's a proposition . . .

"Let's put Kenny out for a punt. Two tries. If he catches it, no practice on Monday; if he doesn't, extra conditioning drills."

Whoa. When you say "A day off," whether people are Black, white, rock, country, or hip-hop, they get interested. Open to the public, players and fans drew closer. They wanted to see if I'd fumble or rise to the moment. Steve Weatherford dropped back and punted the ball for me to receive. That first one? An absolute bomber, flying so hard it's over my head by miles. Even the players were like, "Come on . . ."

We were down to the second punt.

When that ball came off Weatherford's foot, I could see it was coming fast. I watched it arc out, come down. I reached up to get my arms out and hands ready to pull it to me.

The ball hit my hands, hard. But I had it. All I had to do was hold on.

On the sidelines, the players erupted. I looked down, that ball was firmly between my hands. Talk about ecstatic. I'd caught a punt from a major NFL kicker. Reggie Bush actually threw a water bottle all the way across the field in celebration.

Knowing Sean, if I hadn't caught it, it would've been business as usual. But he wanted to set me up to be a hero, part of the team in my own way. The kind of stuff you dream, but even when it happens, you still feel like you're dreaming.

All the players surrounded me, high-fiving, slapping my back. A lot of them came to the show, whether they were country fans or not, because in that moment, we were in it together.

My season winds down around the time football's getting started. When Jahri Evans, a young player from North Philadelphia, only needed half of his skybox, I figured, *What the hell?* I'd come to love New Orleans—the food, music, vibe—so why not take half a suite?

It would be reason to go to the Crescent City when the Saints had home games.

Suddenly, I had an anchor. I'd take road friends, musicians, but especially my father, John Staley, and Jim Cogdill. We were a gang who loved football, delicious food, cocktails, and a damned good time. After all those weekends at Cogdill's pool, I was able to return those moments.

By now, our Vibe Room was colonized with painted chairs, a real bar setup, backdrops that had pictures of friends and moments across the journey. Sean took our idea and installed his own Vibe Room down the hall from the Saints locker room in the Superdome. When we'd wait for Sean after the games, we could hang there with movie stars, politicians, civic leaders, other coaches.

Being in New Orleans with someone like Sean is like being in Key West with Jimmy Buffett. Low-key, but the entire city opens up in ways it doesn't for anyone else. One night, Sean, Jon Gruden, Mike Tirico, and I walked into a restaurant late, straight into the kitchen, and saw a table set up for us.

A black-haired man with flashing eyes and a thick accent, wrapped up in a heavy white apron, kept asking me how I wanted my steak prepared. I was tipsy and annoyed. Why wouldn't he let me talk to my friends? Sean was watching, eyes laughing in a way I didn't get.

What I didn't get, of course, was the man was Emeril Lagasse. Because that's Sean's world.

Emeril and I shared so many friends—Sammy, Shep, Willie—that we fell into conversation. We've been pals ever since. Some of the delicious things he's fed us makes me hate training when I'm in New Orleans, eating my very specific diet.

New Orleans was Sean's magic carpet. All the historic restaurants, places where music lived, were his. After a December 23 game, we headed to Pat O'Brien's. Time was melting. Food kept appearing, drinks were refreshed.

Until . . . I still don't know *how* late it really was—no one was checking their watch—Sean's then-wife appeared in the bar. Livid. Maybe I can't blame her. She took one look at all of us, lasered in on her roaring husband, took his elbow firmly, and announced, "It's Christmas! *You're* coming home."

Seven sheets to the wind, we laughed hysterically. She was right. Sean knew: It was time to leave. I had to be in East Tennessee for Christmas morning.

God may love a drunk. But He made hangovers to teach them a lesson. A couple hours later, no idea how much we'd had to drink, I was in more pain than I knew how to process. I got to my Grandmother Lucy's house, who said, "Let him be," as I crawled into her guest-room bed.

My Uncle Butch agreed. "Let him sleep it off."

My mother was as furious as Sean's wife was. It had been one of those years where "gone" was my return address, and she'd hardly seen me. For my family, Christmas is big. I missed it, passed out cold in my grandmother's bed.

You can't apologize for something you don't truly regret. I felt horrible, but I wouldn't have done anything different. Instead, I slept and slept, knew I wouldn't die, knew Sean and I had a whole lot more life to live and stories to write.

In 2010, the Saints went to the Super Bowl. Having been on the journey with the team, I was bringing my dad and Jim, Boat Captain Ben, my friend JW, and a few other pals from the Virgin Islands. After the season, I wanted to close the circle.

Sean, thrilled to have taken the National Football Conference title, wanted that first Super Bowl win. We were talking about the afterparties, especially if the Saints won. That's when he told me what the act the team's management wanted was going to charge them.

I get it. Private shows are big money. But for a team that faced down Katrina a few years prior, for a team who had ascended to this unthinkable level? I was silent. Sean asked, "You there?"

"Yeah, I'm thinking," I answered. "I mean, you didn't ask me. But if you get my band guys tickets to the game, we'll do it."

"Do it?"

"Play your afterparty. Win, lose, whatever. Get my guys tickets, and you've got a band for your party."

"You're serious?"

"Yes, Sean. I feel like we've become part of this season. We should be there."

"Done."

Pacing is important. Everywhere you go, someone's going to put a drink in your hand. If you're not playing or coaching, it's a massive party for a few days before the game. Game day, it's crazy.

We decided to go over to Collins Avenue, where ESPN was broadcasting live. It was a scene. I knew a bunch of guys from the sports networks, and it would be cool to say hi. Park on a side street by the hotel, roll in.

The ESPN folks knew the Colts' Peyton Manning, my friend from his days as UT's quarterback, was playing my running buddy Sean Payton's Saints. *NFL Sunday Countdown* wanted to put me on. It was good TV, because maybe I'd slip up and say something that got traction.

When Chris Berman and Mike Ditka asked me who I thought would win, my answer was "I just want one of the Paytons." Pretty quick, right?

My dad met Mike Ditka, which made me happy. Ditka was his guy, the dominant player and coach from his era. Watching them talking—coach-to-coach in a way—was another circle closing.

It was chaos, so we decided to head for the stadium. John, my bus driver, was probably cussing under his breath, edging my tour bus toward the causeway, dodging people in the street, cars jumping out of their lane. Finally, we hit the interstate.

We had the music up, ESPN on the TVs. That's when the texts started flying in.

"Look out the window!"

"Look to your left!"

Pulling beside us, with a massive police escort, was Sean Payton on the Saints' lead bus. Grinning from ear to ear, waving and shaking his head. The team's bus, with a presidential escort in front, alongside, and behind rolling up on us? All the cars in South Florida, the traffic for the game. What's the chance?

Their police escort turned on the sirens, and they took off. We fell in behind them.

When Sean started the second half with an onside kick that was unprecedented, it set the tone. By the time Tracy Porter intercepted Peyton's throw and ran it back for a pick-six, the game was done.

We were in the suite when we realized it was over. You could see the shock, then the joy on the field. They'd done it! The Saints had won their very first Super Bowl. They'd beat a damned good team to do it.

In the suite, it was pandemonium, and then some. You can't explain that rush, seeing something incredible happen to your good friends. It was gonna be some kind of party, and we were the house band.

There was a party on my bus, for sure, when we pulled in at the loading dock at the Intercontinental Hotel. The feeling of total happiness for my friends was overwhelming. Life has so few moments like that. I wanted to hang on to the feeling as long as I could.

Thump, thump, thump. The door popped open. There in the stairwell stood Sean. He bounced up the steps, holding the Vince Lombardi Trophy, which he plopped down on the couch.

We erupted. The trophy gleamed, as bright and official as it is on TV.

When people think of Sean and me, they think of us raging. But Sean was also a refuge where I could disappear into his family. A few years he invited me to his house on the Gulf in Florida to decompress. One year, Malchijah Bailey, who helps navigate my world, and I flew to Turks and Caicos for two days off. Great hotel, the water was beautiful.

Two hours after we got there, Bailey got a text. Hugh Hayden wrote, "Tomorrow's Sean's birthday, and we're throwing a party for him in Florida. You guys should be here."

"Let's go to Sean's," I said. We packed and were gone in less than an hour.

Sean is a philosopher, a psychologist, and one helluva of motivator. I learned a lot about how to live in those moments at games, as well as hanging at the beach.

That spring after the Super Bowl, I went to visit. We were about to go down to the beach. Sean says, "Hey, wait a minute. I want to show you something."

I stood there. He went upstairs and came down with a small box. "What's that?"

"Open it. You'll see."

Inside was a Super Bowl ring. From Super Bowl XLIV, 2010. It had my name on it.

"You're kidding."

"Kenny, you were part of it."

THE ROAD, RADIO, POETS, AND PIRATES

Our *Flip-Flop Summer Tour* ended in Atlanta—two nights at the amphitheater. Last nights are always pranky, end-of-the-school-year stuff. Dave Matthews was playing the second night across town, but he was off that first night. He wanted to come over.

Joe Walsh was in town, too. Mr. "Rocky Mountain Way" was coming to the show, to hang out, sit in, whatever. Farmer, me, Wannebo, the band, Robin Majors, Jill Trunnell, and our tour coordinator lost our collective minds.

Joe Walsh, with that scalding guitar tone. Coming with Smokey Wendell, his best friend.

"He wants to play," I said.

"I wonder what?" someone in production asked.

"Whatever he wants," I joked, but wasn't kidding. If Joe Walsh wanted to get up onstage, he could play anything. I didn't care.

"Man, 'Funk 49,'" Farmer said. "That would be awesome."

Second to last night of the tour, people aren't expecting a rager.

"Jill, can you send a runner to Walmart and buy every pot, pan, spoon, kitchen utensil they can find."

She cracked a big smile. "We sure can."

She knew what I was thinking. Farmer, Rome McMahon, the rockers did, too. This was going to be epic.

When Joe and Smokey got there, I asked about coming out for the encore. Make it a big moment. He could see all the stagehands watching. He nodded, looked at Smokey.

Between Dave Matthews sitting in for our Steve Miller/Bob Marley medley and his own "Where Are You Going," the crowd was pumped.

Coming offstage at set's end, Joe was standing there, guitar strapped on, pirate grin across his face. Nobody plays kamikaze guitar like Joe Walsh.

"Ready?" I yelled as the cheers amplified. His eyes said it all.

The band and I raced back out, leaning into a serious rock vamp. Then a lick everybody knew blasted out of the speakers. Throwing my arms to stage left, I announced, "Ladies and gentleman, the next president of the United States of America, Joe Walsh . . ."

The roar doubled as Joe hit the stage. Cranking out the national anthem of rock and roll decadence, "Life's Been Good," we swerved straight into "Life in the Fast Lane." Joe was killing it, jamming hard with my band.

The crew, our guests, Pat Green who was opening, everyone crammed into the sides of the stage. They were all geared up for our surprise for Joe.

"Funk #49" was the third song. One of our high school and college "songs," the James Gang's classic has this swaggering, salty feel.

As Joe got to the big ride, where the percussion solo takes over, everyone burst from the wings and flooded the stage with all that kitchen gear, banging away with complete abandon, all the chaos and clanging bound together by that seven-note, one-chord riff.

Joe couldn't have been more shocked—or delighted. We played five songs. It was every kid's garage band fantasy.

2007 was tricky. Road life was raging hard, we were having a ball. I was thirty-nine years old, coming into my own and feeling able to make cool things happen for my friends.

Uncle Kracker had a birthday when we were in Vegas. I took this crazy suite at the Bellagio with an actual barbershop inside—and someone came up to shampoo and cut Matt's hair. There was booze, music, carrying on. While Kracker was tilted back, shirt off, a giant cake was delivered; out of that cake, a tiny stripper emerged.

We were never a crew to go to the clubs where women danced. But for a moment like that, for Kracker's birthday, how could we not? Crazy, off-the-hook, rock and roll shit: just to say we did. We were celebrating this reality of "We get to do this."

And there are the traditions.

Anyone who's come to a show knows the moment: Ed Wannebo—my production manager for almost twenty-five years—brings out the nightly margarita. For stadium shows, he can be found at 3:00 p.m. on the fifty-yard line with a bottle of champagne, calling play-by-play on the day: the weather, what's going on among us. Then, head tilted back, he howls, "Release the hounds." Magically, the doors open.

We're in this together, the nightly salute at the end of the show where everyone lines up, first stage right, then stage left: It signals our respect for one another and our life. To salute each other, this says "Job well done" in a tangible, public way.

My road family are a talented bunch. A few years, they actually formed their own band for our final tour party. Mostly Crue was so good, I put the band on as the final show's opening act and No Shoes Nation loved them.

Tom's Grille, the much talked about burger joint on the back of the stage, was started to solve a problem. Tom Nissun, my stage manager, realized that what started out as practicality has become a source of community building. Over the years, the grill's become the place everyone wants to gather, even Reese Witherspoon and Vince Vaughn at the Rose Bowl.

The Vibe Room is also now legendary—often borrowed with many attempts to replicate, but never the same. I wanted radio guests, friends, musicians who weren't playing to have somewhere they could hang. Designed as an almost secret speakeasy, you had to be an insider to know where to go. Look for the wooden pirate wench I found outside a store in Fort Lauderdale and insisted they sell to me. She suggests freedom, signals adventure. Enter for adult beverages, scrims with pictures of guests over the years, moments at sea, cold plunges. Twenty years line those walls. Leave with new friends, catching up with someone you've not seen in a long time or the idea "You're on the list."

When Buffy Cooper was out with Gretchen Wilson or Montgomery Gentry, she was a world-class radio promotion exec; she was also the ex-wife of Rick Rockhill, Capricorn's head of country promotion. She knew me before it all started.

That year I was starting the show by entering from the back of the venue. To sneak me out to the soundboard, I was put into a road case and rolled out to the front-of-house monitor platform. Knowing Buffy for so long, I thought I'd pull her into my world.

I asked Farmer to see if Buffy wanted to roll out to front of house in the road case. There was room enough for a couple people. Why not let her experience rolling through the crowd?

Buffy was all in. She laughed as we bumped down the hallways, out onto the field, and under a curtain. That vibe of "Hell, yeah" is one of the reasons when the time came, I hired her to run radio for our management. She understood our culture.

Jill Trunnell came to help us through rehearsals in 2005. She'd worked with Elton John, the Eagles, so many people. We called her back for those first stadium shows in Pittsburgh, DC, and Boston because she fit in, had our free-spirited vibe. We never let her leave.

A major fun broker, she's the ringleader. She helped spearhead Mimosa Sunday on those rare Sundays we play shows. She made the Kentucky Derby into a backstage holiday, complete with juleps and hats for everyone on tour. Later, she staged the Kenpuppy Derby with local dog shelters, a backstage race with some of the cutest puppies, to promote pet adoption.

We started having yearbooks in 2003, because Carolyn Snell, our sponsor rep, decided "this is like school, we should have a yearbook." Our yearbook had several editors in the early years, with Helena Pygrum helping Carolyn.

With people leaving, it ultimately fell to Jill. Armed with a camera, she became a one-woman layout department. Supplemented with pictures from band, crew, and Allister Ann, who shoots most of my album covers and documents a lot of my adventures, Jill creates a visual record of our road life. Working directly with Jostens, the company that produces most of America's high school and college yearbooks, she delivers a coated stock book that weighs between five and seven pounds.

Over the years, she's trussed up and hung off every major stadium to get those overhead shots, kept us in line, and made crazy requests work. She loves music as much as anybody and injects our tour with a real energy and light.

We were heading to San Francisco. Joel Selvin, the *San Francisco Chronicle*'s longtime critic, asked Steve Miller if he'd consider coming out and playing with us. Miller had a private show the night before we played the baseball stadium. I was hoping he'd stay over.

Word came back: "Miller is in."

Steve rolled up for sound check in the coolest blue 1968 Pontiac Firebird convertible, exactly like you'd expect. His guitar guy was waiting, and they made their way up to the stage like they owned the place. Every crew guy was in awe, the band members were ready.

That year, I had a four-piece horn section. Steve dialed in on Jim Horn, who's played sax with the Stones and John Lennon. They spoke briefly, then Steve turned to me.

"What do you wanna play?" he asked after we'd talked about where we grew up—him in Texas, so he understood the music—and the reality of playing stadiums, which he'd done in the '70s and '80s.

"We do 'The Joker,'" I said. "Usually with 'Three Little Birds.' 'I Go Back' name-checks 'Rockin' Me.' That song really hits home."

"Let's do those."

Tim, Daryl, Farmer, and David Ogle were all standing there. Here was the guy who defined driving to and from school in the flesh.

When Steve Miller came onstage the next night, the surprise took the crowd over the top. A local Bay Area hero, he was a big piece of San Francisco. Artists whose songs time-stamp life do that.

Any time I hear "The Joker," I'm still transported to Hickory Star Marina on a houseboat with David Farmer. Lifeguards, young bucks, that was that moment—and it's stayed with me. Even now.

It's the same when I hear "Born to Run." I'm in my high school football locker room, ready to run onto the field. Friday night, all anticipation, the adrenaline of it.

Later I realized the power of his characters and places.

I didn't see Bruce play until I was in college. I'd seen a lot of shows, but I wasn't prepared for this freight train of energy. This man, who'd written all these songs, wasn't giving me a part of himself, but every speck of his being.

He had a different voice, louder and broader, like a Southern Baptist preacher in the way he spoke and sang. It wasn't only the music, but how he delivered his message. Strong, sensitive when it needed to be, and raw.

Bruce was soul. Watching him, I realized music really was possible. He wasn't rich, but blue-collar, writing songs about his friends. He showed me a very different way to do music. Different from all the rock shows I'd been to, this was more passionate than anything I'd ever witnessed.

He felt more connected from the heart, more melodic in nature. It was authentic in a very specific way. He wasn't begging people to love him; he came to love them. Like that Baptist preacher, he was there to save them.

It was a revival, a full immersion baptism. I wasn't sure what that meant for me as a kid playing for tips, but it showed me how I wanted to do that. The way he moved people and exploded what was wrong in their lives stayed with me.

Writing about these characters, it was personal. That I could do: represent my friends and who we were, what we were living. I wanted to be real beyond the happy stuff. That's why I finally recorded Bruce's "One Step Up."

The night before I played the Pittsburgh Steelers' stadium for the first time, Bruce played the University of Pittsburgh's events center all by himself. These were my first real stadium shows, so it felt important to see him reach into this intimate space. We got in the car and moved across an urban Rust Belt campus.

Before the show, I went to pay my respects.

We made small talk, like you do. I wanted to let him get ready. We started to leave. Maybe because it had had such a huge impact on my journey, I turned around.

"Can I ask . . ." I said tentatively. "Would you play 'One Step Up'?"

He looked at me thoughtfully. I didn't realize he hadn't played the song since 1988, let alone on that tour. I only knew what it meant to me.

Sitting on a road case at the side of the stage, the show felt enormous. One man, some guitars, a piano. It struck me how great songs can be stripped down to this and hit you every bit as hard. I was reaching a major life shift, the beginning of my stadium life, and here was this man who'd done it all.

When he started talking about getting a letter about this song, how much that note had meant to him and the song's impact, I realized he was going to play it. My blood rushed through me because this was a moment of passage. What I'd written about his song's influence on me had meant something to him.

Over the years, Bruce had a way of showing up at the right time.

We were playing Holmdel, New Jersey, and we got word: Bruce Springsteen was on his way.

Getting on his motorcycle, he rode from his house and pulled up right next to my bus. He understands the impact he has. But it was more. It felt like he might've understood I was struggling. Beyond visiting with the band and crew, he took me aside, asked me how I was doing. We were talking about the pace of life, some of the venues.

"You know," he said, not trying to tell me anything, but sensing I could use some perspective, "you can write a piece of a song down on paper, put it in a drawer, and walk away. Three years later, you can open that drawer, the song will still be waiting on you.

"Life isn't like that. Your life is more fluid. It moves on."

He didn't have to say anything more.

I let everyone be excited, felt their happiness getting to meet "the Boss." Larry Mullen Jr. from U2 showed up as well. It was time to get my pack on, head to the stage.

Bruce turns to me, as we were leaving the bus, and says, "Well, let's go see what this is all about."

Bruce and Larry went out to the mixing board and watched the show. Afterward, he told me he loved that we had a horn section, that there was such power and joy up there. It was 2007, so much was to come; but in that moment, Springsteen saw something he recognized.

The answer was yes when the call came for Bruce's 2013 MusiCares Person of the Year. A fast room to raise money for MusiCares, which helps people in the music business who are in trouble, Jackson Browne, Neil Young, Eddie Vedder, Patti Smith, and many more rock, roots, alternative, and even Latin superstars were signed on to perform.

You don't think about that until you get there. Bruce had made such an impact on musicians in so many genres. For me, honoring him was what mattered.

It's one thing to sing songs from *The Tunnel of Love* on a bar stool at ETSU. Now the person who wrote and recorded "One Step Up" is five feet away as I'm singing his song. There was Bruce and his wife Patti Scialfa, Jackson Browne, Sting, all listening to me sing this song I'd sung hundreds of times.

Why I was so scared, I don't know. That was the most nervous I've ever been onstage. Only me, my guitar, and my piano player Wyatt Beard. I couldn't look down, so I looked over everyone's heads and sang to a spot on the wall.

From Bruce, I learned by watching: Don't give a piece of you, give every cell in your body, every bit of your heart.

WE DO!

I would go to the very top of every stadium I played. That seat as far from the stage as you can possibly get is the one I seek. I've sat there, quietly, for ten, twenty minutes, taking in the physical distance from that seat to the stage. Emotionally, I'm measuring how far it is to reach to that person. When I'm moving across the T, I'm thinking about how I can connect with whoever is sitting in that seat.

Megan Moroney told me she was once that girl in those nosebleeds; how she and her friends bought the cheap seats and had the time of their lives. She was a University of Georgia student, didn't know being on that stage was possible, but it sparked her imagination.

Doing stadiums never becomes commonplace. Watching NFL games, I know every inch of those stadiums—and think about the visiting team's locker room, the tunnel the home team rushes through on game day. When I get to a city, I reflect on what that team means to the people, how much passion their fans invest in them, win or lose.

Over the years, we've seen all kinds of things. In Pittsburgh, they start tying up their boats almost a week before we get there. Some jokingly called it No Shoes Navy. One year, there was a band on top of a houseboat docked near Heinz Field, playing our songs; when I heard about it, we loaded up the gator, whipped down to where they were docked. Clayton, Wyatt, and I got up and sang "How Forever Feels" and "Old Blue Chair" using their gear.

Melvin Fults, our drum tech, played steel drums on "When the Sun Goes Down" for years. Robin Majors, who got his start running sound for the Marshall Tucker Band, would hit the stage with harmonica for a few songs. Even Mac McAnally came out those summers Jimmy Buffett didn't have him on lockdown. To sing "Back Where I Come From" with Mac, or later "Down the Road," raised my game a whole other level.

Booked to play Wildwood, New Jersey, a free show on the beach, I had a horrible sinus infection. Jon Gruden called to check in a few minutes before the show. As I tried to explain how sick I was, that voice barked in my ear, *"THAT's why you're a goddamn superstar!"*

Ever the coach, he was pumping me up. Reminding me, there's a level of fight that separates teams, players, and artists from the pack.

Every tour would end with a trip to the Virgin Islands. Some years, I'd charter a massive jet; others we'd fly commercial. When it was all done, I wanted everyone to feel the same unwind I did. Sun and chill all day, celebrate what we'd done together at night. Mostly, we try to embrace that idea of "Nowhere to go, nowhere to be" after months of building those stages and bringing our best whether sick, sad, or whatever turmoil people sometimes found themselves in.

"Who lives like we do? WE DO!" was our battle cry.

We would shout it from wherever we congregated to kick off the tour. We would cheer those words before shows, anytime something good happened, before passing out yearbooks the final weekend. It was a truth about how we made up this gypsy pirate life, and we shouted it full voice anytime we needed a reminder or wanted to say "thank you" for what our lives out here had become.

MOMENT OF FOREVER

Could it get any better? Depends on how you measure. In 2007, Willie Nelson was curious, thinking Buddy and I might be good producers. He loved the job we'd done with "Lucky Old Sun." It struck something inside him, and I understood. I listened to our recording of the Ray Charles standard all the time.

Considering he'd been produced by Don Was and Booker T. Jones, I was flattered. We made all the records together, so that was the team he loved. They'd have generational commonality and references that you can't fake. Buddy knew songs, pulling sessions together. Add my song sense, a few of my musical ideas, and it could be something special.

No one sounds like Willie. He'd made music on his terms, creating the art in his soul since even before the days of "Waylon and Willie and the boys."

On the plane to Los Angeles, it got real. Buddy and I were meeting Willie at his bus at Shutters on the Beach, the breezy, white clapboard hotel in Santa Monica. I was excited, both nervous and happy.

I've always believed when you get past the hits, there's a real power in album cuts.

I want to hear Jackson Browne sing "Running on Empty," but even before I was living the life, "The Load Out/Stay" hit me in my soul. Jackson captured my imagination and pulled me close to the music, to a life I hadn't lived yet. Same way with Jimmy, and the idea of the seeking old man in "He Went to Paris" or the smuggler past his prime in "A Pirate Looks at Forty."

Willie embodied all those things. Done right, we had an artist who'd take those risks.

Pulling into the parking lot, Honeysuckle Rose was parked right where they said it would be. Willie may have houses in Texas and Hawaii, but his home is on that bus painted with the iconic Native American on his horse.

Stepping on Willie's bus, all polished wood and leather, it's welcoming, but more you're walking into someone's favorite rooms where people relax and really spend time together. Willie was ready, smiling and excited to talk songs: the ones we'd brought, the things he'd written.

Song people live for great melodies, smart lyrics, a hook that'll never let go of you. Demos don't always spell out what's there, but you know great when you hear it.

Willie played us "Over You Again," written with his sons Lukas and Micah, a song with real smoky tension that became the opener.

Buddy pulled out Kris Kristofferson's "Moment of Forever," about facing aging and holding on to the perfect season of love, which became the title cut.

I had Guy Clark's "Worry B Gone," a song about chilling out with a little smoke or drink. Guy was a songwriter's songwriter and Texas legend, but "Worry" embodied Willie's approach to life. I also offered "I'm Alive," a song I'd written with Dean Dillon and Mark Tamburino about being grateful in the exhaustion, even wreckage, for how beautiful life is.

The recording sessions were unlike anything Nashville had seen in years. Rather than the 10:00 a.m., 2:00 p.m., or 6:00 p.m. session start times, which we used mostly to know when we'd begin the day, this was about the hang. Songs were charted out, the players listening to demos and talking about what they thought their parts should be. But it was looser, a lot more laughter and following the moment musically.

Willie told stories, made jokes, and that would double when Hank Cochran, who was a struggling songwriter in the '60s alongside Willie, stopped by. It was lived history from two Country Music Hall of Fame inductees. They'd written two of Patsy Cline's biggest hits—Willie with "Crazy," Hank with "I Fall to Pieces"—but were laughing about pranks they'd pulled like ten-year-olds.

People were dropping in to soak up the music. Word about the vibe was spreading. Connie Bradley, who ran ASCAP in Nashville and was called "the best friend a dreamer ever had," dropped in to listen. Herky Williams, longtime publisher, golfer, and friend of the Outlaws, was there, too. Even Universal Music Nashville chairman Luke Lewis, who'd signed Willie to Lost Highway, came for the stories.

Moment of Forever wasn't a statement album, but it was serious. Good writers, classic songs, a little tongue-in-cheek vintage Willie. Even Randy Newman's "Louisiana," which felt slow and humid like the Mississippi in the heat of summer, had a real earnestness to it. Three years after Hurricane Katrina devastated New Orleans, I wondered if it was Willie's idea to sing a song about the Mississippi flooding in 1927 to remind people how devastating Katrina actually was.

LUCKY OLD SUN

If nobody saw the success of *Songs from an Old Blue Chair* coming, they couldn't deny the way it impacted people who heard it. When I said I wanted to make another "island record," the label people were more receptive.

Recorded over time, when there's a song that needs to be captured, we go in. No master plan or design, simply a postcard to be written.

We'd recorded "Lucky Old Sun" with Willie Nelson a few years prior just because. That was the reason he'd thought about working with us for *Moment of Forever*.

I'd first heard "Lucky Old Sun" as a little boy on Willie's *Sound in Your Mind*; it had stayed with me as a perfect life moment. Our duet was so pure, I'd drive home after flying home from shows and sink into his performance.

Those 2:00, 3:00, and even 4:00 a.m. drives listening to "Lucky Old Sun" were the closest thing to being on my boat in the Caribbean. That peaceful space in the fast forward of it all was its own velocity.

We'd recorded Dave Matthews's "Gravedigger" on *Moment of Forever*. I'd played Dave Willie's album, because what songwriter wouldn't be honored to have Willie sing their song, especially one so smart and reality-checking? He recognized "I'm Alive," which was also on there.

Dave and I'd been crisscrossing the country, playing the same venues, even sharing our audience. When he visited on a rare Dave Matthews Band night off in 2007, the next-to-final night of our tour, we connected on a different level.

"We're putting you to work," I said. "Players who come see us, we make join us."

"You are?"

"Yes. 'Where Are You Going' is one of my favorite songs. You're going to sing it with us."

People who think country is so separate don't understand: People don't care what it's called. When Dave walked out, the audience loved him as much as they did us. We were blurring lines, making it heart and songs.

As I was thinking about this album, I knew Dave appreciated the blessings in the exhaustion of the road, too. Touring hard and creating new music, he gave the time and focus required. He was the perfect person to sing "I'm Alive" with me, because I wanted anyone who feels worn down by life to know they're not alone.

Every morning you get to choose, not what you have to do, but how you're going to feel about it. Sometimes jumping into the water off the side of my boat when I woke up was all the reminder I needed; but we all need reminders.

Dave agreed. His vocal sounds knowing and one with the world.

Conversational, I'd wanted to create a second verse that paints the vastness of hope when you're looking at the night sky. A note to self that no matter how crazy, exhale and feel the beauty in life.

Those commonalities that feel so isolated amaze me when I least expect it.

Dale Morris lived in Boca Raton, Florida, where he helped me fall in love with boats. Sometimes we'd go up the Intercoastal to a restaurant, tie up, have our dinner and a bottle of wine, then float home looking at the lights shining on the water. Sometimes we'd sit, tied up at his boat slip, simply listening to demos.

Whether I was with Farmer and his dad out on Norris Lake early in the morning, trolling for rockfish, or all of us getting crazy on the *Hey Now*, there was something about being on the water. My first boat—a used forty-five-foot SeaRay with a hundred hours on it—was so liberating because it took me away from everything.

Dean, Scotty Emerick, and I were in the British Virgin Islands, staying on the boat, maybe trying to catch some songs. We were talking a bit, Dean stretched out on the back couch with his legs crossed. He was eating a bag of Doritos, and I could tell he was in deep thought.

"How do you feel on this boat?" he finally asked.

"I feel free" was all I could say.

He continued to study me. Then he started to sing, "Vessels of freedom . . . Harbors of healing . . . Boats . . ."

That was it. That's how "Boats" started, and we stayed there for a few hours, writing a song about how boats can be an emotional anchor no matter what you're going through.

I was in Anegada, where I could tell this couple wanted to talk to me. They didn't want to intrude. Finally, they worked up the nerve. I figured it would be a typical fan interaction. I was wrong.

"We're sorry to bother you," the man began. "But we have to say thank you."

"Thank me?"

"Yes, you know your song 'Outta Here'?"

"I do," I said, wondering where this was going.

"It became our life blueprint," his wife continued.

"We quit our jobs, sold everything, and bought a boat. We decided to start living."

They told me their whole life story. I looked at them, so proud because you could tell how fulfilled and happy they were. This was their best life.

When we were writing "Boats," it was a man whose wife had passed, so he and his daughter sailed down to the islands. Another true story inspired us. They went through a terrible storm, literally, but it was also the storm of their life.

I could see this coming out of Dean's mouth. Sitting there, looking out the window at the water, Dean goes, "Came out alive on the other side."

We name boats because of emotional things. My first boat was *Sixth Gear*, because we got really drunk on it a lot. Later, we had to change the name many times because Ben got tired of chasing people off the boat. Then when Willie and I recorded "Worry B Gone," I named my next boat after that for all the reasons you could imagine.

That song brought *Lucky Old Sun* into focus. Rather than a deep dive into the details of my island life, I wanted to look over the bow and create an album for all the seekers and castaways like me. I'd met too many people whose stories told me they were listening, but even more they were seeing themselves in *Songs from an Old Blue Chair*.

There were maps to healing, escape, and how people literally sail through life. "Way Down Here," "Nowhere to Go, Nowhere to Be," and "Spirit of a Storm" spoke to the restlessness and the need to drift without having to be anywhere.

That freedom, even trying to give the label something to work with, made these records something that was pure music. What did we want to do? How did the songs speak to one another? What did it say about the kid from the mountains who'd fallen in love with the Caribbean? How much more were those islands like my home than so many places I'd been?

I called Mac.

"What are you doing tomorrow?"

"I don't know," he replied.

"Wanna come down to the studio? We're cutting one of your songs."

People recording Mac McAnally songs is a pretty regular thing. I wasn't a hero.

"Which one?" he asked, intrigued.

"I don't know," I replied. "I know everything on your *Simple Life* album. Why don't you pick one?"

"Um, okay . . ." Clearly, this wasn't how most people did it.

When Mac arrived the next morning, I told him the story of driving to Canada for Svetlana, listening to his cassette all the way there and back. He thought that was wonderful. Thinking for a bit, he said, "Well, then why don't we do 'Down the Road'? That kinda suits what happened."

"I don't have kids," I agreed about the song he'd written early one Christmas morning, waiting for his children to wake up. "But if I did, this is what I'd want to say to them."

Few things feel as good as a Mac McAnally song. Warm, reassuring melodies that pull you in and lift you up at the same time. It didn't matter to me which song we'd cut; I wanted to get into the studio and sing one with Mac.

Like "Back Where I Come From," "Down the Road" recognized we take our values with us wherever we go. Who we are remains, but as life moves us forward, it's about not forgetting. When the label heard that—and the reggae/calypso "Everybody Wants to Go to Heaven," which became a video with The Wailers, who would give us a final a cappella tag—they had what they needed to sell this record.

Those two songs would be No. 1 while the album was out, The Wailers even doing the CMA Awards with me and playing an unannounced set at Tootsies the night before. As powerful as all that was, the true soul of *Lucky Old Sun* was actually everything else.

THE WALL

In 2009, we ended our tour in Indianapolis. I actually felt like I couldn't do this anymore. I was mentally, spiritually, physically empty. Maybe beyond empty, the reserve half gallon was gone, even the fumes had been burned.

On the road, nonstop from 1993 to 2009, that's a lot of highways gone down, meet and greets, nights onstage when it's good, those rare nights when you're fighting for it. That was a lot, then a lot more was packed into all of it.

Midway through final mixes for *Hemingway's Whiskey*, I was concerned; usually music would bring me out of whatever kind of life funk was happening. This time, nothing.

Inspired by a few here and there, some of the things I'd written, nothing was pulling me out. The album was done, but somehow, I was numb.

I didn't know how I was going to keep doing this, how to get past feeling like a robot. About to go onstage at the sold-out Colt's football stadium, I felt frozen emotionally. Aware of how much I love the people who come to our shows, it threw me.

The last song we did was "Better as a Memory." I sang the first line, "*I move on like a sinner's prayer, I let go like a levee breaks . . .*"

And that's all I could do. Emotionally, I let go; it was too much. I started crying. The audience didn't know what was wrong. The band didn't understand what was going on. The crew didn't have a clue. But I was thinking, *It's over.*

I let the crowd sing it. Let them take the song, carry it for me.

Catfish, my longtime guitar tech, came up and gave me my guitar. He could see that I was really upset; he didn't know what to do, either. When I walked offstage, I wasn't certain what would happen. But I was so tired, I had no idea where or how to begin, where that moment was going to lead me.

Momentum is strange. Once it starts moving, it picks up force. For so long, if I said I needed time, people would say, "We know, but just this one thing . . ." Being creative, living like that, isn't possible if you're being honest with yourself.

I didn't tour in 2010. It was strange because that was all I'd known. Like a baseball team, six months on, six months off. My life was the tour bus, catering at 4:30 p.m., meet and greet at 7:10 p.m., video intro at 8:57 p.m. Then do what we came for.

I thought about the deal I'd made with myself in West Palm Beach, after my first headlining show. That contract with my soul to give this everything; whatever it took, required, or could make it better, I committed. Was this everything? *Had I given it all away?*

Listening to *Hemingway's Whiskey*, I knew I wasn't going to let what I built erode because we let good enough happen. The record was made and mixed; we were ready for a fall 2009 release. Meetings were scheduled at the label to start setting the album up.

I called Buddy. "The record isn't done."

"It's not . . .?" he said, half quizzical, half thinking maybe I'd found a great song.

"No," I said very seriously. "It's a good record, but it's not what it should be."

He took it in. Buddy is a man of few words, a lot of thought, and great instincts.

"We're not done. I know we've worked our asses off on this record, but we're not done."

"You got any ideas?" Buddy asked.

"Not yet."

It's hard to tell someone I respect as much as Buddy Cannon something like that. But I knew. Had I not taken that year—and it took me being so emotionally and mentally empty that the idea it was over felt real—because I had to recharge, *Hemingway's Whiskey* wouldn't have been what it was. I wouldn't have been who I was when it came out, either.

BOYS OF FALL

Casey Beathard called me, saying, "I'm sending you a song."

He sent me songs all the time.

"Someone passed, but I think you'll really like it. I wanted to make sure *you* want to pass on this one."

Casey doesn't presell like that. That was all I needed.

Sixty seconds later, the email arrived. I opened the file, hit play, that first line . . .

"*When I feel that chill, smell that fresh cut grass . . .*"

I was stunned. Right there, ten words took me and my senses to places I'd been. It was me in the car leaving football practice; me and all my buddies excited the first time we ever put our helmets on for a game in Pee Wee Football. It was me and my dad, walking into Neyland Stadium where everything was so much bigger than life.

When I heard it, I thought, *Oh my God, this wraps its arms around every bit of those emotions.* It wasn't a football song, it was THE football song. The bond, the trust that you share. Not everybody gets to go on to play in the NFL, or even college football.

That was the beauty of this song. When people think about their glory days and what it was like, people think about what they went through on the field. But it's those parents in bleachers, the community that turns out. It was a life song, a lifestyle song into how people are connected.

Casey knew because his whole life was football. His dad, Bobby Beathard, was a general manager for the San Diego Chargers and entrenched in the NFL. That's why he knew what he had written: a song that touches all the senses of loving this game. From our conversations, he knew what football meant to me, and he knew I was the person to sing this song.

I called him back. "Yeah, I'm not passing on that."

Casey'd sent me a guitar-vocal demo. That's all there was. I didn't want to overdo it—let the vocal lead the track and the instruments support the emotion in it.

Don't overcut. Don't overproduce. Let the song be.

When we went into the studio to cut it, Barry Beckett was on my shoulder, going, "Don't cut the hit out of it."

Even more, don't cut the heart out of it.

I understood from the inside out why this song mattered.

I had no idea it would save my creative life. This song was for anyone who'd ever been touched by high school football. There would be challenges—even in this imploding I hadn't seen coming—getting a slow ballad about something some people would think was niche played. It wasn't going to be as easy as "Summertime" or "Livin' in Fast Forward."

Because the album wasn't done, we'd need a single that could buy us time. "Boys of Fall" had been recorded at this point—and was something I was proud of. Because of moving the album, we could release the single early enough it had a chance to speak to people as football season was arriving. I could continue working on the album, at a pace that made sense as I hit pause on touring.

It wasn't a typical first single. But if we went with something else, it would be spring when we released "Boys of Fall." That made no sense. I called the label to let them know what I was thinking. They said, "This is a bad idea. We need something more universally accepted."

It hit me: They'd never played sports. They didn't understand how much gets tied up in watching your high school's team play; how much goes into it for the young men playing on the team. Had they been out on those fields, they would've understood.

I heard them out. Then I explained, "This is the single."

I never doubted it, never regretted it. I don't even remember if it was a No. 1 record, but I know how many places I go—places where nobody cares about country music—they know and love "Boys of Fall" and that universal pride it offers up.

Once the decision was made, the video concept was to reflect the heart of the game. Rather than "stage" something, we captured high school football teams at their fall practices, scrimmage games, hometowns. I wanted a collage of all the phases that comprise a season. A crew went to Gibbs High School, where I played, as well as Battleground Academy in Franklin, Tennessee, where Casey Beathard's son CJ, now in the NFL, was playing.

We went to Celina, Texas, too. It's as American small-town as you get.

Seeing those kids putting everything into it, you realize grown-ups hold back. At that age, the players give everything. To capture the passion of all the people this song was about, we shot the local fans, college and NFL stars, coaches, too. Watching the raw footage, I thought about my coaches who'd stewarded our growth as men and as players.

I called Sean Payton. He'd started preseason, but this was important. What if Sean went home to deliver the speech before Naperville High School's first game? What would it look like to have Shaun Silva and his guys in the locker room for that?

"You want me to *what* . . ."

"Give the speech to the guys in the locker room before they run out on the field."

"In the middle of my preseason? Because, I do have responsibilities."

"I know. And I understand if you can't. But I have to ask. It's what the song deserves."

I'd sent Sean "Boys of Fall." He'd listened.

"You will literally have to fly me in, then fly me right back out."

"Done."

Sean put the players in the clap-three-times drill to anchor them in the present.

"Twenty-seven years ago," he told these students, in awe of the NFL coach who'd come from their hometown, "I sat on one knee in this locker room, getting ready to play a game. I walked in the locker room today, it still smells the same.

"It takes you back real fast.

"One of the things that caught me was how fast twenty-seven

years goes by. There's so many people who live vicariously through you. I would give anything tonight to jump in one of these uniforms with you guys.

"That feeling goes away. It doesn't come every Friday night. It comes when you get married, your first child is born. But you don't get it every Friday night. That's what I miss.

"You seniors, you're focused on college, what you're going to do after school. You're focused on tomorrow, aren't you? You've got plenty of time for tomorrows.

"These tonights, they're going by fast.

"You focus on tonight. This is about you guys, the guys in this room that care about one another . . . who know there's only so many more of these nights left. This is about you.

"They're a faceless opponent. They happened to draw the short straw tonight.

"Now get your asses ready to play. Win on three . . ."

Sean didn't make one note for his speech. He spoke from his heart as the man he became to the boy he was. When Shaun Silva showed me the footage, I was blown away. What needed to be said: Sean Payton nailed.

When I went to play the video for the label, I think they were expecting a highlight reel: fast-paced, quick-cut highlights, a chest-thumping, aren't-we-the-shit deal. This was very emotional: They saw the heart and soul of the game, from the trenches, the sidewalks, and the diners. This is what high school football in small towns looks like.

They still weren't jumping up and down. It was July 2010, the height of summer. When people heard it was "a football song," they expected a fight song. In the middle of something full of testosterone, this was something very different.

◆ ◆ ◆

Unexpected, but powerful. I didn't realize fifteen years later, I'd meet NFL players, who love different kinds of music, Beyoncé, rappers, hard *hard* rockers, and they'd have no idea who I am. But say "Boys of Fall," and they know. Whether you were raised in a big city, a suburb where trees hadn't grown in yet, or somewhere agriculture-based, everybody had those emotions, pride, hardcore practices, and coaches who made you more.

Rather than world premiere on *Entertainment Tonight*, I wanted to take this mini-movie to people who would understand at their core.

I'd met John Walsh, who worked at ESPN, at a *Sports Illustrated* pre–Super Bowl party in Miami. We'd kept in touch. As the song and video were coming together, I sent it to him. John was impressed, especially with Sean's speech.

"That's interesting," I said. "I'm thinking about making a documentary film on this."

John replied, "I think that would be a great idea."

We talked some more. He agreed to debut "Boys of Fall" on *SportsCenter*.

"If you want to try to do this, keep in touch. Maybe we're a home for your documentary."

We went to the New Orleans Saints' training camp, interviewed Sean, the way we would all the coaches, about the game and football being his life. He had fun, saw what we were trying to do.

Then Sean introduced me to Brett Favre. Next thing, we're in Brett Favre's living room in Mississippi. We flew to Tallahassee, Florida, to interview Bobby Bowden; kept going south to Joe Namath's place in Jupiter, Florida. We talked to Tony Dungy, Jon Gruden, Bill Parcells, and Nick Saban.

People were telling one another about what we were doing. We were invited to Oakland to spend an entire day with John Madden. His property was like a huge warehouse—large-screen TVs and memorabilia everywhere. He even cooked dinner for us, then we went to his office and did his interview. It was a special day.

I was working on *Hemingway's Whiskey*, too. But this experience? We were going to the homes of these people who'd given so much of themselves to this sport; talking to people I'd seen while watching TV with my father. I knew what these people opening their souls to us meant. It was feeding me in a way music wasn't, but it reminded me what that spark is that needs to ignite the fire inside each of us.

Inspiring to hear these men talk about life, not just football, but how the two things intertwine. I would leave each interview thinking about the wisdom. We were with Joe Namath at his house, where he really opened his heart.

"You can isolate yourself in the business," he shared. Something I could be guilty of. Here I was in Joe Namath's house, and within his interview, he took this tangent away from sports. He talked about the principles you take into life.

Looking me in the eye, he offered, "Life is a team game . . . It's the *big* game."

Sitting there, stunned, I didn't want to cry in front of him; but I really needed to hear that. It was God sent to me. I knew it was.

Shaun Silva and I finished up, got in the car. We looked at each other, awestruck. We both said, "That was one of the most amazing things I've ever heard" at the same time.

We heard it from Joe Namath, who was as big a rock star as Mick Jagger when we were growing up. Those things I didn't see coming.

When Shaun and I finished, John Walsh sat through all three-and-a-half hours of our first cut. Every bit of it. Walsh introduced us to John Dahl, who helped get it cut down and finished.

We were on the West Coast, John Dahl came, watched the whole film. He said, "I know what to do with this."

We went from there. What I thought was something they'd air a few times that year still has a life to it. High school football, after all, is eternal. That's where my working relationship with John Dahl began.

For *Boys of Fall*, we'd interviewed one of my childhood heroes, Condredge Holloway, about having football in his life. It wasn't a big piece of what made air. John Dahl called me up after *Boys of Fall* debuted on ESPN.

"We saw Condredge Holloway's interview in *Boys of Fall* and had an idea," he said. "One of our big campaigns next year is the Year of the Quarterback. We're going to have a lot of content around quarterbacks and what they've meant to the game. Would you be interested in making a film on Condredge Holloway?"

The football stuff had fed me, refueled me, reminded me who I was at my depths. Making films is hard work. Condredge Holloway was the first Black quarterback in the Southeastern Conference. Was this something I should be doing? *Hemingway's Whiskey* called.

"Let me think about it for a second."

Two, maybe three seconds later, I called back. "This is an amazing opportunity. I'm in."

Suddenly, I was back. All the passion, all the energy had returned.

What started as a song that Casey Beathard knew I would understand turned into something more. Never mind I was lost, exhausted, not sure where to turn. From the moment I committed to "Boys of Fall" as a single, that song led me every step from the video with Sean's speech, to a longer form documentary and beyond—all the way back to the journey I'd committed so completely to as a kid at ETSU.

GRACE

There was a show on TV called *Let's Make a Deal*. People would show up to be contestants, hoping host Monty Hall would pick them to compete for prizes. New cars, new kitchens with all the appliances, expensive watches. You had to pick.

One of two things: color TVs and washer/dryer sets *or* what was behind Door No. 3, knowing it might end up being the Jelly of the Month Club.

I've always been attracted to what's behind Door No. 3. That idea of the big unknown, the massive thing you can't see always appealed to me. The seeker inside has chased the unknown all my life.

When you're a dreamer, you can't not take Door No. 3. That mentality fuels you. Seeking inspiration, wanting to find out has a risk involved. Some Door No. 3s don't work out. But Grace Potter?

She's the epitome of why Door No. 3 is always better than playing it safe.

"You and Tequila" showed up in my email in the middle of the night. Matraca Berg had been drinking red wine with a friend, listening to demos. They were drunk enough to send it across the internet into my inbox.

I remember listening, thinking, *Damn* . . .

That idea of a person you can't quit because they're so addictive is real. You can't resist, only overdo it to the point of poisoning yourself hit me. I called Matraca, asked if there was a demo with a man singing it; she had one. Hearing Tim Krekel sing it hit me even harder.

We cut it really simple. That pull between what you want and knowing you shouldn't made "You and Tequila" burn into people.

We were about done with *Hemingway's Whiskey*. I wanted something to make it shine. Buddy Cannon and I were talking about who might sound good. Clint Higham, my comanager, even reached out to Irving Azoff about the Eagles, since this sounded like a classic Laurel Canyon song.

Then the woman who sent me the demo asked, "Why don't you get Grace Potter? She captures that haunted and haunting feeling."

What makes Grace Potter the ultimate Door No. 3 was the mystery. My fans were asking, "Who the fuck?" while her fans, we joke, were saying, "Why the fuck?" The ultimate hippie songwriter/rock girl. Once she was suggested, as much as it made no sense on paper, I knew she was the person we needed.

◆ ◆ ◆

I listen to a lot of music at night in the Virgin Islands. No light pollution, so you can drift in the sounds. I'd been given Grace's live CD. "Apologies" poured out of the speakers.

Motionless on a chaise lounge when I heard Grace's voice—so soulful, but beautiful and real—I was floored. Nobody in my life had heard this voice except my friend. I felt blessed.

She wrote her own songs. She had a band but wasn't overproduced. Really listening, it was all about how she played that B-3 organ, but especially how she sang those songs.

I looked up at the sky and exhaled. I knew we were aligned. She sounded like coming home.

When we put her on "You and Tequila," all she knew about me was "She Thinks My Tractor's Sexy" because the Eagle in Burlington, Vermont, had played it to death.

I needed to see if it was even possible. Grace had finished a European tour, traveled twenty-four hours with no sleep, and was literally just landing in America. We laugh now, but she listened to the demo on the rental car shuttle having cleared customs.

She was tired. She missed her family. *And* we needed her in Nashville within forty-eight hours to make the deadline for mastering, or we'd have to move the record. Her manager wasn't optimistic. My friend insisted, "Give her the song."

Thirty minutes later, we had a yes. Thirty hours later, Grace Potter landed in Nashville in a flowy leopard-print dress, walked into Blackbird Studio, and changed both of our lives. Brash, smart, and funny, she oozed music. She told wild stories, made some people blush, and asked us what we were thinking.

Buddy suggested, "Get in the booth and put your headphones on. See how it feels to you."

Probably warming up, she was humming. Then that "oooooohOOOOOHohhhh" she does on the record rolled out.

"Do some more of *that*."

Two or three takes later, we were done. We'd talked longer than she was in the vocal booth. Even before it was mixed, we knew it was something. That's the thing: You know.

It was my birthday. I asked her and her boyfriend if they'd like to have dinner. We went to the Sunset Grille, sat outside on the patio and laughed. We came from musically different places; her idea of country music was Willie, Townes Van Zandt, and Lucinda Williams. But we were of the same heart, same small-town, family-oriented life.

She was tired, so we didn't hang long. When I got up to leave, she followed me out of the restaurant, jumped in the passenger seat of my car, and announced, "I don't know what the future holds, but we're going to be friends for life."

Grace Potter knew things. I've always believed there are things in our lives that were predetermined—set into motion by some larger power. Grace was absolutely one.

That heart that Grace brings to everything she does was a skeleton key in my world. Any time she takes a stage with us, people are transfixed. Her voice transcends from Red Rocks to awards shows to stadiums.

For the "You and Tequila" video, we spent two days in Malibu, rolling around the canyons, seeing the cliffs and the ocean, drinking tequila, and talking about life, love, what you dream, and how hard it can be getting there. Not just a serious musician, but a songwriter who finds those real-life slices, she has a real sense of fun, too.

Anyone who's ever seen that video assumes we were having sex. Even Mom thought we were sleeping together, but that wasn't true.

That chemistry comes from our gypsy souls, our desire to chase music where it takes us and disappear into places we can be still.

Though the Nocturnals had never played stadiums, only massive festivals like Bonnaroo and Mile High, Grace was game to do our 2012 stadium tour. Playing in broad daylight, Grace brought such rock passion, she took hostages every show.

We went to the Rock & Roll Hall of Fame in Cleveland where the dress she wore on VH1's *Divas* was displayed, and I took her picture. We hired the Franklin High Marching Band to pour onstage playing "Happy Birthday" during our Nashville stadium show. And there's that New England connection, so having her whole family with us at Gillette Stadium made it an actual homecoming that year.

Rock and roll friendships are strange: They exist in the air, almost rootless. Over the years, Grace and I have told each other our deepest secrets, talked each other through tough stuff, and tried to show up for the other. I've told her things I wouldn't tell anyone else, because rather than judge or saying "How did you let that happen?" she asks, "How can I help?"

I'd do the same for her. It's tricky wanting so much for the people you love. You don't want to tell them what to do or where to go. When she was getting married, I flew all the way to St. Barths to have dinner with her the night before, then right back to play the Dallas Cowboys' stadium. One day off, but I was worried she was making a mistake; not because she didn't love Mattie, but because I could see two great people who probably weren't meant to be together forever.

I couldn't quite tell her, but Grace swears she knew without me saying a word. We drank a few bottles of really good red wine, had a rager, saw the sun come up, and I got back to the tour. She always tells me how generous that was. I think it's what you do for people you love.

On a day off in California, Grace called me to come over to her house on Lookout Mountain. She'd written a song called "Stars," started it that morning, and she wanted to play it for me. One of the prettiest things I'd ever heard, I told her I wanted to produce her on it with Buddy. Really simple, so all that wonder shined through.

Her voice and the song are everything: Stay out of the way, let the heart rise. She was putting out *The Lion the Beast the Beat*, which was more eclectic, so this wouldn't feel out of place.

Shortly after, we went to dinner at the Sunset Tower, this historic old Hollywood hotel on Sunset Plaza. Catching up, laughing and talking trash in a beautiful dining room, it was perfect.

Diana Krall and Elvis Costello were having dinner a few tables over. She got up and played something on the piano. Listening to Diana Krall was a moment. We knew it.

Me, being me, I started prodding Grace to play "Stars." The song was new, but I knew it was striking. I kept saying, "You *have* to go do this. You do."

She wasn't so sure. We'd fallen into a conversation with Steve Buscemi about his film *The Interview*, which is just him, Sienna Miller, and one single shot—one of the smartest movies I've ever seen. He started working on her, too.

At dinner, I'd explained when I went to the islands, I'd listened to "Apologies" repeatedly on my boat, looking up at the stars over the water. I told them "Stars"—which I always took as a song about someone who'd passed, but was really someone who wasn't there anymore—moved me the same way.

Thirty minutes later, she went to the piano. Standing there with Malchijah Bailey, Steve Buscemi, and Dmitri Dimitrov, the legendary maître d' who keeps the place flawless, for support, Grace started singing "Stars."

I've never seen a bar get that quiet that quickly. She sang "Wild Horses" and "Apologies" and was every bit the rock star—the Stevie Nicks, the Bonnie Raitt, the Linda Ronstadt—I knew she'd been inspired by.

Ultimately, she came to Nashville, and we cut it. We cut "Ragged Company," too, from her first indie record. When we called Willie Nelson to see if he'd duet with her, he loved that song as much as we did; probably saw a lot of his life in it, too.

He agreed. Suddenly, Grace Potter had some country soul on her R&B/disco/rock record.

SHE COMES FROM BOSTON

"Boston," so organically written, showed the essence of a certain type of woman I kept meeting in the islands. I never thought anybody, honestly, would hear it. Those songs on *Be as You Are* were snapshots.

"Boston" established a life of its own. I wouldn't dream of singing it anywhere other than Gillette Stadium. They feel such ownership because No Shoes Nation knows I won't ever perform it anywhere else. We get requests. People hold up signs, but I won't.

It's always a quiet moment because it's intimate. Until . . .

Hearing 60,000 people singing those words is a spiritual experience. The power of that song and the pull it has through the region humbles me. "Boston" is the DNA of their world that seeped into their soul. All the power this community created comes at us full blast.

Everyone in that crowd has a bit of that girl who took off on vacation and stayed a year, two, even forever inside them.

Having lunch at Baxter's on Hyannis Inner Harbor a few summers ago, a boat not thirty yards from where we were sitting was blasting it. They had no idea I was there. Seeing a group of friends soaking up the sun, enjoying the day, and drinking some beers made me happy.

Watching Red Sox games, the music will bleed through the broadcast. Sometimes, I'll hear *"She wears a Red Sox cap to hide her baby dreads . . ."* and smile. Seeking commonality is what you hope for, but seeing it through the TV's looking glass is the greatest.

One of the reasons for that connection is where I grew up. Rural, we had family, hard work, our friends. The local high school football team was a big deal. When you get outside Boston, the towns lean on the same things. That's more powerful than some people think.

There was also the thread of the Virgin Islands. Before social media, when everything wasn't instant, you had mystery and a sense of these places, maybe a friend who lived there. Your curiosity deepened, you wanted to know. You went. Slowly, the New England–island link strengthened.

In 2004, we sold out two nights in Mansfield, Massachusetts. You could feel the groundswell.

Playing Gillette Stadium in 2005 wasn't completely crazy, but it was a big leap from two amphitheaters to headlining Patriots' stadium. Stadium shows weren't commonplace. Some years, I would be the only tour playing those major football stadiums. That wasn't lost on Robert Kraft, who watched it get a little bigger every year.

We have a tradition. Every year, Robert and his son Jonathan Kraft have lunch with me before the first show. At some point in the conversation, Mr. Kraft will say, "I can't believe you're selling this place out! You're from Tennessee, coming to New England! Who saw that coming?"

"I don't question it," I say. I feel the heart inside that audience. "They care about me because I care about them—and they *know* I care about them. They can feel it."

I've come to believe the only difference may be the accent.

Over the years, because the Krafts are about family as much as football, I've felt welcomed into their world. Because No Shoes Nation was named at Gillette Stadium, Robert Kraft hung a banner in the end zone alongside the Patriots' Super Bowl flags.

The Krafts believed in all those kids, too. They didn't see just fans, they saw our culture, the parking lot parties and tailgating. They recognize the passion and understand how much this music and community means to everyone.

Robert Kraft told me many times, "Nothing brings people together like sports or music. We build communities with those things."

✦ ✦ ✦

How many Super Bowls have I seen from the Krafts' box? Some years were brutal. In 2017, when the Falcons had a 28–3 lead in the third quarter, it was somber. What can you say? How do you say it? Nobody wanted to go over to Robert.

I knew what the Patriots were capable of. I stood there next to him.

"This isn't over," I said to Robert, not sure where the words were coming from. But I'd been to their training camp, knew the power of Tom Brady and Bill Belichick, their competitive nature.

"You mark my words: They're not done."

In the end, the Patriots won 34–28.

Heart. Life. Football. Maybe . . . There's a lot of power in passion, execution, doing the work, and having a vision that can respond to the moment. It was one of the most unbelievable final quarters I've ever seen.

When Robert told my father, "We love your son. He's part of our family," that was a big deal. I can't think of a higher compliment someone could have given him.

I met Rory Kennedy through the geography of a table at a friend's house in Los Angeles. We'd gone for a movie screening, then were seated together at dinner. I asked her what she was working on. I was finishing my third ESPN documentary. Realizing she made award-winning docs, I knew she might have insight.

"I think the film's about thirty-five minutes too long," I explained.

Without missing a beat, she shot back, "How long is it? About thirty-five minutes?"

Her very direct question landed between us.

I was shocked, but in the best way. Rather than speak, I burst out laughing. She did, too. I'm not sure it was a test, but, clearly, hardcore teasing is her love language. That she'd lob a comment like that and I laughed said everything. We were each other's kind of people.

She invited me to come to Hyannis Port to meet her mother, Ethel, the day before our Gillette shows. When you pull up to the Kennedy compound and see that yard you've seen so many times in magazines and news clips, the history hits you.

Then, Ethel Kennedy sees you and reaches for a hug, she's so bright and welcoming, her presence eclipses all of it. From the moment I sat down on the couch with her, there wasn't any history. I didn't think about her as an activist, an icon, but someone filled with life, who filled everyone with love.

Walk around the house, you see the black-and-white images of John F. Kennedy, Ethel, and Bobby, waiting on election returns. They're sitting in this wonderful living room, where I was seated, waiting for JFK to win by that narrow margin.

Somewhere in that day—we had lunch, went for a sail in Nantucket Sound, came back and talked, played volleyball in the backyard with all the kids—we fell in deep soul love. Her spirit is so engaging, I wanted to soak it all up.

When we left for sound check in Foxboro, I couldn't believe it had happened. One of those written-in-the-universe things, it was only the beginning. I went on so many sailing trips, as well as Ethel's ninetieth birthday party in Palm Beach.

I'm not political. She didn't care.

When Rory premiered her *Take Every Wave* documentary about our mutual friend Laird Hamilton in New York, she invited me. Blink and you'll miss me working out with Laird, but I wasn't going to miss seeing Rory's work—her films are very thoughtful.

Everyone on the red carpet was buzzing. Hot and crowded, people were packed together. Waiting to go in, Kerry Kennedy came over. By now, I knew most of the family, especially the kids who'd all come to our shows.

"Kenny, I have to tell you, my mom loves you!"

"Well, I love her."

Who knows why? Everything about us clicked. The humor, curiosity, passion for living was our reality. We shared so many laughs and moments, Page Six, the *New York Post*'s gossip column, ran an item headlined, "Are Ethel Kennedy and Kenny Chesney Sailing Buddies?"

She was ninety, having more fun than people a third her age. Nobody loved living, her family, dogs, or causes more.

I was honored when she asked me to perform "This Land Is Your Land" in Arlington National Cemetery, honoring the fiftieth anniversary of Robert Kennedy's assassination. Something so solemn was obviously personal. You don't imagine that request when you're learning about these things in history class.

Rory surprised me when the family asked me to sing at Ethel's funeral.

There I was at St. Matthew the Apostle before Presidents Joe Biden, Barack Obama, and Bill Clinton; the ambassador from Ireland; senators; bishops; and the world—via live stream—to honor my friend. Along with Stevie Wonder and Sting, I was offering—a cappella—a song that defined Ethel Kennedy.

"Every time I was around your mother, she made me feel great, because she felt like sunshine."

Nothing every person in the capacity cathedral didn't already know. But it was true. Putting my hands to my chest in a small prayer, I began "You Are My Sunshine."

WHEN I SEE THIS BAR

Kristi Hansen died. Born in Maine, she was the quintessential island girl. Funny, smart, quick to help any of us, quicker to laugh. One of the core bartenders at Woody's, she knew everyone. She'd moved back to the mainland with her fiancé, Ben, to start raising a family, walked down the driveway to get the mail—and that was that. She was gone.

Thirty-five years old. Six months pregnant with her first child, a brain aneurysm was all it took. Kristi and her unborn daughter, Aria Dulce, would never laugh with us again.

It knocked everyone off their feet emotionally.

One of the original island friends, she was the first to show up at the dock for an all-day sail or hop on the ferry to Duffy's Love Shack for "Power Hour," throw a straw in a big blue Shark Tank cocktail, pay the man, and jump the last ferry back. You knew the locals because they were the ones doing it.

This wasn't supposed to happen. Definitely not now.

The words fell out. When it doesn't make sense, songwriters reach for their guitar. All the images of Kristi, behind the bar keeping us in line, pouring shots and opening beers; dancing on the bow of the *Hey Now*, arms in the air and laughter on her lips. "Happy on the Hey Now" gathered them all up, a song for *a friend of a friend, someone I'm glad I knew.*

It was so simple, then it wasn't.

I had spent some of my time off over the previous years making documentaries, traveling with a backpack, a notebook, and no guitar. It was a different way to live, but I was curious. It's easy, too, to spread out when you've got an anchor like we all had on island. Wherever you wandered, you could come back, and everyone would be waiting with their arms wide open.

People had started leaving, growing up and going back to the real world. But this? This was too final. Instead of everyone heading to Woody's or the Quiet Mon, it was long-distance calls to Maine, Florida, North Carolina, trying to make sense without coming together.

I will always see you dancing, up there on the bow / Living life in the moment, happy on the Hey Now . . . was how every one of us saw our friend. Someone that shining doesn't disappear. As the song says, *You'll live with us as long as memories stay alive, and you left with us so many, Kristi, you will never die* . . .

That first loss in any group of friends makes you pause. Everything so precious and free, most of us take for granted. Busy living, hopefully in the moment, it's easy to forget to stop, take it in, and appreciate it. I had a backpack of songs I'd written in a handful of moments never intended for anything more than the memory; probably let a thousand more go not even realizing.

"Happy on the Hey Now" was grieving our friend Kristi. It wasn't intentional, but there was a lot of intent there. I wanted to hold on to what she meant to us, who she was, but it was mostly pure mourning. It was also mourning my youth and our innocence. We'd lived so much together, but we were growing up. I thought about people I'd met, the characters. I thought about those notebooks in my backpack where the words fell onto the paper the way they wanted, not how they should be.

I was down island when I realized life was changing. I was in a bar where we'd made these memories, thinking about it. Slow afternoon, no one was around. Once again, a song arrived on a pile of cocktail napkins, no idea about the music.

"When I See This Bar" was as real as anything I'd written. Looking around, every nick in the bar or torn picture tied to a friend, a moment, something. Small things, but that was the beauty of being there.

Someone said to me, "Heart, life, music: How you feel in your heart should be how you live . . . and that's what you should fill your music with." When I looked at the words on those napkins, the pages in my journal, I realized, unknowingly, that's what I'd done.

Created with no boundaries, expectations, or timelines, they were written to be *written*. I didn't know I had an album, wasn't thinking how to sell it. Instead, these pieces of my heart I'd found along the way seemed to be where the deeper truth was.

Some of them still didn't have music, but "When I See This Bar" gave me the anchor. I had an emotional center for my record, if that's what this was. When I couldn't find the music, I called Troy Tomlinson.

"I have this song, and I'm stuck."

"Tell me about it," he said.

I explained the phase of life it was living in and the memories. He got quiet, then had an idea.

"You always loved 'El Cerrito Place.' Why don't you send it to Keith Gattis? He understands those kinds of feelings. That's really what he does."

The yearning in "El Cerrito Place" was haunted, not maudlin. A respected player who'd been Dwight Yoakam's bandleader, he understood the power and the kick of the rock side, but he found the song's core.

"That's a great idea."

Keith put his soul into it, changed the song's essence. He heard all the emotions I was too in the middle of. It was really different, edgy, strong. Even slightly angry, but remembering youth and innocence. When you look back, you can take it all in. When I was thinking about all the friends who'd moved on, but also the ones who stayed—*Some are still living the dream, stuck in still life it seems*—my heart sped up knowing we'd shared something so special.

Keith's melody has a triumph to it. When we play it, it's honoring how powerful that time in our lives was. When Eric Church was on tour with us, that was the song he sang with us each night. He knew that passion, too, and really tore into it.

So much of *Life on a Rock* was like that. What wasn't intended became something valuable in terms of vulnerability and opening my world. "That Time of the Day" and "Marley" were a giant exhale. "Coconut Tree" was something silly with Willie. Some friends thought it was about Keith Richards's misadventures in a coconut tree, but I'm not saying.

Life on a Rock celebrated what tourists miss. Lindy was an island fixture; someone everyone saw. A lot of us didn't know how he lived or where he came from. A tall man with a head of dreadlocks and no shoes, he talked a lot to himself. He would bum cigarettes, nod at the locals.

When afternoons were heavy, hot, and humid, sometimes you'd hear the piano rolling out of St. Ursula's Episcopal Church when no one was around. Lindy would go in and play, for himself or the Lord. I heard him one afternoon, stopped in my tracks and really listened.

What made me go home and write "Lindy" down, I don't know. There was something so spiritual in what he was playing. Authentic wasn't even a word for it, Lindy just was.

Six or seven years prior, I'd been asked by Aston "Family Man" Barrett to finish a song The Wailers had recorded but never completed. For a project they were doing that didn't come together, but anything I could do for Aston or Alvin "Seeco" Patterson was my pleasure. "Spread the Love" was a song of hope, even healing.

Unsure what they were doing with it, I called to ask if I could make it part of this album. Talking to "Fam," who'd been there with Bob Marley, was like speaking to the source. Wise, quiet, he took things in.

Word came back. I could have the song.

The Boston Marathon bombing had happened. At a time when fear—I remember being on my bus watching the marathon—struck something so positive, I wanted to offer the message of hope, not hate.

Would The Wailers be willing to do the video? Yes, come.

We'd done the "Everybody Wants to Go to Heaven" video in Jamaica with them, which was beautiful. I'd spent time talking about life, rasta, and their friend Bob. I knew how much deeper life in Jamaica ran, and I wanted to show that.

I also wanted to show hope, bright eyes, and what the future could be. We started the video at Hope House School, me in a roomful of these children in their uniforms who were so ready to take on the world. Fun, curious, they were a reminder to never take learning—or playing—for granted as they teased me, sang in those young voices.

We shot in Trenchtown, made sure to get the culture of the islands and faces of the people who live beyond the tourist zone. There's so much we don't see, and that's where the richness is. I am grateful to Fam and the others for opening those windows for us.

But I am especially grateful for the time we spent at Tuff Gong Studios, where Marley recorded. In a circle, we filmed in the studio. Sweat dripped off us. The words from Psalm 1:51 "Therefore the ungodly shall not stand in the judgment, nor sinners in the congregation

Legendary Coach Bobby Bowden invited me
to participate in spring football practice with Florida State in 2002.
He became a really good friend.

With my high school football coach Randy Carroll during
"The Boys of Fall" video shoot at Gibbs High School.

In the Vibe Room with one of my favorite humans, Jon Gruden.
Preshow at Raymond James Stadium, Tampa, Florida.

Me and Daryl Hobby hanging with one of the best to ever do it—
my friend Nick Saban. Tuscaloosa, Alabama.

The Vince Lombardy Trophy, me, and Sean Payton
onstage after the New Orleans Saints won the Super Bowl.
There are no words to measure how much joy—or rum—we were feeling.

Few things make me as happy as going to sporting events with
John Staley, Jim Cogdill, and my dad.
At a Boston Celtics game, in Boston, Massachusetts.

Best friends. Poncho and Ruby, aka da Ponch and da Ruba Girl.

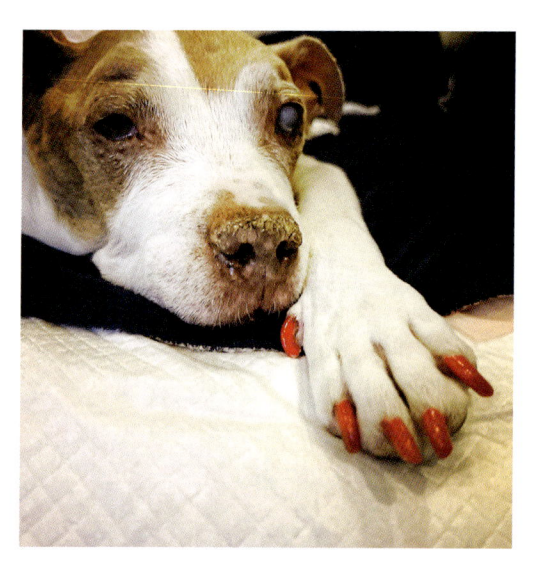

Ruby with her ruby-red nails.

Me and Poncho in the Florida Keys.

Honoring Troy Tomlinson
with the CMA Songwriter Advocate Award.
From the moment I walked into Acuff-Rose
wanting something to happen,
he's been that for me.

I get my love of the sun, water, and music from my mother.
Nobody gets joy or loves like she does.

The Grigsby family comes together. Grandma Lucy (in green sweater)
is right in the middle where she belongs.
She was the center of all of our worlds.

Proud of "back where I come from."

A quiet moment. Waiting on soundcheck.
The night before kicking off *The Big Revival Tour*, 2015.

of the righteous" on the wall of the studio behind us lent a gravity to this moment.

Once again, I was somewhere unthinkable for that college kid hearing reggae for the first time. That rhythm like your heartbeat from another world unites. For this album taking shape, I wanted a bridge to the future. It's not recognizing what was gone, but moving toward a future "Spread the Love" created.

Almost a year to the day after Kristi died, Todd and Chad Beaty sold Woody's Seafood Saloon. It was time, almost twenty years. Some things feel like they will always be there. That blue-painted outside, the perfect dive bar where when you walk in time moves a little slower, was where I'd spent a lot of that slowed-down time.

What people couldn't see—even the ones looking for me—was our lives, screwups, triumphs, helping each other through rough patches. You had to be there for that.

To think that the *Hey Now*'s maiden voyage was 01/01/01. January first, the first full year of the twenty-first century. So many friendships began that day, grew deeper, bonded for life. It was lightning in a bottle what had passed between us.

KJ sent me a text on 12/12/12. All it said was, "It's over."

What was the mathematical chance of that? It would take another century before another group of young people could come together on an island and live as if they were never going to grow up. To be able to exist as if it will always be this way.

Those twelve years, all that happened shaped us. It grounded me when fame hit, inspired me to write songs that reached deeper. More honest and personal, I also told the stories of the people I'd met there.

The day Woody's closed, we filmed the video for "When I See

This Bar" in the middle of the floor, time-stamping it forever. I wore a Low Key Crew shirt and flip-flops like I was stopping in for a beer. We spliced so much footage of all the years we'd been coming to the islands throughout. Boat trips, Christmas hats, shots, conga drums, and all the sunburn we could withstand.

When we hit the line *and a man learning to move on*, the clip cuts to us onstage. The force of where music had taken me showed how far that bar had propelled me. Having Woody's to release and reset kept my priorities and passions in order; it meant more than we could've known.

In some ways, it was the death of Bobby Crouton, *my island alter ego*. That carefree spirit who ran wild was gone. We'd all grown up too much. But we'd been there, dancing on the *Hey Now*'s bow.

That's why songs matter. As the lyric promises, *With songs that fill my memories like a tip jar, that's what I see when I see this bar . . .*

When she was getting ready to leave the island, my friend Jaana Martin signed the shot ski I'd had made with a Boston Red Sox logo. She wrote:

> We lived here
> We loved here
> & we loved each other here.

> 01-01-01 U.S. VI
>
> Today was magic! We all went out on Bob's new boat and we couldn't have ordered a more perfect. Day at sea. The kind of day you wish you could bottle up and take with you where ever you go in life. I've seen a lot of sunsets down here but as we were coming home tonight across the channel, I saw more colors in the sky than I thought was possible! Everyone was quiet on the boat. No music!! Nothing really!! It was just a beautiful silence watching another day slip away and a reminder that there is something much bigger out there than all of us. You feel so alive, humble, and human when you are on the ocean and you witness day turn into night with such style and beauty. What a way to spend the first day of this year with friends, rum, music, and knowing deep in your heart and soul, that at least for a little while, that you were happy, still, and living in the moment.   K.C. 8:32 pm
> New Years Day 2001
> U.S.V.I

REVIVALS

Twenty years since my first album, over a decade since stadiums started to dominate my summers, I was at a crossroads. Following *Life on a Rock*, I was a different person. I wasn't certain how, but I was hungry to press all the things I'd been doing, while letting go of what drags you down.

I'd been in the islands with Shane McAnally and Josh Osborne, purging our souls, writing some songs, laughing about life. We'd written "Wild Child." My next "commercial" album was mostly done. On the plane home, with all our computers out, we were swapping songs.

Shane told me about this song, some artist couldn't decide about cutting it or not. "But I'm going to play it for you."

"No, don't . . . Not if the song's on hold."

We looked at each other. Songs are a special addiction. "Okay, play it for me."

"American Kids" with its three different tempos, the double chorus, and tagline was vibrant.

"I will cut that song an hour after we land."

He knew I was serious. I know what a song like that can mean to someone.

"I don't wanna take a song away from anybody, so I'm going to give them one month to make up their minds. I will give you, give them one month from today to decide."

"American Kids" spoke to everything about who No Shoes Nation is.

I started counting. Every single day. A month passed, I dialed the phone.

"Hey, Shane. Guess what day it is?" He laughed.

"We've got the studio booked, and we're cutting 'American Kids' tomorrow morning."

I'd called Buddy when we'd landed that day, said, "Get the band ready! Wait'll you hear what Shane played me."

We cut it, and "The Big Revival" the same day. It had an edge and energy, but it spoke to the culture and how we—myself, my friends, my people—lived.

To channel that euphoria and freedom, we leaned into hippie youth culture. Shaun Silva, a couple techs, and I flew to California to help paint a school bus bright colors and crazy geometric designs, and set out on an adventure.

The group of people we assembled threw themselves into the mission with the same abandon I felt when I heard the song. If *Life on a Rock* had been a reckoning, *The Big Revival* was an awakening. Some artists find their zone, know what they're good at, and stick with it. I was coloring outside the lines and feeling more alive than I had in years.

Grace finally got her No. 1 country hit. "Wild Child," written with Shane and Josh Osborne, continued exploring my fascination with freewheeling women who follow their dreams. At a time when country music was all about girls in cutoffs, I knew women were so much more. Like Jill, like Kristi, like Emily, like Mary, like Grace, this was a love song to freedom, not tying a girl down.

The best songwriting comes from life.

"FloraBama" came from a sprawling bar on the Florida-Alabama line where I got lost with friends, telling stories, laughing, and being carefree in the middle of a long run of shows. Disappearing into a bar covered with bras, old band promo pictures, boat flags, license plates, sports memorabilia, college pennants was heaven—and that afternoon gave me a song.

Revival closed with "If This Bus Could Talk," an ode written with Tom Douglas to Moby, who'd seen it all. Piano-driven, I conjured corn-dog county fairs, opening for Patty Loveless, Bobby Lowe rolling the bus, and all the drunk philosophizing. A love song to my first bus, it was the adventures that Silver Eagle had witnessed.

NOISE

The Big Revival taught me to trust the unorthodox.

How do you take that lesson and move forward? How about a mid-tempo song about dissatisfaction anchored with an almost Gregorian chant for a first single? "Rich and Miserable" felt like a message that needed to be voiced.

My friend John C. McGinley met me in New York City to play a college professor challenging his students about the meaning of success for the accompanying video. His speech confronted materialism, what we're brokered as a standard for what success is. Not your positive, happy up-tempo country hit.

Watching Johnny address a room full of Columbia students, suggesting that what's been set as the goal may not deliver what they're seeking, I realized how powerful "Rich and Miserable" was. Well-written, it spoke to a spiritual crisis without preaching.

The label had to be thrilled by all of this. Somber, wrestling with being too young until we're too old, I'm sure they thought there had to be better ways to launch a record. Ironically, I was late to the setup meeting.

I was sitting in my car outside the label, texting Clint, "I'll be in in a moment."

Shane McAnally called earlier, and we'd gotten into a conversation about how hard it is to be creative amid all the noise. Constant rushing, an insatiable need for "more, louder, extra" was drowning the space to think.

A song started. We tossed lines back and forth. Everything we were feeling, frustrations and increasing volume turned into waves of words; verses and a chorus swirled. I was driving as we played catch, consumed by a song that spoke to the chaos drowning out everything.

Remembering what Bruce Springsteen told me about a song's ability to wait, I told Shane I needed to get into the meeting. I was twenty-five minutes late—and I'm always early.

Ninety minutes later, we wrapped the meeting. I talked through the launch of the "Rich and Miserable" video. When I called Shane, he said an MP3 would be in my inbox shortly.

While I was doing business, Shane, Ross Copperman, and Jon Nite had finished "Noise." It was a sentiment that desperately needed to be released into the universe. I wasn't telling anyone how to live, think, or breathe, but sometimes there's power in knowing it's not only you.

Playing the song across America, I hear people sing their guts out, purging the anxiety this accelerated pace of life compounds on a daily basis.

To this day, "Noise" remains a song that creates an equal force of response when we play it. Like "Rich and Miserable," success was now making records that said things. Complicated emotions, hard truths, less-than-glossy freedoms, I'd arrived at a place where I made music to a different standard—to be in a conversation with No Shoes Nation.

SPIRIT OF A STORM

I started watching the Weather Channel. Hurricane Irma looked bad, but people in the islands had weathered hurricanes before. They respected them, knew how to put things up, take shelter, ride it out.

Watching Irma bouncing around the Caribbean, a Category 2 or 3 was endurable. But the ocean was warm and the pressure created a perfect storm. More frightening was how quickly it became—and stayed—a Category 5.

I could hear anxiety and stress when I'd talk to my friends down there. Hoping for the best, even if the best was rough, they were trying to keep a positive attitude. They had each other.

Watching from Nashville, I was worried.

"If it gets bad, go to my house," I said, not wanting to add anxiety, but having just redone the windows in my place, I knew it was safer than most. Built into the hillside, all the rooms had reinforced walls. I'd installed 200 mph–rated glass. Why take chances?

"We'll be fine," everyone reassured me. I detected a bit of tension in their voices.

"Okay, but if it gets scary, go to my house, okay? Get everybody inside, away from the windows. Have a party, ride it out. I don't care..."

"Kenny, we'll get through this."

"Yes, you're going to be locked away, deep inside my house."

Hurricane Irma kept coming. The winds topped out at 187 miles per hour. All seventeen friends who ended up in those few rooms will tell you: Every single window got blown out. The rain was blowing sideways, so fast and hard, the men were holding mattresses against the doors, trying to slow the water rushing underneath. They were using any clothing and towels to soak it up.

The power grid was destroyed. Trees and bushes were ripped from the ground. All the boats that would bob peacefully in the water were hurled from their moorings, or where they'd been tied down, landing upside down on each other; some sank, some landed on land. Many buildings were blown away, whole frames and roofs gone.

What started as a tropical storm off the coast of North Africa turned into the worst hurricane since the Labor Day Hurricane of 1935. Irma destroyed the Saints, Barbuda, the Greater Antilles—only the second Category 5 hurricane to maintain that force for over sixty hours.

For those of us off-island, we were in the dark. No calls or texts were going out. When the winds finally stopped, an eerie quiet covered the island. All the support structures were gone. People couldn't pass through the streets; cars and trucks were blown around like children's toys, often miles from where they'd been parked.

St. Thomas lost its airport. The ferry was not traveling. No one knew anything.

I didn't know what I could do.

Talking on the phone with a friend, expressing fear and frustration, they said, "You will make a record and call it *Songs for the Saints*. It will reflect all that those islands are."

How could anyone think something like that at a time like this?

"You'll write a song called 'Love for Love City,' because that is the heart of it all. I bet you start a fund or a foundation. You'll rally No Shoes Nation. You're a songwriter, take that heart and put it to use. That's something you, and only you, can do."

I wasn't sure. This may be how I process, but this was almost too much. Writing gave me somewhere to channel all the terrible nerves I was feeling. Talking to friends, like Ben and Emily who'd moved back to the mainland, no one had heard anything.

When I got the first text from Marty Bruckner, saying "We're okay," the tension burst from my body. I wept tears of relief. They'd been through so much; there was so much more to come—and we knew it.

I had, indeed, written the first few songs. I'd taken "Love for Love City" and "Songs for the Saints" into the studio. I was tracking and cutting in the moment. I wanted to bring all the feelings into the room; wanted the musicians to experience this with me.

Mac McAnally came when we cut "Trying to Reason (with Hurricane Season)." A masterful musician, he was also a Coral Reefer; I knew he understood the soul of Jimmy's song. But then Mac didn't leave. He saw what I was doing—nonlinear as it was—and wanted to be part of the healing.

Healing was everything. "Better Boat" served as a metaphor for anyone at a crisis point. About rebuilding, it was literal to those in

Tortolla, US Virgin Islands, the Leeward Islands, the British Virgin Islands, and the coast of Florida. For me, who'd gone to the islands seeking something I didn't know I was looking for, Travis Meadows's song struck me.

I wasn't there for the storm, but I was changed by what I saw my friends living with and through. I became more patient, more real about what's possible and what to expect. I found myself shifting my attitudes, making even larger circles of gratitude.

Maybe the strongest voice I heard when I first arrived in St. John all those years ago was Mindy Smith. Hours spent on the open-air back of my boat, I'd listen to her *One Moment More*, especially the spiritual "Come to Jesus."

This very broken song of slowly finding the internal strength to keep going required a special voice. Mindy, who'd sounded like an angel floating over the ocean back then, had a tone that offered encouragement, acceptance, and love without judgment.

I brought a US Virgin Islands flag to the studio. Every person who played, sang, engineered, or mixed signed that flag. It seemed important for each of us to sign on to this moment of healing.

Before we were through, literally everyone including my guests would sign that flag.

Running into Jimmy Buffett at a friend's house in LA, we got talking about the devastation in the islands and the Keys. I told him, "I recorded 'Hurricane Season.' What's more appropriate?"

We'd sung it at his Gulf Coast hurricane benefit in Tallahassee. Now it was on *Songs for the Saints*.

"All these years later, it still is," he acknowledged.

"It's crazy."

This album was meant to show listeners the essence of the people who lived in the islands, but really anyone drawn to living on the water. Jimmy loved the islands they call "the Saints" as much as I did.

Before I could even ask, he said, "I'd love to be a part of it."

There was something about what happened that inspired people to help.

I thought a lot about "Love for Love City." Meant as an infusion of positive energy for this region that instilled so much goodness in my soul, I wanted that song to be special. With its reggae undertow, I wanted that life affirmation I'd found in Bob Marley and The Wailers' music.

I reached out to Ziggy Marley. His music shared that sensibility that drew me to reggae. If it felt true to him, maybe he'd sing on it. He did, bringing his voice, with its island lineage, to a song meant for healing.

Ziggy's raspy tone carries a wisdom from the spirit. All the history of where he grew up lives in his DNA, and you can't help but hear it when he sings.

Even before I knew what *Songs for the Saints* was going to be, I knew it had to reflect the spirit of the people who inhabited the Caribbean. Show them we saw them, loved them, but also recognized their resilience and strength.

I would walk outside on breaks, getting updates when I could. The only internet on the island was at Ronnie's Pizza—set up as an emergency outpost. Everyone had to go there to send email, so nobody had much access to the outside world. Commercial planes couldn't get in; they were running out of food and supplies.

I had a plane and I had friends. I went to work. Who knew I would talk to the head of FEMA? Getting certified as a humanitarian effort so we could land, doing the next right thing. The first flight down was packed with medical supplies, dog food, and water, that's how little there was.

Our mandate: No plane flies with empty space. Getting people off the island to St. Thomas wasn't impossible, but it wasn't easy. When the first load—a dozen people, plus Cookie, my island dog—took off, they broke down.

Anderson Cooper called, asked if I could add anything to their coverage. He wanted to give us his CNN viewers, to spread the message. My friends were getting ready to come to Nashville.

"Maybe one of them would like to tell people?" he suggested. "If you've never been there, people can't imagine how beautiful. I think seeing them, if it's not too much, could put a face on this unthinkable disaster."

Having seen New Orleans post-Katrina, losing my house in Nashville's flood, I knew what he meant. I trusted Anderson, who'd been fair with me on *60 Minutes*, and knew if St. John was leveled, rebuilding wouldn't be easy.

"Let me see what I can do."

Kate Hannah did the interview with me—a blur even now watching it—with so much grace. All I could think about were the vans pulling up to my front door, the very exhausted bodies of my dear friends climbing out of them.

When they saw me, we all broke down. They were safe.

Being barricaded in the house, they'd had no idea. Even cutting through fallen brush and trees to get into town hadn't given them a sense. It was when the helicopter to get across the water to the plane rose that they saw the destruction.

Low Key Bob, Quiet Mon Kenny, Jordon Holt, Seth and Peter Bettinger, Blaise Bruckner, Chuckles and Rosemary, Mandy Lemley, Anne Bequette, Ashley Coerdt and her son Storm, and Kate. Ribs sticking out, my island dog Cookie was lifted from the van, unsure and disoriented.

My friends came as a pack. They wouldn't leave Cookie behind.

Whether they ultimately went back or not, their lives had passed before their eyes. You could see the trauma, ghostly present, when you really looked at them. Some came with health issues, others with children.

I'd been in the studio all day, singing these songs written to remind people of their buoyancy and resolve. Getting people drinks, taking what bags they had, and helping situate everyone on couches, inflatable mattresses, sleeping bags, and every bed in my Nashville house—the fragility of life was evident.

These were people I loved. All it takes is a few moments.

Determined not to cry in front of them, to be the beginning of the healing, there were hugs, deep hugs, listening to what they wanted to share and not digging for details that might trigger them. We were together. For the islanders, they were disoriented, but safe.

Cookie was riddled with worms, but even more, the shock was too much. For four days, she never settled in, never ate the way I hoped and drank only some water. She was so happy to be with us; she'd look up when I'd pet her and wag her tail, but something wasn't quite right.

Five days after arriving, Cookie and I had a few deep minutes. I kissed her good night, went to my bed, and fell into the deepest sleep. She watched me go, then crawled into Jill's lap on the big recliner. Cookie died in the arms of someone who loves dogs the way gamblers love Vegas. Cookie knew she was safe, so she decided it was time.

Jill sat in the recliner for a few hours. She knew my heart, knew how much I'd been through trying to move people to safety. When she told me right after sunup, she'd already let a couple key people know: Kenny is going to want to go to St. John.

That's what I did. I had to take Cookie home. We had her cremated, and I took her ashes. This was not how I envisioned going back to the Virgin Islands.

My dear friend Maria Rodriguez piloted the helicopter I used a lot. She met me at the St. Thomas airport. We didn't really talk. She was exhausted because their helicopters had become one of the lifelines for the British Virgin Islands, St. Croix, and Puerto Rico.

I saw the devastation from above. Biblical, no other word captures it. A level of destruction no man could cause. Flying over, it looked like the world was ending, or had ended.

Ghost streets, quiet except for the sounds of chainsaws and people working on cleanup. John McGinnis, Ben Bourassa, Justin Bartosh,

294 / HEART ♦LIFE ♦MUSIC

and Marty Bruckner, who were a big part of the Love for Love City efforts, met me and told me what they had been doing. It was a lot to take in. Many people lost businesses, but more importantly, lives were profoundly changed. So many were displaced. Fishermen lost boats; the *Hey Now*, which Low Key Bob had sold a few weeks before, sank in the storm.

Knowing I would have to leave before dark, I was amazed by the resilience. Everyone was stressed and concerned, but there was hope in the exhaustion. It's called Love City for a reason.

Breaking away for a few minutes, Ben and I took Cookie, walked past all these sailboats thrown up on the beach and in the streets. The stern of one boat had impaled the side of a restaurant. Midday, it was dark gray and kind of miserable as we got to Cruz Bay, where we scattered her ashes on the water.

Emily Bourassa teased me about that when she heard. "Kenny, but Cookie hated the water . . ."

GET ALONG

After all that, I knew I wanted to give the world as much positivity as it could handle. *Songs for the Saints* came from a tragedy, but it delivered hope and thriving. When John Esposito, then chairman of Warner Nashville, said he'd put out this record, that I'd pledged all the proceeds from it to our Love for Love City Fund, I wanted to empower him and make it less of a work project.

Music is Esposito's drug of choice; he's quick to turn someone on to a band they've never heard of. I like setting people up to win; I wanted him to know this album turned on positive energy, creating community and things that felt good. At a time like this, making people feel better seemed important.

"Get Along" was built around a street preacher with a *Bible* in one hand, a bottle in another. An anthem of nonjudgment, it was a life plan to create a better world for anyone listening. Simple directives to treat people well and pull life to you, its aggressive down-home sound cut through on radio like a light saber.

There's an unwritten rule: Never compete with yourself. The idea of having a duet with David Lee Murphy, the original hillbilly rock star who'd written "Livin' in Fast Forward" and "Pirate Flag," out at the same time seemed suicidal. Surely, one record would die.

"Everything's Gonna Be Alright" captured two pals at a bar getting schooled by a barmaid about the power of positivity. Reassuring, but also reality fixing, the duet didn't sound like "Get Along," but it offered that same come-together attitude the world was craving.

Never mind David Lee was on an indie label, what that song said was something people needed to hear. Even more than escape, real people want to find ways to be reassured that most times the worst won't happen.

I believed in "Everything's Gonna Be Alright" so much, I said, "Put it out." We had David Lee come out on the road with us all summer to sing the duet in our show, as well as "Dust on the Bottle" and "Party Crowd" from his artist career in the '90s. Dressed in his faded Wranglers, he was so authentic the audience responded.

Even before "Everything's Gonna Be Alright" was a hit, by the second chorus, you'd hear No Shoes Nation singing along—demonstrating people want to know there's a better way of facing what's coming.

They're still two of my biggest songs.

DA PONCH AND DA RUBA GIRL

It was a few days before Christmas, 2011. The doorbell rang.

Standing there, with a ball of caramel curls in her arms, was my therapist.

"What's this?" I asked, as much to her showing up as the small bundle looking around.

"You need to learn to attach to something," she announced. "Merry Christmas."

With that pronouncement, she held the puppy out to me. Uncertain, I wrapped my arms around it, looked at her without a word.

She smiled. "You'll see. This is going to be great."

She turned, got in her car, and drove away.

I looked at him. He looked at me. There we were, completely unsure of what should happen next.

I stepped back inside, set him down. I'd never really noticed dogs much. I was moving too fast. I loved my friends' pets—Cookie down in the islands—but this was different. I knew that much.

This Goldendoodle looked up at me, like, "Okay, now what?"

I laughed, realizing I was completely unprepared for this moment. But it was here; if nothing else, I could get him a bowl of water.

Half of me wanted to call my therapist and say, "Come get this dog." But part of me looked at that face, curious, ready to play, and thought, *I can't reject this little guy.*

The next day, I was in the aisle at PetSmart, buying one of everything because I wasn't sure what I needed. I didn't know, didn't care, because I was going to figure it out.

That's how Poncho—aka "Da Ponch"—entered my life.

Not long after, Mary Nolan, the woman I'd been seeing, wandered into Proverbs 12:10 Animal Rescue, where she encountered a red-nosed pit bull terrier so badly abused she cowered in the back of her space. Hearing the unthinkable story of what had happened to this sweet girl, there was only one thing for Mary to do: adopt her.

Ruby needed saving, and Mary had the perfect heart for the task. Suddenly, it was me, Ponch, Ruby, and Mary; we were a family. For Ruby, it was a second chance to have the life she'd always deserved. For Poncho, it was having a best friend and running buddy every day of his life. For me, it was an opportunity to learn a very deep lesson in conditioning and bias.

When Ruby arrived, I wasn't so sure. Pit bulls were something I didn't realize I was afraid of, but I was. There was a tension about her that crept into my body, something I'd absorbed without ever thinking about it. Prejudice often isn't something people knowingly choose; for me, it was a filter I saw through because of things I'd heard about the breed.

The truth is: dogs are precious and loving. People who abuse them, no matter what breed, can scare an animal so badly it will go to any length to protect itself. In the end, dogs want to love and be loved—loyalty above all—and have fun if they feel safe.

Watching Poncho and Ruby play, seeing Mary love Da Ruba Girl back from all the bad things that had happened to her, I saw not just transformation, but the innocence that Ruby started from. Talk about a learning experience.

Over the years, those two dogs romped and played and chased balls, waves, and each other for hours. They loved the ocean. The house I was living in had acres of woods and land; they'd tear off on an adventure and be gone for hours. They chased every deer, every squirrel, herded the turkeys, and whatever else they could find.

Mary would be worried. I'd say, "They'll be back." Hours passed; they always returned. They'd look at each other, filthy dirty, heads down a little and out of breath, but they shared this secret of whatever they'd gotten up to. They knew they were in trouble, but it was worth it.

Ruby, especially, was protective of us. One day, Cheryl Bevis, my then-assistant, came into the house laughing. She put her things down on the counter, said, "You all have to come see this. . ." and led us outside.

How it happened, I'll never know. But there was Ruby with three head of cattle—two cows and a steer—corralled in the front yard, just walking back and forth, not letting them move. She'd secured them! Maybe her proudest moment.

Where they'd come from, we had no idea. What to do? I wasn't sure.

Finally, Jamie Raley went to the Tractor Supply for supplies to build a temporary fence. Jamie managed to figure out who owned them. Until then, we gave Ruby a break on guarding the house. That's the devotion a dog will provide if you let it.

Even after my relationship with Mary shifted—and that's another reality: trying to protect people you love's privacy, because they didn't sign up for anything beyond loving this person who chases a dream—we had Ruby and Poncho to consider. They'd never been apart since they'd met. Whether we moved on or not, our dogs shouldn't have to suffer.

Funny thing about the way we love animals: It's bigger than whatever humans experience. Even though we'd shifted, we would always share our dogs. It wasn't that Poncho was mine and Ruby was Mary's; they were best friends, and they were "ours."

Joint custody is too rigid a label. We shared Da Ponch and Da Ruba Girl.

Laughing over trouble they got into, watching them play, or just being still and sleeping together, there was no denying we were a family. Ruby, though, started slowing down, was tired all the time. We'd seen it, hoped it was something easy to fix, whether anemia and needing different food or some basic infection.

Going to the vet to get to the bottom of it, Mary called with bad news: Ruby was filled with tumors; there wasn't much we could do. The vet actually asked about putting her down to save her suffering. It was a horrible conversation.

Mary said, "She doesn't seem ready to go. Her appetite's strong. She was happy to see me, wants to play."

Love is powerful. I trust Mary about all these kinds of things.

"Bring her home," I agreed. "We don't know how long. But let's make however long it is wonderful."

Instead of grieving, our lives became *how do we fill her—their— time with so much bliss*. Poncho was worried about his best friend, too. We decided to give both of them the most fun, most special experiences we could for as long as it was possible.

For two months, every day was puppy play day. Toward the end, and we could tell it was coming, Mary and I got on a plane and took Ruby and Poncho to California. Of all the oceans in the world, Ruby loved the Pacific the best. Maybe those wild waves matched her heart; she felt calm lying there, listening to the surf and absorbing the energy of the ocean.

She spent the weekend sleeping in the sun on the porch, trotting the beach, feeling the wind on her face, and sniffing the salt in the air. She was happy and at peace. Watching the sun bleed out over the water, we'd all sit there, saying nothing. Grateful to be together, Mary and I knowing the inevitable was coming.

We were making the best of something that was going to trample our hearts. Whether Da Ruba Girl knew it or not, we'll never know. But I swear you could see joy and contentment in her eyes as it grew dark. This was her happy place, and we were all together.

With time growing short, we tried to make as much space as possible to be with the dogs. Mary even painted her nails ruby red. Life has a way of creeping in. Mary had gone to Ohio to see family; I was in Costa Rica. The kids were at an incredible overnight camp for pets that's wide open and lets them romp and be their best doggie selves.

After a full day of walking in the woods, treats, and playing together, Da Ruba Girl and Da Ponch were put in their room. Like they always do, they cuddled up together. It was December 4, 2022.

Maybe she didn't want to put us through it. Maybe she decided it was time.

But Da Ruba Girl closed her eyes, went to sleep, and slipped into heaven. She passed right next to her very best friend in the world. It had been a perfect several weeks.

Mary got the call. Devastated, she had her friend Tara call me.

Although we knew it was coming, we were still destroyed. Poncho was lost and stayed sad for a long time.

Ruby taught us all so many lessons. About moving beyond what you know, how love is so much bigger than you can ever believe, how it transcends things mere people can't get beyond. Everyone who met her was better for it.

Sitting in the wonder and grief, I thought about the song I'd written as a Christmas gift for Mary so many years ago. Anyone who listens to No Shoes Radio already knows "Da Ruba Girl" by heart.

> *You needed her, she needed you*
> *To hold, to help fill a space*
> *Last in line, last cage at the rescue*
> *Was a love that no one could replace*
> *Lying there like a lost string of pearls*
> *Was Da Ruba Girl . . .*

WEGMAN

When you live in the wind, you meet all kinds of people. My Key West friend Richard Hatch, whom I've known so long, I can't remember meeting him, said, "You have to meet this guy."

Nothing could've prepared me for David Wegman—artist, adventurer, sailor, inventor, poet, philosopher, witness to history, and seeker. With a white pirate beard and a presence that says, "I've done things you wouldn't dare dream," he had the most curious eyes and a smile that challenges you to take off on some great adventure. When he rode up on what was a mail delivery bicycle from the '60s, it was clear this man had a rhythm of his own.

Arriving in Key West in 1971, he built his first sailboat from a Cuban refugee boat that had no motor; sailed it toward the Dry Tortugas on his twenty-fifth birthday, ran into a hurricane and was tossed sideways for ten days until he ended up on the West Coast of Florida. An artist, he painted signs—and pictures—above Howie's at 109 Duval Street; got his five-year-old daughter a business license so she could run her own fruit stand.

Whimsy and a happy heart drove him. Without art or music lessons, he became a touchstone for all kinds of gypsies and creatives. He got another boat, sailed around the Bahamas and Virgin Islands for a couple years; opened a second painting studio above Le Select, the legendary burger bar in St. Barths, which he still works out of.

A few years later, he got on his beloved *African Queen* in St. Barths, sailed to the Virgin Islands to get supplies, and embarked on an eight-year sail around the world. He jokes it would've been three years "but it's a big world." He handwrote a newsletter for his friends as he traveled, leaving directions to send mail to general delivery, whatever port he was heading to, be it North Caledonia, the Philippines, somewhere on the coast of Africa.

Just gone, chasing the sun, the wind, the magic. He had a place in Maine, family in Indiana, but his return address was the sea. To love the water that much, it spoke to my soul. That peace you feel when the water is all you see, the waves their own rhythm, Dave felt it, too.

You could see that in his eyes. The youngest eyes I've ever seen, that calm that comes from the ocean poured from them, with a kindness and curiosity that added adventure to everything.

And adventure was drawn to the man who'd scavenge broken guitars from the trash and make instruments, who'd jam with his crew of musicians on an eighty-two-foot ship in St. Barths loud enough to inspire Bob Dylan on a boat named the *Water Pearl* to row over, come aboard, and play into the night. Before our paths even crossed, we had common ground: David Wegman was on Jost alongside Keith Richards the night the power went off at Ivan's Stress Free Bar. Undaunted, they went to the beach and swapped songs and a joint until the lights came on, then played with Ivan for hours.

Memorialized in a painting, which I bought, the delight in such a strange turn of a moment is what makes David the romantic broker of everything I wish to be. While I built a life around music, seeing the world for over thirty years on a bus flying down the highway, there were all the meetings, schedules, putting business and responsibility over the magic. David with his pirate wink just sailed, or played his guitar, or created his art; when he was ready, he'd pull up anchor and on to the next place or port.

There's a simplicity to following dreams unencumbered that I crave. I tell my closest friends I'm jealous of David, because I am. He pulled the ultimate magic trick. In April 2025, The Studios of Key West mounted his art in an exhibition—A *Fifty Year Retrospective: David Wegman*. Pictures of ships, mermaids, beauties, historic places in the Caribbean and Key West, as well as a night at Ivan's when the power went out.

Like the Chicken Preserve, an artist enclave where musicians passing through may crash for a few days or fellow artisans, writers, and such may live in residence, the glorious chaos defines him. Random objects, bold colors, free-range chickens, a massive fan by where David sleeps, so many paintings and maps hanging everywhere, mangrove trees that cover an open yard where movies are screened, potluck meals are convened and jam sessions happen, strings of prayer flags crisscross original pirate flags of David's making, art supplies fill the studio, and a kitchen that could be forty years old hold this life that is so rich, joyous, and driven by creativity.

When Oprah Winfrey challenged me to do a bucket list thing, I told her I wanted to take my grandmother flying for the first time.

Grandma Lucy had never been on a plane; never seen Key West or the ocean from the sky. I wanted her to have that sense of wonder and freedom, to see what I loved so much.

She held my hand a little hard when we took off, but coming into the Keys, seeing that blue water, her eyes got so big. I could feel her delight, and I knew she loved seeing the world through my eyes. We landed, had lunch, ate the biggest slice of key lime pie, and she took it all in with a child's awe. My Grandma Lucy in the Keys.

David Wegman is the other side of that ability to love and have such deep but innocent wonder. Everything inspires him, touches him in ways that show all of us something more.

Having bought the painting of Ivan's before the show, I flew down to Key West to drop off the money, hug David, and thank him for being. Places to go, my team couldn't believe I'd make a trip like that when so much had to be done; but this was an artist at life as much as painting, making instruments, sailing the world, and I wanted to honor the creator.

I thought it was going to be a quick trip, say hello and be gone.

Three hours of laughter and stories later, I found my very accelerated, highly motivated nervous energy completely wound down. Like sitting on the front porch with my grandparents, David understands the pace life should be lived, and he brings all of us to that rhythm.

Realizing I had to go, he understood. Wished me well, happy travels. Coming from David Wegman, he's someone who knows everything about what that means.

HERE AND NOW

Brian Noland, president of East Tennessee State University, didn't come for a concert. ETSU wanted to give me a degree. I wasn't sure. An honor, but me? Even an honorary doctorate. I barely graduated from ETSU. When music kicked in, I became a very average student.

Then he told me they wanted to honor Jack Tottle that same night to recognize the fortieth anniversary of the program he'd started. Now *that* deserved a doctorate. Tottle had taught me so many of the fundamentals of everything my life was built on, and he was being honored for thinking beyond conventional academics.

October 21, 2023. Count me in.

Going back to somewhere you were learning to dream suspends time. When the plane landed, we got in the car and started moving; I remembered that twenty-year-old kid trying to find his voice.

Everything was so electric and alive, the positive energy I talk about all the time was exploding inside me.

The biggest difference: I was wearing a suit. I intended to respect the occasion. I wanted to be the man I didn't know I would grow up to be. Lots of dreamers chase songs down different alleys; a few make it. Luck, destiny, the idea you meet certain people; I've already said I'm sure it was written in the stars.

Jack Tottle is proof. He started a program so unique, it's the only one of its kind. A passionate instructor, he put up with, even encouraged, a student who didn't appear particularly gifted because he saw my desire to learn. He couldn't have thought I was going to grow up and have a successful career; he loved how much I loved the music.

Pulling onto the campus, I marveled. This was real.

Inside, there would be interviews, taking pictures. I really wanted to see Jack Tottle, who'd moved to Hawaii. Evidently being one of the most revered mandolinists, authors, songwriters, and academics wasn't enough to keep him in the mountains. Like me, Jack Tottle wanted to be near the sea.

Walking through the hallways to our holding area, I could hear the plinks of banjo, that sound of a bow being drawn across a fiddle. The ETSU Bluegrass Band was going to play for an almost full house who'd turned out to honor my friend and mentor. I smiled, thinking about the nerves some were probably feeling. I knew those nerves.

Standing in the back of a school building is a great equalizer. I may've joked I was going to make everyone on tour call me "Dr. Chesney," but I was excited in a way that took me back. Seeing Jack Tottle, who'd given me the confidence to have this dream, taking me to Russia with gifted student musicians, not only showed me how far music can take you, but proved music created common ground where it shouldn't exist.

This man, white hair, but eyes shining, was still creating community through music. How many lives had he given an extra layer of meaning? I would be given my degree first, so I could be part of bestowing his doctorate—something I never would've believed.

Talking to the current ETSU Bluegrass Band, they were as serious as we had been, as intent on honoring the program as I was. Seeing a doghouse bass, I nodded. You don't see those every day, and it takes a special kind of musician to play it.

I asked if they'd take a picture with me. The students laughed. I knew a secret: One of them might have a dream so determined, they could change how bluegrass is made, go in a new direction. I think about the musicians who've passed through the program. It's entirely possible.

You can't know in that moment. Jack Tottle taught me you don't have to. Trust fate and the future. Show up, do the work. Keep showing up even when it's not working. Be smart. Get educated and find the answers. But mostly, dream.

Dream, because you never know.

Kelsea Ballerini sent me a drunk text, asking if I'd sing on her song. My response was "Let me hear the song."

Kelsea grew up where I did, how I did. If anyone understood the musical truth inside me, it would be Kelsea. "Half of My Hometown" was a slam dunk. Anyone who's lived in a small town understands: No matter what you do, half the population's going to think you blew it. That goes double if you're chasing a dream they can't get their head around.

What I loved about singing the song with Kelsea, beyond the common roots, was I felt her dream would come true. I knew she'd go places no one she went to school with could imagine; that she'd have number one records, be one of *TIME*'s 100 Most Influential People, perform on *Saturday Night Live*, create music that offered a new dynamic.

I didn't know that specifically, or how it would happen. But I recognized the light in her eyes, the way her voice inhabited the conflict of knowing you want to go but not quite letting go of all the things and people you love. She had it.

When the song went No. 1, I was proud. I was happy for her.

It was the story of her life, her dream—and what she faced to get here.

At this point in my life, there's as much joy looking to the future as looking back. I know the songs I've got sitting on ice, already recorded, ideas to write. More than being what I've got ahead, it's seeing the future coming on strong.

When Megan Moroney was booked to open the *Sun Goes Down Tour*, I almost regretted the decision. "We're going to watch this lovely girl bleed out onstage," was all I could think, knowing stadiums are tough, tougher at 5:00 p.m. in direct sunlight.

It wasn't that Megan wasn't a good songwriter. She had a presence and love for music you could feel. Adaptable, she'd figure it out. I also knew the last act to be successful in that slot had ten No. 1s. This wasn't about her, but reality.

If that first set in Tampa was slightly tentative, her second show was stronger. By her third stadium date, Megan hit that stage like she'd designed it. All the young women—and a lot of young men—knew all the words. Suddenly, everyone was singing loud enough you could hear them. It was a love fest in cobalt blue.

I've never been so glad to be wrong.

Megan took the days we'd have off and booked her own shows. She was unstoppable, playing 3,000-, even 5,000-seat buildings to make sure her fans got to hear all the songs she wasn't playing with us.

What we didn't see coming with Megan was how much fun she was going to bring us. Every now and then, someone comes with fresh eyes who can't get enough. She's on the side of the stage, soaking it in, laughing out by the buses with a bunch of our crew, flying by at 3:00 p.m. to start her own meet and greets with a smile on her face that reminds everyone how lucky we are to do this.

And when she came rolling down the T at Gillette Stadium in my clothes—*my clothes*—wearing my palm leaf hat on a motorized child's tractor? I couldn't catch my breath because I was laughing so hard. To see someone so shamelessly pranking, it reminds you what it's all about out here.

Take the music, not yourself, seriously. Be in on the joke, laugh and grab all the joy you can every single moment. Dream dreams so big you don't know what they are. She talked about seeing us from the cheapest seats you could buy in 2018, and all I could think about was me so broke at Buffett I couldn't buy a beer. Then chase them when they arrive.

When she came down to the islands after playing *Dick Clark's Rockin' New Year's Eve*, she'd had a year that's the speed of light. I wanted to tell her to inhale, take a lot of pictures, keep a decent journal. Before I could share that, she told me she had a present for me.

Maybe the greatest gift a songwriter can give anyone is a song.

"You Had to Be There" was her ride from sitting with friends in the nosebleeds to seven years later. For anyone who's dared to imagine what that leap would be, all they had to do was listen. At sunset, she played it for me—and she jokes we played it 8,000 more times. About the way chasing music excites you, sharing the adventure with someone who is as hungry and wide open as you were when you were starting to have success—she nailed it.

To see someone with all that charisma, talent, savvy, work ethic, passion, and even sparkle, who's not afraid to put it all out there and share her heart with the fans is a rare thing. She's got that lust for all of it, with a fearlessness that lets her go places—like riding that tractor with her sneaky smile—very few would.

To me, that's everything. To know how to not just create that kind of fun, but give it away to everyone around her, I knew she and I were spirit animals in the same cosmic zoo.

Megan said she had to have a few Painkillers before she asked. She should've known the answer was always yes. Of course, I would sing on her song. I'd been there. I knew.

Time moves, whether you're paying attention or not. I'm learning that now. I don't like it, not one bit. Not because I'm afraid of getting older, but I hate losing people I love. I don't like funerals, but I go. I hate picking up the phone and realizing someone who's been a mentor, a brother, a friend, or a champion like Connie Bradley, who ran ASCAP in Nashville for years, won't answer.

When the call came from the Rock & Roll Hall of Fame to come to Cleveland and sing for my friend Jimmy's induction, it was a lot to take in. How much I loved Jimmy's carefree being, his curiosity, the way he treasured things most people never noticed, not to mention how his songwriting, those character sketches held together by truth, had inspired me.

I'd never wanted to be Jimmy Buffett, as the less generous critics insist. I wanted to do for people in East Tennessee what Jimmy did for folks in Alabama where he grew up. Like Jimmy, I wanted to take people far away from their problems for a few hours, make them forget and feel happy, calm, and alive.

To sing for him in front of all those rock stars and heavyweights was a lot of emotional space. Mac was going to be there with me.

As I was getting to yes, word came: We would be singing with James Taylor.

Only Jimmy.

I flew to Cleveland, Ohio, in the bitter cold, something he and I both hated. I had a lump in my throat almost the entire time. I wanted to be there, and I wanted to show up with my heart open.

There's something about being in a small rehearsal space. There, on two tall stools, sat Mac and James, plus a few businesspeople waiting. Three songwriters noodling on guitars, talking about their friend who was gone. Moments like this, you're humanized.

James Taylor is one of the kindest people. His voice up close is as warm and familiar as it is rolling out of your car speakers. I remembered the first time I heard "Sweet Baby James." Now here we are.

The next day, it wasn't nerves exactly, more a desire to do right by the moment. In a world of marketing, this was holy. James, Mac, and I felt the same.

Live TV. No going back. We'd worked out our parts, but never forget nerves and emotions. Or technical glitches.

Mac had gone out front to sit for part of the dinner. I stayed back with my thoughts. Sometimes it's easier for me, especially when it's important, to focus.

When Mac came back, he had a hint of a smile. He'd told us he was bringing Jimmy's guitar onstage, the one he played night after night. It would be in a stand by Mac, as if it were another brilliant night with the Coral Reefer Band. What would be more fitting for a poet, pirate, raconteur, and ambassador of fun?

"I've got something," Mac said, like a boy sharing a secret.

Pulling a small jar from his pocket, he smiled.

"It's Jimmy . . ."

Did I say it? James? I don't know. That moment, we knew those ashes were someone we loved.

"Savannah gave me this," Mac said.

Even in death, Jimmy Buffett, flyer of seaplanes, surfer, author, rogue, father, friend, and Key West folkie, found a way to not miss the party. On the night he was to be inducted into the Rock & Roll Hall of Fame, Jimmy was in the house.

UNTHINKABLE NEWS

The days your life changes don't seem any different.

Gray. Cold. Below freezing, with enough snowy-sleety particles, they'd canceled school. It was the kind of day I hate.

I'd had a meeting scheduled, and moved it to the house. It's as easy to put eight people around the table as it is to slog through the traffic. That's when I got the call that Clint and Joe needed to see me for a few minutes before I started; they were trapped in traffic.

I didn't think anything about it. I told Jamie Raley, "You may have to finish getting this set up yourself." It was a casual meeting, people were on their way.

When Clint and Joe came through the door a few minutes later, their faces seemed flushed from the cold. I walked out of the kitchen to hug them. Behind them was Sarah Trahern, the head of the Country Music Association. I've known Sarah for thirty years.

I figured she must've seen the guys, wanted to pull in and say hi. It's not like Sarah comes over to the house. We'd met when she'd moved to Nashville for a cable network and I was signed to Capricorn; she'd triaged one of the worst TV experiences of my life, which we laugh about now.

"Maybe we should go over here," Joe suggested, tilting his head toward the room off to the right. High ceilings, it's filled with slouchy chairs and a grand piano.

"Yeah, great," I agreed, following. I wanted to get dinner on the table for my guests.

Clint and Joe were looking at each other. Their faces seemed to say, "You tell him." All I could think was someone must be sick.

Joe, who's in the Country Music Hall of Fame as one of the most iconic executives in the history of Nashville, began talking to me about what that meant. To be elected into the Hall, one must have made an indelible contribution to the genre, created something that changed everything—and there are many ways that impact can be felt.

Oh, no. It's Joe . . . was all I could think.

Clint looked like he had tears in his eyes. Joe's a mentor to him.

Joe kept talking about the process of how someone gets on the ballot, how selective it is, what it means to be voted any year's single inductee in grave tones. I looked around this gray room, made grayer by the day. Inhaling, I thought, *This isn't the way to get bad news.*

Looking at their faces, trying to really connect in this moment, even with Clint's eyes welling up, no one looks like someone's dying.

Then Joe says, "I think you ought to sit down."

I sat.

They looked at each other. It struck me, but it was like going through a plate glass window in very, very slow motion. Turning to Sarah, whose smile seemed as if it was going to burst, I half-mouthed the words, "I got in . . ."

She nodded. "Yes. You have been voted into the Country Music Hall of Fame."

Reality hit me. All over. In the heart, the head, the throat, the gut, my shoulder blades: everything in my body and my soul felt this wave hit of something any artist truly hopes for, but most wouldn't have the ego to expect. No words.

"In."

It was all I could say. Then I started to laugh. I waited for them to tell me it was a joke. It was too soon. It wasn't my time. I went numb. Again. Emotions cycling, because after all of it, who dares to imagine their name alongside Hank Williams, George Jones, Willie Nelson, Kris Kristofferson, Merle Haggard, Dolly Parton, and yes, Joe Galante?

You can crazy dream something all your life, think you know how it will go. I can tell you: "No, you don't." Not that I had a plan or notion, nor had I played it out in my mind. But I now know I've never experienced anything like hearing the words: *You've been voted into the Country Music Hall of Fame.*

In the rush of emotions—gratitude, shock, euphoria, disbelief—they started talking. I can't even tell you who said what, only that they were explaining:

"This is secret. No one can know."

"There will be a press conference to announce, that's when it's okay."

"Everyone will work with your team to make it great."

"Don't tell anyone, because people get excited—and it slips."

But I do remember everyone laughing with me, the joy as we all hugged each other.

At some point, they each said, "I'm so proud of you." And I was so proud of—and for—them. Because so many people worked so hard, sacrificed over the years to get us here.

Then I went full millennial: "Let's do a selfie."

Extending my arm out, our arms wrapped around each other, everyone cheered. What's not to love about a moment like this? Sarah left. Clint still had this massive smile, the college kid from a farming town in Northern California who thought he could get me some gigs, and Joe, the label head who'd signed me because Dale asked him to and stuck with me when Music Row didn't believe, was glowing.

Talk about a moment. Every one of us had faced so much to get here.

Ever practical, Joe reminded us we couldn't tell anyone. I walked back to the kitchen with a real spring in my step. Gray day mood lifted, I dug into my steak and broccoli—because it was time to get into shape for Sphere in Las Vegas—as everyone else enjoyed a delicious pasta dinner.

Spirits were high around the table. I'm not sure anyone realized why. But it didn't matter. I was going into the Country Music Hall of Fame, the highest honor you can achieve, thirty-five years and five weeks after putting my car on I-40 West, making that move with a few contacts, a big dream, and no idea what lay ahead.

I gave it my heart . . . pulled my life through it all . . . and let it drive everything about my music.

THE HALL REVEALED

I get up early. Always have. I won't say the day of the Country Music Hall of Fame inductees press conference, where they announce the three people who will be that year's newest members, was unlike any other morning; but I will say driving the streets of Music Row, where so much is gone, heading down Broadway, which is unrecognizable now, was a lot of time travel.

All the places I'd been—the Turf Club, Gilley's, the George Jones Car Museum, Mac's Country Kitchen, the Pie Wagon, the original Country Music Hall of Fame—I could see as my Jeep rolled down those streets. Ghosts and memories, good times and so many songs sung.

I shook my head. That magic trick? The thing nobody saw coming? I *knew* nobody saw me coming this morning.

Secrets are hard to keep in Nashville. Some folks on my team get so excited, they blurt. Some people we didn't tell. But I knew—driving down Demonbreun to make the turn into the loading dock and down into the garage—the secret had held. Nobody had said a word to me about anything around the Hall.

I'd come by myself, wanting to take it all in. Be with my memories, dreams, thoughts about all the people who'd been part of my journey. It had been a helluva drive downtown.

Security met me, took me up a special elevator to the back of the Hall's holding areas. They have dressing rooms, staging areas, hallways leading to several places in the Museum and Ford Theater. Getting off the elevator, it struck me: This is real.

I'd had my speech for several days, reading it over, thinking about what I would say. I wasn't going to take it out of my pocket because I wanted to speak from the heart. But I had a sense of what I wanted to share about my journey.

Looking down that hallway, like a million hallways I'd been in for special events, benefits, awards shows, I shook my head. There would never be another day like this.

They showed me into my dressing room, marked "Contemporary Inductee." The CMA took the secret seriously. I knew people would be coming in to brief me about the flow of the event.

Vince Gill, already in the Hall, was hosting. He came in to congratulate me. The look on his face showed he understood all the emotions I was feeling, because there are so many emotions you can't identify them.

If you think it's "triumph" or excitement, it's not that simple. Writing this now, if I could only pick one, it would be gratitude—for all those people who helped me along the way, who believed in me when no one else did, those who didn't and made me resolved to prove them wrong, musicians who'd given me their talent, and songwriters who taught me, inspired me, even gave me their songs.

It's so many other things, too. Overwhelm, awe, exhaustion, grief for the people who aren't here to share it, as well as pride for what this music has meant, the people who are part of this with me, peace—because there is something that makes you feel peaceful realizing you are here.

Tony Brown, the producer who'd made iconic albums with George Strait and Vince Gill, as well as Steve Earle, Patty Loveless, and Lyle Lovett, was going in as the Executive. Black hair and beard, he came up to the door with a smile that seemed like he'd won the lottery.

"Hey, man, I'm so happy for you," he said to *me*. "You so deserve it, buddy. This is great."

On a thin gold chain around his neck, I saw a charm that said "TCB" with a lightning bolt. It hit me, this man had *played* with Elvis.

I asked about being on the road. "With Emmylou and the Hot Band," he said, "it was steak, chicken, whatever you wanted. With Elvis, it was Diet Pepsi and some water . . ."

"Wow."

"Yeah, but we had Ronnie Tutt in the band, played drums, and James Burton."

"That's crazy. And you were playing with him toward the end."

"Last show in Indianapolis, June 26, 1977."

"Were you with him when he played Knoxville a couple weeks earlier?"

"Sure was. Knoxville Coliseum."

"My mom was at that show. I'd wanted to go, but I guess they thought I was too young."

Tony Brown: I'd parked his car all those years ago. My mother had seen Tony play with Elvis. It was surreal.

Clint and Joe got off the elevator, both in suits, grinning. After hugging me, Joe, who was inducted in 2022, said, "This is the easiest thing you're ever going to do."

I thought that was hilarious. He continued, "There are so many things that will happen between now and then, and you will be enriched by them. But it's all charted out, and it all leads to October."

October was the Medallion Ceremony, where they unveil the brass plaque that will be hung in the Rotunda. They hang a medallion on your neck, make it official, tell people the story, and have your music sung by very special artists to celebrate your work.

Someone explained the route to us, how we would walk, that we needed to keep moving because "you will be going through a portion of the museum, and there will be people. They have no idea it's you, but obviously, they'll recognize you. And you have to keep moving."

I nodded.

They run their events precisely. Sarah Trahern wearing a yellow dress was welcoming everyone, saying this was one of her favorite days of the year. Country Music Hall of Fame head Kyle Young followed her, explaining the gravitas and meaning of inclusion.

Joe Galante always stressed the world *indelible* when it came to inclusion in the Hall of Fame; contributions that couldn't be erased, that changed the genre in ways that shifted the music, business, audience forever. I was starting to understand why that had been so important to him.

I listened, taking it all in the same way I listened to Jack Tottle, Dale, Beckett, Jerry Bradley. This was knowledge, a moment to really absorb. Listening to Vince talk about Tony Brown, who'd produced Gill's breakthrough *When I Call Your Name*, you realized that friendly man who was so filled with creativity had played with legendary artists, changed many artists' careers, as well as songwriters like Dean Dillon and executives like Renee Bell.

An escort started gathering up the people who were going behind the curtain with me. There was a TV crew from CBS's *Sunday Morning*, filming a profile for this book, waiting for us to make the walk, ready to start in front of us, then shoot from behind.

"You ready?"

Here it comes. I put my black cowboy hat on, the one we call Darth Vader because it transforms the guy from East Tennessee into a country star. I stepped forward, started walking, and knew—to steal from *Almost Famous*—it's all happening.

Putting my head down, my team and I moved through the now-empty halls, out a double door with a cameraman walking backward and into the museum. We hadn't gone more than eight, ten feet when a lady looked at her friend in shock; I heard someone say, "Oh, my God! It's Kenny Chesney. He's going into the Hall."

I sure was. The cameraman moved to the side, fell back behind, and captured us slipping in behind the media who were intently listening to Carlene Carter and John Carter Cash, whose mother, June Carter Cash, was the other inductee. They were as happy as I was for them. The cheers were awesome when they finished.

Vince Gill returned to the stage to introduce the Contemporary Inductee.

Vince had a way of personalizing what was written, making a reference to how vast my influences were. You could feel the energy on the other side of the curtain gathering; people were realizing who it must be.

I looked down, taking it in. Walking behind the black pipe

THE HALL REVEALED / 329

and drape, I had been studying the faces on the wall. Elvis, Merle Haggard, Wesley Rose, Patty Loveless. So many legends whose songs had defined moments and eras, working-class culture and dreams. Many of them had defined my dreams, fueled my desire to tell stories, capture those experiences people miss that say everything about who we are.

Vince was talking about the music I'd made, the albums and some of the songs, and what they meant. It was strange hearing so much boiled down into such a clean recounting. I had no idea when you take the truck stops, practical jokes, great songs you don't get to record but can't believe you heard before anyone else, young artists you believe in and watch make it, the heartbreak of things you leave behind, crazy lessons learned from all those experiences, that it would sound like this.

All I ever knew was I wanted to find the next great thing to do. I never considered how it all fit together beyond knowing it was a foundation built to last. I put my hands in my pockets, looked beyond the edge of the curtain, and saw so many faces I knew in that Rotunda. Some of those people, including Troy and Renee, I'd known even before I had a record deal.

When Vince introduced me, I walked into the light and up to the podium. When people say things can hit you all at once, all over, it's true. I know I knew my speech. I know it was in the teleprompter. I know I even got most of it right.

I do know I meant every word that I said, and I mean every word in my speech. Rather than give you the words of an overwhelmed artist joining his idols and friends without any of the emotion, this is what I would've said, if I had delivered my speech as written.

> If you'd told the little kid who went to see Alabama in a field less than ten minutes from where we lived in East Tennessee that one day I'd be standing here, I'd've thought you were crazy.
>
> I mean, if you'd told the kid going to Russia with the ETSU Bluegrass Band who actually played at the Carter Fold with Dr. Jack Tottle in that program—or the young man who walked into Troy Tomlinson's office hoping for a publishing deal at Acuff-Rose, the one getting signed to Capricorn, then BNA Records, I'd've told you, you were dreaming.
>
> *But the beauty of country music is . . .*
>
> *Even though it tells some pretty strong truth, country music runs on dreams.*

I'm a pretty big dreamer, and I've dreamed some big dreams people didn't see coming . . . because all I ever wanted to do was bring people together, sing songs that reflected *their* lives and spread as much love and positive energy as I could . . . because that's what music should do: Make people feel better because that's what my heroes did for me.

Standing here, knowing this isn't a dream, that it's real, is surreal.

I am humbled . . . grateful . . . proud . . .

ACKNOWLEDGMENTS

I struggle with thank yous, cause if you are in this book then you are a big part of my life and this journey, so I collectively give you a hug and say thanks for everything. I love all of you, and my life was forever changed by your friendship, passion, and love for what we do. We are connected because we all share a dream, and for that I am incredibly grateful.

Grateful especially to Dale Morris and Clint Higham. I love you, I dreamed with you, and I've learned from you both. You've been in the trenches and on the top of the mountain with me. I'm so grateful we all experienced the journey in this book together.

I want to thank Holly Gleason, who has lived a lot of this journey with me, who's been a voice of reason, a creative compass, who raised my SAT score, and who has also been in the trenches with me for a long time. I love and appreciate you, Holly—and I'm convinced you were the only person to tell this story with heart and care. You brought my journey and dream to life on these pages, and I thank you. I know in my heart we were supposed to do this together. It was written down somewhere.

Thanks Mauro DiPreta, Liate Stehlik, Ben Steinberg, Kelly Rudolph, Heidi Richter, Melissa Esner, Allie Johnston, Jennifer Eck, and everyone at HarperCollins for believing in my journey and helping me bring this very unique story to anyone who might care or be inspired. I have loved working with you, Mauro, because I could tell from the beginning you cared and understood the culture we've built. Your heart was invested and I thank you for that.

Thanks to David Vigliano and everyone at Vigliano Associates.

Thanks to Buffy Cooper, Kyle Quigley, Mike Betterton, and Ebie McFarland for everything you do and have done. Keeping all of it together is no small feat.

Thanks to every member of my Road Family. It's impossible to put on these pages all the fun we've had and continue to have, all the life lived, all the faces seen. Rolling down the highway and living this dream with all of you has been the highlight of my life. Who Lives Like We Do? WE DO.

Maybe every artist says their band is the best alive. I believe that about Rosie & the Revival. We have all taken our own unique journey over the years to get ready for this moment where we get to play music together. Each of you has made me better: You gave me energy when I thought I had none. You bring your talent, love for music, and hearts to the stage every night, wide open and on fire. Thank you and then some to Wyatt Beard, Kenny Greenberg, Danny Rader, Harmoni Kelley, Nick Buda, and Jon Conley for creating so much joy in my life.

So many people have made a difference. Special thanks go to:

All my island family and friends who've inspired me and my creativity more than you could ever realize. For all the boat trips and sunsets shared, the laughter, the stories, the friendships, the happy hours, all the rum and Red Bulls we drank, and for all the authentic life lived so completely. All I can say is, "Damn that was fun!"

Rande Gerber, Cindy Crawford, and Virgil for everything.

Jamie Raley for the many jobs you do and for your friendship.

All the songwriters who have changed my life with their songs, shared creativity and passion, as well as anyone at any radio station who has ever shared that music with the fans!

Jon Anthony, Tommy Massad, and Kizzi Barazetti who bring all this music, my songs and the places I wander to life every day on No Shoes Radio.

Jennifer Witz, Jim Meyer, Scott Greenstein, Steve Blatter, and everyone at SiriusXM for giving No Shoes Radio such a wonderful platform. More than radio, it is the heartbeat of our audience.

All my family back in East Tennessee who weren't mentioned in this book. Don't worry. You will be in the tell-all book. Haha! I love you all . . .

Thanks also need to be given to Jess Rosen, Casey Wasserman, Jim Morey, Renee Allen, Allister Ann, Danielle Laures-Bouharoun, Bob Crout, Shane Tarleton, Ainsley Barry, Cheryl Bevis, Ryan Lassan, Jennifer Kemp, Ash Summerford, Ben Kline, Tony Castle, Shannon Finnegan, Reid Shippen, Justin Niebank, Greg Guidry, Bob Thomas, David Haase, Fred Hurst, Marty Bruckner, Brian Long, Dan Murphy, Kassie Epstein, Jess Enos, and Kathie Orrico. Each of you has touched my life in a singular, important way—and I want to acknowledge your impact.

And finally, one more thought for Joe Galante . . .

Don't ever tell anybody outside "THE FAMILY" what you are thinking.

With all the gratitude a heart can hold,

                      Kenny
                      Key West, Florida
                      2025

Holly Gleason thanks:

Kenny Chesney for always wanting to create magic, even distilling a life beyond imagination. Renee Bell, Clint Higham, and Scott Kernahan for trying to make that first meeting happen, and Joe Galante for closing the deal.

Laurel School in Cleveland, Ohio, for teaching a dyslexic kid how to work beyond limitations, as well as Mauro DiPreta, whose instincts helped shape a very big life. The Library of the Four Arts, Swiftys, Howleys, Cucina, and Dontee's Diner for the refuge in Florida, and Margo Café, Bongo Java, Baja Burrito, and the Waffle House in Nashville for the hours of sitting, writing, or staring into space. Dandelion in Vegas for the cold brew jet fuel for the final weeks of *Heart Life Music*. Mr. Corliss and Very Important Paws for being here when I got home.

Along the way, Rob Simbeck, Michael McFarlane, Bobby Patterson, Michael McCall, David Ritz, Andrea Billups, Malchijah Bailey, John Hobbs, and Delaney Groth offered insight; Dave Marsh remains the compass. Generous conversations with Karen Cloud, Troy Tomlinson, Sean Payton, Tim Holt, David Farmer, Jill Trunnell, John Staley, Wyatt Beard, Kenny Greenberg, Ed Wannebo, Grace Potter, Mac McAnally, Steve Miller, and people I'm forgetting filled in details, blanks, and a sense of the moment.

Scott Ambrose Reilly, Greg Harris, Mojo Nixon, Jeremy Tepper, Steve Earle, Shelby Morrison, Dan Baird, Louis Arzonico, and the Toad Liquors for inspiration beyond the obvious.

Dave Vigliano for pointing us to Mauro, who was the man for this mission. Allie Johnston created order in a Sphere-dominated world. Eric Rayman, you made sense and simplicity from something that was anything but standard.

Twenty-five years ago, a frustrated artist who burned with passion sat with me at a picnic table in Cuyahoga Falls, Ohio. Michael Stanley, the rock god of Cleveland, saw his set, said, "They look at him like they looked at me"—and I realized: This is Every(young)man.

To watch him crystallize the twenty-first-century experience of coming of age in the flyover was an ongoing thrill. Whether in college bars, three nights at Gillette Stadium, the kitchen rhythm section in Atlanta, or somewhere in the Caribbean, you created space for so many people to dream their dreams, too.

Telling this story with all the moving pieces was no small task. But watching you, Kenny Chesney, make it happen has been a joy.

To the Gopher, we're a long way from Blossom.

RIGHTS AND ATTRIBUTIONS FOR PHOTOGRAPHS AND LYRICS

Interior Photo Credits

All photos courtesy of the author, except the following: Shaun Silva: 21, 275, 276, 278; Jay Cooper: 32; David Farmer: 36, 265; Tim Holt: 40, 43, 93; David Lowe: 51, 98, 109; Marcia Beverly, Courtesy of Capricorn Records/Amantha Walden: 63; Ron Keith, Courtesy of Capricorn Records/Amantha Walden: 73; Sandra Morgan: 79; Courtesy of the author and Capricorn Records/Amantha Walden: 84; Alison Stewart: 89, 186; Chevy Nash: 120; Emily Bourassa: 132, 202, 240; Jill Trunnell: 146, 220; Glen Rose: 157, 162, 163, 172, 179, 182, 193, 203, 211, 221, 226, 228, 236, 260; Helena Pygrum: 190; John "JW" Walsh: 217; Allister Ann: 233, 284, 315; Mary Nolan: 267; Isaac Therrien: 271; John McGinnis: 294 (top), 295, 296; Holly Gleason: 309; Zach Farnum: 318; Malchijah Bailey: 330

Insert 1:
Courtesy of the author: 1, 2, 3, 4, 5 (top); Tim Holt: 5 (bottom), 6; Glen Rose: 7, 8

Insert 2:
Glen Rose: 1 (top), 3 (bottom), 5 (bottom); Steve Simenson: 1 (middle); courtesy of the author: 1 (bottom); Emily Bourassa: 2 (top); Allister Ann: 2 (bottom), 5 (top), 6 (bottom), 7 (top and middle); Marty Bruckner: 3 (top); Buffy Cooper: 3 (middle); Jill Trunnell: 4 (bottom), 7 (bottom); Helena Pygrum: 6 (top); CeCe Dawson: 8

Insert 3:
Staci Wilkshire: 1 (top), Shaun Silva: 1 (bottom), 5; Jill Trunnell: 2 (top); David Farmer: 2 (bottom), 6 (bottom); Nick Hoffman: 3 (top); Mary Nolan: 3 (bottom), 4 (bottom); courtesy of the author: 4 (top), 7 (top and bottom); Ford Fairchild/Country Music Association, Inc.: 6 (top); Allister Ann: 8

Lyrics Permissions

"Better As A Memory"
(Scooter Carusoe/Lady Goodman)
© 2007 Scrambler Music (ASCAP) / Midwest Midnight Music (BMI). A division of Carnival Music Group. All rights reserved. Used by permission.
© 2007 New Rezume Music (ASCAP). All rights administered by WC Music Corp. All rights reserved. Used by permission.

"Boats"
(Kenny Chesney/Dean Dillon/Scotty Emerick)
© 2008 Songs Of Universal Inc. / Basuare Music. All rights administered by Songs Of Universal, Inc. All rights reserved. Used by permission.
© 2008 Sony Music Publishing (US) LLC. All rights obo Sony Music Publishing (US) LLC administered by Sony Music Publishing. All rights reserved. Used by permission.
© 2008 Florida Room Music (BMI). All rights administered by Me Gusta Music. All rights reserved. Used by permission.

"Boston"
(Kenny Chesney/Mark Tamburino)
© 2005 Sony Music Publishing (US) LLC.
All rights obo Sony Music Publishing (US) LLC administered by Sony Music Publishing. All rights reserved. Used by permission.
© 2005 Songs Of Universal Inc. / Basuare Music. All rights administered by Songs Of Universal, Inc. All rights reserved. Used by permission.

"The Boys Of Fall"
(Casey Beathard/Dave Turnbull)
© 2010 Sony Music Publishing (US) LLC and Six Ring Circus Songs. All rights obo Sony Music Publishing (US) LLC and Six Rings Circus Songs administered by Sony Music Publishing. All rights reserved. Used by permission.
© 2010 Dixie Stars Music, V Bulls Music, and Six Ring Circus Songs. All rights on behalf of Dixie Stars Music administered by Concord Music Publishing, LLC. All rights reserved. Used by permission.
© 2010 V Bulls Music (ASCAP). All rights on behalf of V Bulls Music administered by Anthem Music Group. All rights reserved. Used by permission.

"Da Ruba Girl"
(Kenny Chesney)
© 2022 Songs Of Universal Inc. / Basuare Music. All rights administered by Songs Of Universal, Inc. All rights reserved. Used by permission.

"Happy On The Hey Now (A Song For Kristi)"
(Kenny Chesney)
© 2013 Songs Of Universal Inc. / Basuare Music. All rights administered by Songs Of Universal, Inc. All rights reserved. Used by permission.

"The Tin Man"
(Kenny Chesney/David Lowe/Stacey Slate)
© 1993 Songs Of Universal Inc. / Roots And Boots Music. All rights administered by Songs Of Universal, Inc. All rights reserved. Used by permission.
© 1993 Sony Music Publishing (US) LLC, EMI Longitude Music, and EMI Full Keel Music. All rights obo Sony Music Publishing (US) LLC, EMI Longitude Music, and EMI Full Keel Music administered by Sony Music Publishing. All rights reserved. Used by permission.
© 1993 Reservoir 416 (BMI). All rights administered worldwide by Reservoir Media Management, Inc. All rights reserved. Used by permission.

"When I See This Bar"
(Kenny Chesney/Keith Gattis)
© 2013 Songs Of Universal Inc. / Basuare Music. All rights administered by Songs Of Universal, Inc. All rights reserved. Used by permission.
© 2013 Sony Music Publishing (US) LLC and Publisher(s) Unknown. All rights obo Sony Music Publishing (US) LLC administered by Sony Music Publishing. All rights reserved. Used by permission.

Soldier Field, Chicago, IL, 2024